MOTIVATING & INSPIRING STUDENTS

STRATEGIES TO *AWAKEN* THE *LEARNER*

Robert J. Marzano   Tina H. Boogren

Darrell Scott   Ming Lee Newcomb

555 North Morton Street
Bloomington, IN 47404
888.849.0851
FAX: 866.801.1477

email: info@marzanoresearch.com
marzanoresearch.com

Visit **marzanoresearch.com/reproducibles** to download the free reproducibles in this book.

Printed in the United States of America

Library of Congress Control Number: 2016911419

ISBN: 978-0-9913748-7-8

20   19   18   17   2   3   4   5

Text and Cover Designer: Rian Anderson

Marzano Research Development Team

Director of Content and Resources
Julia A. Simms

Editorial Manager
Laurel Hecker

Production Editor
Ming Lee Newcomb

Editorial Assistants / Staff Writers
Elizabeth A. Bearden
Christopher Dodson

Marzano Research Associates

Mario Acosta
Tina H. Boogren
Robin J. Carey
Bev Clemens
Sally Corey
Michelle Finn
Douglas Finn III
Jane Doty Fischer
Jeff Flygare
Jason E. Harlacher
Tammy Heflebower
Lynne Herr
Mitzi Hoback
Jan K. Hoegh
Jeanie Iberlin

Daniel Joseph
Bettina Kates
Jessica McIntyre
Rebecca Mestaz
Diane E. Paynter
Kristin Poage
Cameron Rains
Tom Roy
Mike Ruyle
Roberta Selleck
Julia A. Simms
Gerry Varty
Phil Warrick
Kenneth C. Williams
David C. Yanoski

Visit **marzanoresearch.com/reproducibles** to download the free reproducibles in this book.

Table of Contents

Reproducible pages are in italics.

CHAPTER 3 Self-Actualization 29

CHAPTER 4 Esteem Within a Community 63

CHAPTER 5 Belonging 95

CHAPTER 6 Safety 117

CHAPTER 7 Physiology 137

About the Authors

Robert J. Marzano, PhD, is the cofounder and CEO of Marzano Research in Denver, Colorado. During his forty-nine years in the field of education, he has worked with educators as a speaker and trainer and has authored more than forty books and 250 articles on topics such as instruction, assessment, writing and implementing standards, cognition, effective leadership, and school intervention. His books include *The Art and Science of Teaching, Leaders of Learning, The Classroom Strategies Series, A Handbook for High Reliability Schools, Awaken the Learner, Managing the Inner World of Teaching,* and *Collaborative Teams That Transform Schools.* His practical translations of the most current research and theory into classroom strategies are known internationally and are widely practiced by both teachers and administrators. He received a bachelor's degree from Iona College in New York, a master's degree from Seattle University, and a doctorate from the University of Washington.

Darrell Scott is the founder of the Rachel's Challenge organization. He has spoken to over five million people in live settings around the world and reached millions more through TV channels such as CNN and programs such as *The Oprah Winfrey Show, Larry King Live,* and *The Today Show.* He has authored or coauthored numerous books, including *Awaken the Learner: Finding the Source of Effective Education, Rachel's Tears: The Spiritual Journey of Columbine Martyr Rachel Scott, Rachel Smiles: The Spiritual Legacy of Columbine Martyr Rachel Scott,* and *Chain Reaction: A Call to Compassionate Revolution,* and meets with politicians and educators regularly to discuss issues of school violence.

Tina H. Boogren, PhD, is a former classroom teacher, English department chair, teacher mentor, instructional coach, professional developer, and athletic coach. She has presented at the school, district, state, and national levels and has been a featured speaker at Barnes and Noble Educators' Nights and the International Literacy Association Annual Conference. Dr. Boogren was a 2007 finalist for Colorado Teacher of the Year and received the Douglas County School District Outstanding Teacher Award seven years in a row, from 2002 to 2009. In addition to writing articles for the National Writing Project's *The Voice* and *The Quarterly*, she authored *Supporting Beginning Teachers* and *In the First Few Years*. She is a contributing author to Richard Kellough's *Middle School Teaching* and Robert J. Marzano's *Becoming a Reflective Teacher*. Dr. Boogren holds a bachelor's degree from the University of Iowa, a master's degree with an administrative endorsement from the University of Colorado Denver, and a doctorate from the University of Denver in educational administration and policy studies.

Ming Lee Newcomb is a production editor at Marzano Research in Denver, Colorado and a coauthor of *Teaching Reasoning: Activities and Games for the Classroom*. She has experience mentoring groups of students at the high school level and tutoring students at the elementary and postsecondary level. She has published education policy briefs with the National Conference of State Legislatures, served as an editor for *Leviathan Magazine*, and written articles for the *Catalyst Newspaper*. She holds a bachelor of arts degree in English with a concentration in fiction writing from Colorado College.

About Rachel's Challenge

Rachel's Challenge is an organization responsible for a series of empowerment programs and strategies that help students and adults prevent bullying and allay feelings of isolation and despair by creating a culture of kindness and compassion. The programs are based on the writings and life of seventeen-year-old Rachel Scott, the first student killed at Columbine High School in 1999. During her life, Rachel reached out to those who were different, picked on by others, or new at her school. Shortly before her death she wrote, "I have this theory that if one person can go out of their way to show compassion, then it will start a chain reaction of the same. People will never know how far a little kindness can go." Rachel's Challenge was founded by Darrell Scott (Rachel's father) and Sandy Scott (Rachel's stepmother) when they realized how Rachel's writings and drawings resonated with her friends and classmates.

Although Rachel was a typical teenager with ups and downs, she believed that she would someday change the world. The Scott family tells her story to inspire others toward kindness, compassion, and forgiveness. More than twenty million people have been touched by Rachel's story. Each year, at least three million more are added to that number. In the last several years, Rachel's Challenge has received hundreds of unsolicited emails from students stating that, after hearing Rachel's story, they reached out for help as they were contemplating suicide. Some even say that Rachel saved their lives.

Rachel's Challenge is a nonprofit, nonpolitical, nonreligious organization based in Littleton, Colorado. By turning the story of a tragic death at Columbine High School into a mission for change, Rachel's Challenge makes a worldwide impact by helping create safer learning environments for students.

About Marzano Research

Marzano Research is a joint venture between Solution Tree and Dr. Robert J. Marzano. Marzano Research combines Dr. Marzano's more than forty years of educational research with continuous action research in all major areas of schooling in order to provide effective and accessible instructional strategies, leadership strategies, and classroom assessment strategies that are always at the forefront of best practice. By providing such an all-inclusive, research-into-practice resource center, Marzano Research provides teachers and principals with the tools they need to effect profound and immediate improvement in student achievement.

CHAPTER 1

Research and Theory

Motivation and inspiration both contribute to an individual's personal drive or desire to do something. As such, the motivation and inspiration of students is a topic of discussion among educators at all levels. Over the years, there has been a chorus of calls to recognize the positive effects of motivating and inspiring students in the classroom. Consider the following statements about the need for motivation and inspiration.

▶ "Good teachers can inspire students, and effective teachers continue to hone this skill by improving their understanding of student psychology and the culture of the classroom and school" (Colwell & Hewitt, 2016, p. 5).

▶ "In a culture obsessed with measuring talent and ability, we often overlook the important role of inspiration. Inspiration awakens us to new possibilities by allowing us to transcend our ordinary experiences and limitations. Inspiration propels a person from apathy to possibility, and transforms the way we perceive our own capabilities. Inspiration may sometimes be overlooked because of its elusive nature. . . . But as recent research shows, inspiration can be activated, captured, and manipulated, and it has a major effect on important life outcomes" (Kaufman, 2011).

▶ "When performance in mathematics was predicted and prior achievement was controlled, motivation but not intelligence contributed to the prediction. Since mathematics performance is often thought to be highly cognitive in nature, the importance of motivation is most interesting. This result is especially important considering the potential malleability of motivation via educational processes. Compared to intelligence or more specific abilities, motivation may be more easily influenced by situational factors, such as salient classroom goals. . . . Thus, when teachers aim at improving students' performance, enhancing their motivation might be as important as the conveyance of knowledge" (Steinmayr & Spinath, 2009, p. 88).

▸ "Some teachers, those we might call our great teachers, have a knack for moving students up . . . motivation levels. . . . Somehow these teachers are able to inspire students to work harder than they were initially inclined to work. . . . They are the ones who elicit such comments from students as

  ▸ I liked coming to class. I hated being absent.

  ▸ She turned us on to history and made it come alive.

  ▸ I never worked so hard in my life.

  ▸ I didn't expect to like that class, but I really did.

We might reasonably conclude, therefore, that it is possible to inspire students to become more fully active learners. Clearly, some teachers manage to do it" (Harmin, 2006, pp. 4–5).

▸ "Research on student motivation seems to be central to research in learning and teaching contexts. Researchers interested in basic questions about how and why some students seem to learn and thrive in school contexts, while other students seem to struggle to develop the knowledge and cognitive resources to be successful academically, must consider the role of motivation" (Pintrich, 2003, p. 667).

▸ "In terms of education, it has become ever more apparent that . . . intrinsic motivation . . . leads to the types of outcomes that are beneficial both to individuals and to society" (Deci, Vallerand, Pelletier, & Ryan, 1991, p. 342).

▸ "Do we as teachers sell inspiration short? We know what inspiration, or the lack of it, means in our own lives. Why do we let ourselves forget that our pupils are made as we are and that they are not always moved to their best efforts by our exhortation, our fervent persuasion, our nagging and scolding" (Spitzer, 1951, p. 136)?

Clearly, educators have long recognized the importance of motivation and inspiration. However, just how to evoke them in students is neither a simple nor obvious task.

Motivation and inspiration were strong themes in the book *Awaken the Learner* (Scott & Marzano, 2014), which posited that K–12 schools primarily focus on knowledge and skills to the detriment of their students. The current education system fails to take advantage of the vast array of available resources and strategies related to motivation and inspiration; this may be due to a systemic failure to recognize the positive influence that these strategies can have on students, both academically and personally. This book is designed to make some of these resources readily available to K–12 teachers by providing a comprehensive model of the nature of motivation and inspiration as well as specific strategies to elicit them in the classroom.

Hierarchy of Needs and Goals

A prevalent model that researchers use to explain human motivation involves the pursuit of specific needs and goals. That is, motivation and inspiration occur when we perceive that an activity or opportunity will help us meet a specific need or goal. Conversely, they do not occur when we perceive we will not be able to accomplish a specific need or goal. From this perspective, understanding human needs and goals provides a window to the inner workings of human motivation and inspiration.

Many discussions of needs and goals assume a hierarchic structure (Alderfer, 1969; Elliot & Church, 1997; McClelland, 1987; Vallerand, 1997, 2000; Vallerand & Ratelle, 2002). The model presented here is based on Abraham Maslow's well-known hierarchy of needs (Maslow, 1943, 1954). The hierarchy originally had five levels: (1) physiology, (2) safety, (3) belonging, (4) esteem within a community, and (5) self-actualization. Later versions (Koltko-Rivera, 2006; Maslow, 1969, 1979) included a sixth level: connection to something greater than self. The six levels of needs and goals are arranged into a hierarchy because each level is generally not available without fulfilling the needs related to the levels below it. Figure 1.1 depicts the hierarchic organization of all six levels of the model.

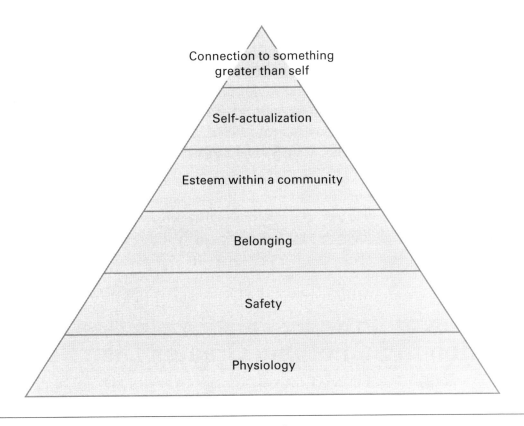

Figure 1.1: Maslow's hierarchy of needs and goals.

To better understand the hierarchic nature of the needs and goals in figure 1.1, consider the topmost levels, which involve connection to something greater than self and self-actualization. These levels can only be accessed with a solid foundation of the levels below them—that is, they only occur in individuals whose needs related to physiology, safety, belonging, and esteem within a community have been met.

It is important to note that while Maslow directly referenced *needs* and only alluded to *goals*, both terms make sense. We use both terms somewhat interchangeably, though it is probably more accurate to think of lower levels of the hierarchy as needs and the higher levels as goals. However, there is certainly no clear-cut dividing line between the two.

The extent to which students are motivated and inspired in a particular classroom is a function of the extent to which the classroom attends to the needs and goals in the hierarchy—particularly needs and goals related to the top two levels. Metaphorically, one might say that students in any given situation are constantly asking themselves the following questions.

- ▸ **Level 1:** "Am I physiologically comfortable in this situation?"
- ▸ **Level 2:** "Does this situation make me feel safe?"
- ▸ **Level 3:** "Does this situation make me feel like others accept me?"
- ▸ **Level 4:** "Does this situation make me feel like I am valued?"
- ▸ **Level 5:** "Does this situation make me feel as though I am living up to my potential?"
- ▸ **Level 6:** "Does this situation make me feel like I am a part of something important?"

To illustrate how this affects motivation, imagine students in a typical classroom. If they cannot answer "Yes" to the level 1 and level 2 questions, their thoughts will be focused on basic physical needs related to physiology and safety rather than what is occurring in class. If students cannot answer "Yes" to the level 3 and level 4 questions, it is probably accurate to say that the students might be able to attend to what is occurring in class but are probably disengaged to a significant degree. Schools tend to focus on issues related to the bottom four levels, which deal with foundational human needs. However, these levels do little to enhance students' motivation and inspiration, which manifest in levels 5 and 6 of the hierarchy. This is depicted in figure 1.2.

As depicted in figure 1.2, when a situation meets our needs related to physiology, safety, belonging, and esteem within a community, we are engaged and attentive. Inspiration and motivation, however, occur only when students have the opportunity to meet goals related to self-actualization and connection to something greater than self. Stated differently, students must answer "Yes" to the level 5 and level 6 questions as well as the questions for levels 1 through 4 to be truly motivated and inspired in class. Thus, effectively motivating and inspiring students relies on a thorough understanding of all the levels of the hierarchy. Here, we present a brief description of the research and theory behind each level, beginning with the top level of the hierarchy.

Connection to Something Greater Than Self

Connection to something greater than self represents the topmost level of Maslow's hierarchy of needs. Theoretically, this is the highest level of human motivation and inspiration. While not articulated in Maslow's (1943, 1954) original hierarchy of needs, he made reference to this sixth level in later writings (1969, 1979). To differentiate connection to something greater than self from self-actualization, Maslow defined needs and goals related to self-actualization as an individual's inclination to fulfill his or her *own* potential. Needs and goals related to a connection to something greater than self represented an individual's desire for a higher purpose and to help *others* move up the hierarchy of needs. In Maslow's (1969) own words:

> The fully developed (and very fortunate) human being, working under the best conditions tends to be motivated by values which transcend his *self*. They are not selfish anymore in the old sense of that term. . . . It has transcended the geographical limitations of the self. (p. 4)

Maslow was not the first person to articulate this difference. In Victor Frankl's (1959/2006) famous work, *Man's Search for Meaning*, he reflected upon the lessons learned during his time in Auschwitz during World

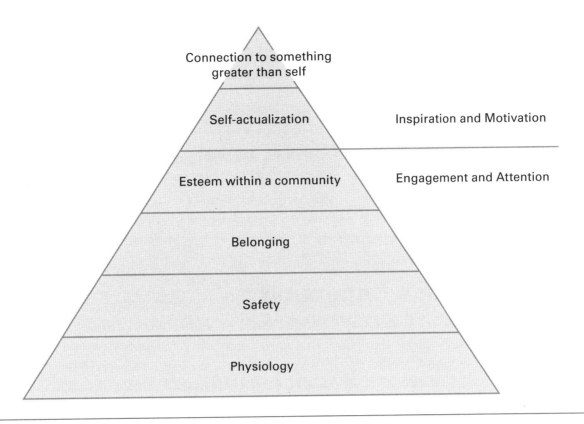

Figure 1.2: The hierarchy of goals as it relates to inspiration, motivation, engagement, and attention.

War II and noted, "The true meaning of life is to be discovered in the world rather than within man or his own psyche" (p. 110). Frankl emphasized humans' proclivity to seek a connection to something greater than self, and it is likely that Maslow's creation of a sixth level of his hierarchy was influenced by Frankl's work.

Regardless of its origins, Maslow (1969) called the state of feeling a connection to something greater than self *transcendence*, which he associated with a sensation of oneness with the world and moments of understanding outside of ordinary experience. As individuals repeatedly fulfill their goals at this level, they often also experience humility, wisdom, or a creative outpouring. Once individuals experience transcendence, they will attempt to prolong that state. However, only a small percent of the population ever truly sustains this connection over a long period of time; Mother Teresa, Mahatma Gandhi, and Martin Luther King Jr. might be considered examples of those who have. This is not to minimize the impact that brief experiences of connection to something greater than self can have on an individual. Indeed, even if they are rare or not sustained for long, we should seek out and cherish such moments when they occur.

Self-Actualization

Maslow (1943) defined needs and goals related to self-actualization as "the desire to become more and more what one is, to become everything that one is capable of becoming" (p. 382). In other words, they represent the desire to pursue self-identified goals. Goals related to self-actualization can be described as *global motivators*, as individuals will work tirelessly to achieve goals they have personally identified as important. Inherent in their definition, needs and goals related to self-actualization vary widely from individual to individual. For example, in order for one student to experience self-actualization, he may need to express himself creatively through visual art or music, whereas another student might be driven to reach her potential as an athlete. Regardless of the focus of the goals, all efforts to this end involve "the full use and exploitation of talents, capabilities, [and] potentialities" (Maslow, 1954, p. 150).

It is important to note that self-actualization marks a transition within Maslow's hierarchy from needs and goals related to deficiency to those of personal growth. The lower four levels—(1) physiology, (2) safety, (3) belonging, and (4) esteem within a community—define needs an individual must meet in order to avoid negative physical or psychological sensations. On the other hand, needs and goals related to self-actualization and connection to something greater than self articulate an individual's desire for personal growth. It is not coincidental that the goals at these higher levels also mark a shift from engagement and attention to inspiration and motivation, as shown in figure 1.2 (page 5).

Esteem Within a Community

Individuals' esteem within a community is highly dependent on their own *self-representations* or *self-concept*—the way they think about themselves. Researchers generally distinguish between self-esteem, or "global self-representations," and "specific representations, such as academic self-concept" (Peixoto & Almeida, 2010, p. 158). For example, a student's academic self-concept could differ drastically from his athletic self-concept, as he might excel on the racetrack or baseball diamond but struggle during school hours. Students' academic self-concepts can be even further divided: a student may have a high self-concept for her abilities in mathematics and science but a lower self-concept for her abilities related to language arts or history. These specific self-concepts contribute to students' esteem as a whole. As Cynthia G. Scott, Gerald C. Murray, Carol Mertens, and E. Richard Dustin (1996) explained:

> Both academically and interpersonally, students' self-esteem is affected daily by evaluations not only from school personnel but also from peers and family members. Because of the multitude of academic and social roles that students assume, they must constantly evaluate and reevaluate their knowledge and skills and compare them to others. (pp. 286–287)

Thus, recognizing the various communities in which students regularly participate can be useful when trying to understand and meet their esteem needs.

Maslow (1943) postulated that esteem can emanate from two sources: (1) self-esteem and (2) esteem from others. Needs related to self-esteem, he posited, involve "the desire for strength, for achievement, for adequacy, for confidence in the face of the world, and for independence and freedom" (p. 381), while esteem from others involves a "desire for reputation or prestige . . . recognition, attention, importance or appreciation" (p. 382). It is important to note, however, that people tend to consider self-esteem a higher version of esteem derived from others, as esteem derived from others is "dependent on external validation," which can "create stress, hostility, and conflict" (Crocker, 2002, p. 608).

As stated previously, esteem within a community is a type of deficiency motivation. When individuals' esteem needs are not met, they will focus on fulfilling those needs before moving on to needs related to personal growth (self-actualization and connection to something greater than self). As such, regardless of whether esteem is derived from the self or from others, a sense of esteem is critical to confidence and, when underdeveloped, has been correlated with psychological issues such as depression (Sowislo & Orth, 2013).

Belonging

Needs and goals related to belonging drive the social behaviors of humans and compel us to seek out fulfilling, affectionate relationships with others. In order for belonging needs to be met, individuals' relationships must be two-directional and elicit feelings of acceptance and connectedness.

The need to belong is so important that, when unfilled, it can have drastic negative effects on students' mental and physical health. To illustrate, consider this letter from a student in Illinois:

> As I started my 8th grade year, things got tougher. School got harder, friends got meaner, and I felt like there was no one I could talk to. Soon after that, I started cutting. It became a regular thing for me. Feel sad, grab scissors, feel better. (Rachel's Challenge, 2015, p. 7)

Clearly, feelings of belonging (or the lack thereof) immediately affect the emotional health of students. When left unaddressed, such feelings can cause destructive behaviors, sometimes evolving into suicidal thoughts:

> In my school, I'm known as the "loner," the "emo;" people just don't care enough to get to know me. I once dreamed, but the way I've been treated caused me to give up. This has had such a negative effect on me, I suffer from depression. I developed a plan for suicide and almost carried it through. (Rachel's Challenge, 2015, p. 31)

The previous quotations are featured in *Saved by a Story: Letters of Transformation and Hope*, a book that compiles thank-you notes received by Rachel's Challenge (2015). The booklet contains dozens of letters from students who, when their needs for belonging went unmet at school, physically harmed themselves, attempted suicide, or bullied other students. Once these students felt they belonged at school, their negative outlooks were transformed, as exemplified at the end of the letter from the student in Illinois:

> I realized there are people who care about me, and people I care about. I realized that I could die tomorrow, and that I didn't want to leave this world thinking I had no one. (Rachel's Challenge, 2015, p. 7)

Such examples highlight the importance of a sense of belonging, particularly because meeting such needs mitigates negative mindsets that may contribute to students' dangerous behaviors. In an analysis of previous research on the topic, Xin Ma (2003) found that a sense of belonging among students was positively related to the following factors.

- Engagement in class
- Persistence with difficult work
- Positive attitudes toward other racial-ethnic groups
- Students' expectations of academic success
- Intrinsic interest in academic work
- Higher course grades
- Teachers' ratings of students' academic effort

The same study found that a sense of belonging was also negatively correlated with high school incompletion rates and student involvement with gangs, substance abuse, and delinquency.

Safety

Safety needs fall into the second-lowest level of the hierarchy. *Safety*, in this sense, can be defined as a feeling of order, fairness, and predictability that ultimately reduces or eliminates physical or emotional harm. In other words, after individuals' physiological needs (level 1 of the hierarchy) are met, they will seek out spaces where they feel secure. Teachers should also note the difference between actual and perceived safety. *Actual safety* relates to the real or genuine danger that individuals might encounter, whereas *perceived safety* relates to people's opinions about how safe they are. Regardless of whether students feel or actually are unsafe, the effect is the same: they will endeavor to meet their safety needs by trying to escape or reduce the real or imagined threat rather than focusing on academics (Maslow, 1943, 1954).

While some people would argue that U.S. schools are becoming less and less safe, research indicates otherwise. Schools are better equipped now than they have ever been to ensure students' safety. Some have metal detectors at their entrances, and many have school resource officers. The total victimization rate for students between the ages of twelve and eighteen has decreased since 1992, as has the total number of student homicides per year (Robers, Zhang, Morgan, & Musu-Gillette, 2015). Furthermore, from 1995 to 2013, the percentage of students who feared going to school because they felt a threat of attack or harm decreased from 12 percent to 3 percent (Robers et al., 2015). In sum, most schools do a very good job of keeping their students physically safe and contributing to students' perception of safety. Despite this, there is still work to be done. It is notable that in 2013, 5 percent of students avoided at least one activity or place during school hours because of a perceived threat to their safety (Robers et al., 2015).

Physiology

The lowest level of Maslow's hierarchy involves the most basic of human needs related to physiological comfort. When unmet, the ability to focus on any of the higher levels of the hierarchy is inhibited. For example, if an individual is too hungry, thirsty, or tired, he or she must eat, drink, or sleep before focusing on anything else. From an evolutionary perspective, these needs ensure that an environment meets the minimum conditions for survival. Generally, schools do a fairly good job of providing for students' physiological needs. Cafeterias provide sustenance, and school buildings are heated during the winter and often cooled during warmer months. Many schools have resource officers, administrators, and counselors who actively monitor students to ensure that their physiological needs are met and who work with students, parents, and outside entities when they are not.

Despite this attention, much of the scope of students' physiological needs falls outside of the schools' direct control. For example, in a survey of a thousand U.S. educators, three out of four public school teachers taught students who regularly came to school hungry, and four out of five of those educators identified the problem as recurring on at least a weekly basis (No Kid Hungry, 2015). Katherine M. Keyes, Julie Maslowsky, Ava Hamilton, and John Schulenberg (2015) found that eighth-grade and high school students get less sleep than their counterparts did years ago and that only around 14 percent of adolescents felt they got enough sleep each night. These statistics point to the frequency with which certain physiological needs go unmet among students, which in turn translates into behavioral or learning problems.

Research and Theory in Practice

The hierarchy of needs and goals presented in this chapter provides a framework K–12 educators can use to create schools and classrooms in which students are motivated and inspired. Chapters 2 through 7 each contain strategies related to a specific level of the hierarchy, with chapter 2 containing strategies related to the highest level of the hierarchy (connection to something greater than self) and chapter 7 containing strategies related to the lowest level (physiology). Each chapter ends with a section containing a summary of its strategies, general recommendations for implementation, and a vignette showing how the recommendations might manifest in a classroom. Teachers can use the strategies and recommendations for all the chapters together to ensure all students are not only engaged and attentive but also motivated and inspired during class. While this book presents a complete model for responding to students' unmet needs at all levels of the hierarchy, teachers might choose to focus on one level of the hierarchy at a time, especially if they notice that their students need extra support at a particular level. To get a better sense of students' needs across a school, the appendix (page 158) contains a free reproducible survey that schools can use to determine how effectively they address students' needs at each level of the hierarchy.

CHAPTER 2

Connection to Something Greater Than Self

Connection to something greater than self is the highest level of human needs and goals. While a sustained connection is not easily acquired, teachers can design their classrooms to provide opportunities for students to begin forging such connections. Here, we consider seven topics related to connection to something greater than self: (1) inspirational ideals, (2) altruism, (3) empathy, (4) forgiveness, (5) gratitude, (6) mindfulness, and (7) Rachel's Challenge.

Inspirational Ideals

In order to inspire students in the classroom, educators must first address a very basic question: What is inspiration? Inspiration is fairly easy to identify when it is being experienced firsthand. For example, consider an individual reading a story about a woman who overcame poverty, started a multimillion-dollar company, and now donates much of her wealth to benefit underprivileged communities. It is likely that the individual reading this story would be moved or even experience a sense of awe or wonder—clearly, the individual would be inspired. The cause of inspiration, however, may not be so easily articulated. As Todd M. Thrash, Andrew J. Elliot, Laura A. Maruskin, and Scott E. Cassidy (2010) explained:

> Many of the experiences that individuals find most fulfilling—peak experiences . . .
> creative insights . . . spiritual epiphanies . . . and emotions of awe and elevation . . .
> —cannot be controlled or directly acquired, because they involve the transcendence
> of one's current desires, values, or expectations. Indeed, life would likely seem bland
> if one's strivings were never interrupted and informed by such experiences. We pro-
> pose that *inspiration* . . . is central to each of the above experiences. (p. 488)

Foundational to Thrash and colleagues' (2010) description of inspiration is the concept of *transcendence*—going beyond our current circumstances. Experiencing transcendence, and therefore inspiration, is a function of gaining access to our *ideals*—the way we would like the world to be. Examples of commonly held ideals include the ability to overcome difficult circumstances, the power of hard work, and the intrinsic goodness of others. These ideals are not always at the forefront of our minds. Rather, they form a subtle network of hopes and dreams. Inspiration occurs when people see evidence that one or more of their ideals could actually be true. For example, the story of the philanthropic entrepreneur might provide evidence for the ideal that great wealth can be used to benefit others or that people can overcome negative circumstances outside their control. A person holding these beliefs would transcend his or her current circumstances by recognizing that one or more of his or her ideals are in operation in the larger world. This is the essence of inspiration. It is also important to note that while some experiences of transcendence or inspiration are momentary, moments of transcendence, however brief, can have long-lasting effects that drive individuals to act on their ideals and make them reality.

Fostering inspiration in the classroom begins by presenting students with examples of persistence, bravery, altruism, and so on. Teachers can then use these examples to help students become aware of and identify the underlying ideals they represent. Educators can provide examples in a variety of formats including movies, stories, and quotations.

Movies

Movies can be a source of inspiration for both students and teachers. Movies to inspire teachers might include *Dead Poets Society, Lean on Me, Freedom Writers, Mr. Holland's Opus,* and *Good Will Hunting.* For students, inspirational movies might include *Rudy, Remember the Titans, Up, The Blind Side,* and *The Help.* Table 2.1 contains a short list of movies which might be appropriate for classroom use along with the ideals they exemplify. Visit **marzanoresearch.com/reproducibles** for a comprehensive list of inspirational movies.

Table 2.1: List of Movies and Ideals They Exemplify

Movie	Example Ideal
Cool Runnings	Hard work and companionship can lead to success, even against the greatest of odds.
Remember the Titans	People can learn to overcome their differences to care for one another, even if at first it seems unlikely.
Seabiscuit	When people stop believing others' negative expectations of them, they can go on to do great things.
Forrest Gump	Good things happen to people with a positive attitude.
Whale Rider	Even when others doubt your abilities, you can prove yourself through fearlessness and hard work.
Billy Elliot	People who follow their dreams are rewarded, even if their dreams run counter to the expectations of society.

Before having students watch a film (or selections from one), teachers should provide a context and a purpose for viewing the video. To illustrate, consider a middle school teacher who wants to show excerpts of the movie *Remember the Titans*. The teacher might first address the context of the film by talking to students about segregation as well as the Supreme Court's 1954 ruling in *Brown v. Board of Education*. The purpose, as articulated by the teacher, should always focus on ideals that are represented in the clip and be age- and subject-matter appropriate. As such, the teacher might preface the viewing by defining what an ideal is, describing how ideals relate to inspiration, and asking students to think about this concept. As students watch, the teacher might pause the film occasionally to get students' reactions about how characters treat each other and how these relationships change. After watching *Remember the Titans*, the teacher could lead a discussion about the film's depiction of the hostility toward African Americans during the reintegration of schools in the South. The teacher could then ask students to articulate ideals they felt were shown in the movie. For example, a student might generate the following list of ideals.

- People can learn to overcome their differences to care for one another, even if at first it seems unlikely.
- People can go on to do great things, even after they experience tragedy.
- Hard work does pay off, even if it is difficult and not rewarding initially.
- Setting an example by doing what is right can have a huge positive impact on a community.

After each student has generated a few ideals, the teacher can ask students to respond to the following questions.

- Can you describe an instance in your own life when you experienced this ideal in action? How did this make you feel?
- Can you describe an instance in your own life when this ideal was lacking?

Educators can reinforce students' ideals throughout the year by referencing previously identified ideals when appropriate.

Stories

Like movies, teachers can incorporate stories into their classrooms as a way to foster inspiration. While there are many inspirational stories online and in print, one particularly well-known source of inspirational stories is the *Chicken Soup for the Soul* series. Each book in the series compiles short stories and anecdotes about life written by dozens of different authors. The series also contains multiple volumes written specifically for adolescents, such as *Chicken Soup for the Teenage Soul* (Canfield, Hansen, & Kirberger, 1997) and *Chicken Soup for the Child's Soul* (Canfield, Hansen, Hansen, & Dunlap, 2007).

As an illustration of how these stories might be used in a classroom, a teacher could have groups of students choose stories from *Chicken Soup for the Teenage Soul* (Canfield et al., 1997) and explain why they are inspirational. For example, consider the story "The Most Mature Thing I've Ever Seen" (Doenim, 1997), which is about a student defending a new classmate from being teased. In the story, a girl named Lisa is new to a school and feels unwelcome because she is not a member of any of the cliques that assemble around the quad during lunch. As such, she experiences "cruel, hateful stares" (p. 268) from her classmates while trying to find a place to eat. As she walks across the quad, a place other students avoid, she trips, and the other students laugh. A boy helps Lisa up and escorts her out of the quad, which silences the laughter and highlights the cruelty of the other students. Students presenting on this story could give a brief summary of its plot and then read the following excerpt:

> The next day at Monroe High School at lunchtime a curious thing happened. As soon as the bell that ended the last morning class started ringing, the students swarmed toward their lockers. Then those who didn't eat in the cafeteria headed with their sack lunches across the quad. From all parts of the campus, different groups of students walked freely across the quad. No one could really explain why it was okay now. Everybody just knew. And if you ever visit Monroe High School, that's how it is today. It happened some time ago. I never even knew his name. But what he did, nobody who was there will ever forget. Nobody. (p. 269)

After reading the excerpt, the group members could use the quotation to provide evidence for ideals they feel are exemplified by the story, such as those related to the importance of kindness or the impact of one's actions. Alternatively, a teacher might assign all students the same story to read and ask them to use ideals to explain why the story is inspirational. Visit **marzanoresearch.com/reproducibles** for a list of brief stories about inspirational individuals that students can also use to practice identifying ideals.

Quotations

Quotations provide a quick and easy way to integrate inspiration into the classroom, as they are usually explicit or implicit statements of ideals. A valuable feature of incorporating inspiring quotes into the classroom is that teachers can offer them to students with little explanation. For example, a teacher might begin his or her class by displaying an inspirational quote on a PowerPoint slide or whiteboard but choose not to address it directly. Alternatively, the teacher could comment briefly on the quote by providing information about its author and its key ideal or ask students to take a few minutes to think about the quotation's meaning without further discussion.

For a more in-depth activity, teachers can ask students to rephrase ideals embedded in quotations. For example, consider the following quotation from Albert Einstein: "It is the same with people as it is with riding a bike. Only when moving can one comfortably maintain one's balance" (as cited in Isaacson, 2007, p. 565). After reading this to students, a teacher could ask them to work in small groups to identify an ideal from the quote that inspires them and discuss how it applies to their lives.

Teachers can also ask students to examine the stories behind given quotations. With access to the Internet, this is fairly easy to do. To illustrate, consider the following quotation by Dr. Martin Luther King Jr. during his pre-eminent "I Have a Dream" speech at the Lincoln Memorial in Washington, DC, on August 28, 1963:

> But there is something that I must say to my people who stand on the warm threshold which leads into the palace of justice. In the process of gaining our rightful place we must not be guilty of wrongful deeds. Let us not seek to satisfy our thirst for freedom by drinking from the cup of bitterness and hatred. We must forever conduct our struggle on the high plane of dignity and discipline. We must not allow our creative protest to degenerate into physical violence. Again and again, we must rise to the majestic heights of meeting physical force with soul force. (as cited in Council on Foreign Relations, 2016)

After presenting the quote, the teacher might elaborate on the historical significance of the "I Have a Dream" speech and contextualize it by describing the brutality experienced by many protestors during the civil rights movement. Once the class understood the political and social climate leading up to King's March on Washington, the teacher could revisit the quote and ask students to explain why Dr. King's emphasis on non-violence is exceptional. Visit **marzanoresearch.com/reproducibles** for a comprehensive list of inspirational quotations.

Altruism

Providing opportunities for students to practice altruism is a powerful strategy that directly contributes to a sense of connection to something greater than self. Simply stated, *altruism* is the act of assisting others without an expectation of recognition or payback. Such acts can be quite inspiring, as they allow students to transcend their current circumstances and recognize that they can positively impact the world. Depending on the time and resources available, teachers can engage students in long- and short-term projects that encourage altruistic tendencies.

It is important to note that teachers should never actively reward altruistic behavior. In fact, research has shown that rewarding selfless behaviors may actually make it less likely that individuals will engage in such behaviors when rewards are not involved (Chernyak & Kushnir, 2013; Fabes, Fultz, Eisenberg, May-Plumlee, & Christopher, 1989; Warneken & Tomasello, 2008, 2013). Rather, educators should capitalize on students' natural proclivity toward altruism by providing them with opportunities to volunteer and, afterward, prompting reflection on their experiences. These activities encourage students to view altruism positively and heighten their sense of connection to something greater than self, regardless of the degree to which the activities are voluntary.

There are a number of ways students can be engaged in altruistic activities while at school. Participation in volunteer days is an increasingly common practice that helps students experience the positive benefits of altruism. There are a number of pre-established events—such as Earth Day (www.earthday.org), Make a Difference Day (http://makeadifferenceday.com), and Pay It Forward Day (http://payitforwardday.com)—that encourage nationwide volunteerism on a specific date. Teachers or students can also design their own service projects that are specific to the unique needs of their communities and schedules. Table 2.2 (page 16) provides a list of examples of such projects. In addition, teachers can provide lists of local charities that may need volunteers or remind students of service-oriented community events.

Rather than rewarding altruistic behaviors, teachers can guide students through reflection activities that help them see how helping others is a powerful and positive experience. To this end, teachers can use the following questions to prompt discussion after service activities.

▸ How do you think your actions positively affected others?

▸ How does it make you feel to know that you have positively impacted someone else's life?

▸ Has someone done something nice for you without the expectation of receiving something in return? How did this make you feel?

If students doubt the importance of their role in volunteering, teachers can ask relevant community organizers involved in the volunteer day to speak about the impact of the students' actions or, if possible, provide

Table 2.2: Example Service Projects

Length of Project	Example Projects
One-Time Projects	• Donate blood. • Write thank-you letters or create care packages for troops deployed overseas. • Write a letter to a politician about an important issue (for example, Amnesty International has a campaign called Write for Rights that students can participate in). • Collect donations for a specific charity over a length of time and donate them after a specific date (for example, have students collect and donate clothes, blankets, nonperishable foods, books, toys, hygiene products, and so on). • Clean up the neighborhoods, community areas, or parks surrounding the school. • Organize a bake sale and donate proceeds to a specific cause. • Participate in a charity competition event (for example, Race for the Cure or Relay for Life). • Trick-or-Treat for UNICEF (www.unicefusa.org/trick-or-treat). • Spend time with and assist people in nursing homes.
Ongoing Projects	• Tutor younger students. • Participate in mentorship programs. • Provide a service for the school (for example, develop a program in which students reshelve books in the library or clean up trash on campus once a month). • Partner with a local organization and make repeated visits to volunteer there.

Source: Adapted from Amos, 2014.

data and statistics to this effect. Teachers could also provide examples of the lasting impact of other students' altruistic actions on their communities. For example, Isaac McFarland of Shreveport, Louisiana, distributed three thousand backpacks filled with food and hygiene products to homeless students, local shelters, and rescue missions on Make a Difference Day in 2014 (Spradlin, 2015). Following are a few other examples of altruistic actions by students adapted from Lesli Amos (2014).

▶ At the age of nine, Neha Gupta established her organization, Empower Orphans, which focuses on providing education and health care to orphaned children. The organization has helped more than twenty-five thousand children globally.

▶ At the age of nine, Katie Stagliano started planting fruits and vegetables in her garden to help the hungry and eventually founded her organization, Katie's Krops, which has helped feed thousands of people.

▶ At the age of ten, Zach Certner founded SNAP, which develops athletic programs for children with special needs.

▶ At the age of ten, LuLu Cerone founded LemonAID Warriors, which challenges kids to make social activism a part of their social lives.

▶ At the age of twelve, Jonathan Woods established the Under the Tree Foundation, which provides gifts to underprivileged teens during the holidays.

▶ At the age of thirteen, Claire Fraise established her organization, Lucky Tails Animal Rescue, which provides second chances for dogs that would otherwise be euthanized.

- At the age of fourteen, Jordyn Schara founded WI P2D2 (Wisconsin Prescription Pill and Drug Disposal), which helps people dispose of medications in an environmentally friendly and safe way.
- At the age of fifteen, Shannon McNamara started SHARE, which provides thousands of girls in Africa with books and school supplies.

Teachers can share such examples with students to highlight the impact young people and their altruistic actions can have on their communities. As students engage in altruistic behaviors and see this impact first-hand, they are by definition experiencing brief moments of a connection to something greater than self.

Empathy

Empathy is a direct pathway to a connection to something greater than self. When we experience empathy, we transcend our natural tendency to focus exclusively on our own needs and goals. Before teachers can expect students to practice empathy, however, they must understand the meaning of the term. Empathy is often confused with sympathy, and while both relate to others' feelings, they are not the same. When we *empathize* with someone, we attempt to understand his or her perspective or circumstances as a means to connect on a deeper level, while *sympathy* involves commiseration and feeling sorry for others.

Examples of Empathy

There are a number of resources that provide examples of empathic behavior or highlight the differences between empathy and sympathy. To this end, educators can find stories from history and literature and incorporate them into class time. For an example from literature, students could be asked to consider *Charlotte's Web* by E. B. White (1952). In the book, Charlotte, Templeton, and Fern Arable all exhibit empathy for Wilbur when his life is at risk by attempting to understand his situation as if it were their own. This inspires them to take direct actions that help Wilbur rather than simply feeling sorry for him, which would be considered a product of sympathy.

Teachers can also use historical figures to highlight instances of empathy in the real world. Chiune Sugihara is one such example.

> *Chiune Sugihara was a Japanese diplomat stationed in Lithuania at the beginning of World War II. As the Nazis began to take over Western Europe, Jewish refugees fled into Lithuania, bringing accounts of the atrocities of the Holocaust with them. In 1940, the Soviet Union (which occupied Lithuania) ordered that all diplomats return to their countries of origin before the Nazi army invaded. Before Sugihara left with his family, Jewish refugees gathered around the Japanese consulate hoping that Sugihara could issue them the appropriate papers to allow them to leave the country. Sugihara did not have the clearance to issue these visas without approval, but when he asked his superiors, they denied his request. Recognizing that the refugees' lives depended on him, he asked for a twenty-day extension of his post and began issuing visas on his own, despite the fact these actions directly contradicted his orders. Sugihara spent eighteen to twenty hours a day handwriting visas for refugees, and often produced a month's worth of visas in a single day. Ultimately, he issued over six thousand visas to Jewish refugees, which allowed them to escape the country with their lives (WGBH Educational Foundation, 2005).*

Students might be asked, after hearing this story, why Sugihara's actions are more indicative of empathy than sympathy. After students examine fictional and nonfictional accounts of empathy, they can find and explain their own examples of empathy from literature or history.

Attributes of Empathy

When teachers ask students to understand empathy as it applies to their lives, it may be helpful to highlight the following four attributes, as identified by Theresa Wiseman (1996).

1. Being able to see the world as others see it
2. Being nonjudgmental
3. Being able to understand another person's feelings
4. Being able to communicate an understanding of another person's feelings

To demonstrate being able to see the world as others see it, teachers might engage students in the following actions.

▶ **Analyzing competing points of view:** For example, debating as a means to understand multiple sides of the same issue

▶ **Stepping outside their current circumstances:** For example, roleplaying as notable figures (such as the protagonist of a short story or famous figures from history)

▶ **Explaining other people's reasoning:** For example, explaining the reasoning behind specific opinions on a controversial issue

To demonstrate being nonjudgmental, teachers might engage students in the following actions.

▶ **Becoming aware of and avoiding negative or judgmental language:** For example, limiting the use of judgmental language about themselves and others and correcting it when it does occur

▶ **Exploring why judgments are often inaccurate:** For example, identifying a judgment or stereotype and examining how it is incorrect

▶ **Identifying their own judgments:** For example, reflecting on judgments they hold about something (such as a specific character in a book or the difficulty of a mathematics problem) and reflecting on why they feel that way

To demonstrate being able to understand another person's feelings, teachers might engage students in the following actions.

▶ **Using targeted questioning:** For example, asking themselves a question like "If I were in this situation, how would I feel?" and so on

▶ **Explaining how feelings affect interactions:** For example, discussing how feelings and emotions affect an individual's interpretation of a situation

▶ **Examining sympathetic feelings:** For example, recognizing and describing sympathetic feelings and explaining how these feelings could motivate empathetic behaviors

▶ **Practicing reading facial expressions:** For example, identifying the feelings of subjects in photographs or artwork

To demonstrate being able to communicate an understanding of another person's feelings, teachers might engage students in the following actions.

▶ **Reflecting on their own language:** For example, examining how often they ask questions of their fellow students as an opportunity to tell other students about themselves

▶ **Focusing on how others' actions affect them rather than placing blame:** For example, using statements such as "I feel _____ when you _____" (see "I" Statements, page 104)

▶ **Explaining empathic qualities:** For example, explaining others' positive actions using examples, such as "I knew you were paying attention to me because your response question built on my previous answer" and so on

▶ **Reviewing reminders of appropriate communication:** For example, referring to classroom procedures or classroom decorations that outline appropriate communication

In addition to these strategies, teachers can provide students with the following five steps that encourage empathic interactions with one another.

1. **Watch & Listen:** What is the other person saying, and what is his or her body language?

2. **Remember:** When did you feel the same way?

3. **Imagine:** How does the other person feel? And how would you feel in that situation?

4. **Ask:** Ask what the person is feeling.

5. **Show You Care:** Let him or her know that you care through your words and actions. (Taran, 2013)

As students are asked to practice empathic behaviors, they may find that these behaviors become more natural over time. Teachers should also model and reinforce empathy whenever possible to further strengthen students' practice of it.

Forgiveness

The experience of forgiveness can also provide a direct connection to something greater than self. This connection occurs because forgiveness inherently requires individuals to think outside of themselves. Robert D. Enright and Richard P. Fitzgibbons (2000), in their empirical guide about the process of forgiveness, stated:

> People, upon rationally determining that they have been unfairly treated, forgive when they willfully abandon resentment and related responses (to which they have a right), and endeavor to respond to the wrongdoer based on the moral principle of beneficence, which may include compassion, unconditional worth, generosity, and moral love (to which the wrongdoer, by nature of the hurtful act or acts, has no right). (p. 29)

As such, the nature of forgiveness makes it intrinsically challenging for most if not all individuals. When individuals do succeed in forgiving others, they often experience positive psychological and physical benefits (Enright & Fitzgibbons, 2000; Gassin, Enright, & Knutson, 2005; Luskin, Ginzburg, & Thoresen, 2005;

Witvliet, Ludwig, & Vander Laan, 2001). For example, after observing the effects of forgiveness education in schools, Elizabeth A. Gassin, Robert D. Enright, and Jeanette A. Knutson (2005) posited that the reduction in anger stemming from forgiveness leads "to less depression and anxiety and to stronger academic achievement and more peaceful social behavior" (p. 321) among students.

Teachers should help students associate forgiveness with positive and powerful outcomes. To this end, teachers can lead students in discussions about times in their lives when they have forgiven or needed forgiveness from others. Teachers can also provide students with stories of forgiveness, whether personal or from books, movies, or history, as some stories of forgiveness are deeply moving. For example, consider the story of Mary Johnson and Oshea Israel.

> In 1993, when Oshea Israel was sixteen, he shot and killed Laramiun Byrd, Mary Johnson's only son. Although it might have been easier for Mary Johnson to remain angry at Oshea Israel, she chose a different path. During Israel's prison sentence, Johnson reached out to her son's killer, and the two agreed to meet. By the end of their initial meeting, both Johnson and Israel were overcome with emotion and Johnson felt she had sincerely forgiven Israel. Throughout Israel's sentence, Johnson continued to visit Israel regularly, and the two built a strong relationship. After being released from prison, Israel moved next door to Johnson, and the two remained very close. Johnson and Israel regularly expressed love for the other, and Johnson often referred to Israel as her son. As Johnson put it, "Well, my natural son is no longer here. I didn't see him graduate. Now you're going to college. I'll have the opportunity to see you graduate. I didn't see him getting married. Hopefully one day, I'll be able to experience that with you" (NPR Staff, 2011).

After presenting such a story and discussing its inspirational attributes, teachers can directly teach students about the process of forgiveness. For example, teachers could present the Enright Forgiveness Process Model (Enright, 2001) to their students, which identifies the following four phases of the forgiveness process.

1. **Uncovering phase:** Recognizing an offense and its associated negative consequences

2. **Decision phase:** Deciding to forgive

3. **Work phase:** Trying to reframe feelings about the offense or the offender

4. **Deepening phase:** Identifying the positives from the situation as a whole

Each phase in this model is further broken down into component actions. Teachers can explain the phases of the forgiveness process and actions taken during each using the prompts in table 2.3.

Gassin and colleagues (2005) noted that it is important to delve into the true nature of forgiveness to dispel common misconceptions about it:

> Our group thoroughly reviewed philosophical work on forgiveness, which makes clear that forgiveness is offered from a position of strength. . . . Forgiveness does not make one weak or vulnerable; it should be confused neither with condoning (e.g., ignoring or subtly approving) an offense, nor with reconciliation (reestablishing a relationship with an offender). Forgiveness does not preclude *moderate*, *limited* expressions of anger or a search for *reasonable* redress of injustice. (p. 322)

After discussing forgiveness with students, teachers should directly address these common misconceptions. They can do this by asking students to differentiate between forgiveness, approval, and reconciliation, as

Table 2.3: Enright Forgiveness Process Model

Phase	Associated Prompts
Uncovering phase	• Who hurt you? • How deeply were you hurt? • On what specific incident will you focus? • What were the circumstances at the time? Was it morning or afternoon? Cloudy or sunny? What was said? How did you respond? • How have you avoided dealing with anger? • How have you faced your anger? • Are you afraid to expose your shame or guilt? • Has your anger affected your health? • Have you been obsessed with the injury or the offender? • Do you compare your situation with that of the offender? • Has the injury caused a permanent change in your life? • Has the injury changed your worldview?
Decision phase	• Decide that what you have been doing hasn't worked. • Be willing to begin the forgiveness process. • Decide to forgive.
Work phase	• Work toward understanding the offender by viewing him or her in context. • Work toward compassion for the offender. • Accept the pain associated with the offense. • Give the offender a gift (moral or otherwise).
Deepening phase	• Find meaning for the self and others in the offense and the forgiveness process. • Recognize times when you needed forgiveness from others. • Discover you are not alone. • Realize that the offense has positive implications. • Recognize the emotional release, decreased negative effect, and increased positive effect of forgiveness.

Source: Adapted from Enright, 2001. Used with permission.

well as to define appropriate and inappropriate responses to an offense. Teachers should be wary of forcing students to forgive one another after conflicts arise in class, as one can never mandate forgiveness. In other words, teachers can inform students of the forgiveness process and its benefits, but they should also make the distinction that practicing forgiveness is an individual choice in which students must decide to engage.

Gratitude

Exploring and experiencing gratitude is another way to help students connect to something greater than self. Researchers Jeffrey J. Froh and Giacomo Bono (2012) stated that, for students, gratitude "improves their mood, mental health, and life satisfaction, and it can jumpstart more purposeful engagement in life at a critical moment in their development, when their identity is taking shape." In fact, Froh and Bono (2012) found:

> Teens who had high levels of gratitude when entering high school had less negative emotions and depression and more positive emotions, life satisfaction, and

happiness four years later when they were finishing high school. They also had more hope and a stronger sense of meaning in life.

Gratitude helps us see the positive aspects of our lives overall as opposed to a narrow perspective of what is happening in our lives at a specific moment. According to Christopher Peterson (2008), gratitude is at the heart of positive psychology, the study of what makes life worth living. Peterson (2008) noted that the following beliefs underlie positive psychology.

- ▶ What is good in life is as genuine as what is bad.

- ▶ What is good in life is not the absence of what is not.

- ▶ What is good in life is worth acknowledging and exploring.

These beliefs are probably a good place to start with students as they begin to engage in gratitude practice. Teachers could present groups of students with these statements and discuss the extent to which they believe these principles are true and present in their day-to-day actions.

With this discussion as a background, students working individually or in groups can be asked to generate definitions of gratitude. The following list contains a few examples.

- ▶ "An emotion or state resulting from an awareness and appreciation of that which is valuable and meaningful to oneself" (Lambert, Clark, Durtschi, Fincham, & Graham, 2010, p. 574)

- ▶ "Gratitude—a positive emotion that typically flows from the perception that one has benefited from the costly, intentional, voluntary action of another person" (McCullough, Kimeldorf, & Cohen, 2008, p. 281)

- ▶ "Gratitude is the positive emotion one feels when another person has intentionally given, or attempted to give, one something of value" (Bartlett & DeSteno, 2006, p. 319)

- ▶ "An estimate of gain coupled with the judgment that someone else is responsible for that gain" (Solomon, 1976/1993, p. 257)

- ▶ "Hav[ing] something to do with kindness, generousness, gifts, the beauty of giving and receiving, or 'getting something for nothing'" (Pruyser, 1976, p. 69)

- ▶ "By showing gratitude . . . we express our beliefs that [others] acted with our interests in mind and that we benefited; we show that we are glad for the benefit and the others' concern—we appreciate what was done" (Berger, 1975, p. 302)

Once students understand the concept of gratitude, they can be systematically engaged in gratitude-based activities. The following gratitude activities identified by Vicki Zakrzewski (2013) are easily integrated into the classroom.

- ▶ **Gratitude book:** Create a classroom scrapbook with space for students to write and draw about things for which they are grateful. Send the book home with a different student each week so families can contribute to the gratitude book as well.

- ▶ **Gratitude circle:** Begin or end the day by having each student identify one thing he or she is grateful for and why. For younger students, provide examples to help model this behavior.

- ▶ **Gratitude collage or bulletin board:** Have students cut out pictures of things for which they are grateful and post them on a bulletin board or use them to create a class collage.

- ▶ **Gratitude journals:** Once a week, have students write in their journals about three things for which they are grateful and why. This strategy may lose its impact if it is employed more than once a week, as time for reflection is necessary to prevent repetitive entries.

- ▶ **Gratitude letters for the community:** Have students write letters of gratitude to others in the school. For example, students might choose to write to janitors, food service staff, other teachers, or administrators to thank them for their service. Teachers could also expand this activity so that students write to members of their larger community, such as firefighters, nurses, police officers, and so on.

- ▶ **Gratitude paper chain:** Give students strips of paper and ask them to write down one thing for which they are grateful on each strip. Have the class work together to create a gratitude paper chain and hang it somewhere in the room.

- ▶ **Gratitude quilt:** Give students square pieces of paper and ask them to draw things they are grateful for on their squares. Have students mount their squares on larger pieces of colored paper to create borders and assemble the squares into a "quilt" to hang in the classroom.

- ▶ **Gratitude surprise sticky notes:** Give students each a sticky note and ask them to write about something in the school for which they are grateful. Have students post their sticky notes in places where others will see them.

Clearly, a number of these strategies can be used quickly and without much setup. As such, teachers can easily incorporate them into class time as activities for free time at the end of a period or during transitions.

Mindfulness

A definition of *mindfulness* is a deliberate focus on thinking that results in intentionality. The premise behind mindfulness is that people are typically filled with so many thoughts and related emotions that they are often incapable of making the best decisions or noticing what is happening around them. Thus, the simple act of being more aware often increases their self-efficacy.

Mindfulness practice has a strong grounding in research on the positive effects of some forms of meditation. Meditation has been tied to improved academic achievement, with one study finding that 41 percent of students who participated in transcendental meditation experienced boosts in academic performance compared to 15 percent in control groups (Nidich et al., 2011). Additionally, meditation has been associated with better concentration and focus (Paul, Elam, & Verhulst, 2007; Travis, Grosswald, & Stixrud, 2011); emotional well-being, as students who meditated daily were found to have higher esteem and emotional competence than their peers who did not regularly meditate (David Lynch Foundation, n.d.); and reduction in academic stress, absenteeism, and negative or destructive behaviors among students (Barnes, Bauza, & Treiber, 2003; Paul et al., 2007). Meditation may also improve students' physical health, as it has been linked to reductions in blood pressure and risk of cardiovascular diseases among practitioners (Tanner et al., 2009). Although not all mindfulness strategies involve meditation, both practices rely on similar mental dynamics.

Increasingly, mindfulness practice is being integrated into schools as more and more studies show the positive effects it can have on students. As an example, consider Visitacion Valley Middle School in San Francisco. Before adopting the Quiet Time program, an integrated mindfulness program that incorporates two fifteen-minute periods of meditation into the school day, the school struggled with disruptive and poorly behaved students, frequent fighting during the school day, graffiti, and continual confrontations between students and teachers (Kirp, 2014). However, after implementation, the school noticed a drastic change in students' behaviors:

> In the first year of Quiet Time, the number of suspensions fell by 45 percent. Within four years, the suspension rate was among the lowest in the city. Daily attendance rates climbed to 98 percent, well above the citywide average. Grade point averages improved markedly.... Remarkably, in the annual California Healthy Kids Survey, these middle school youngsters recorded the highest happiness levels in San Francisco. (Kirp, 2014)

The following list presents specific strategies from Patricia A. Jennings (2015) that allow teachers to incorporate mindfulness into their classrooms.

▸ **Mindful listening:** During transition times, engage students in specific listening activities that encourage mindfulness. It may be helpful to exclusively use a specific chime or bell for this activity. To begin, announce, "We're going to do a listening activity that will help our minds relax and become more focused. First, let's all sit up nice and tall in our seats with our hands folded in our laps (or on the desk). In a few minutes, I'm going to ring this chime, and we're going to listen to the sound until it disappears. I find that I can focus my attention on my hearing best when I close my eyes. You can try that, but if you aren't comfortable closing your eyes, you can lower your gaze to your hands." After the students seem collected, ring the bell. Once the ringing has stopped, begin class.

▸ **Mindful walking:** During transition periods, instruct students to pay particular attention to the way they walk and how their feet hit the ground (with the heel, then ball of the foot, and then the toes making contact with the floor). Take the class on five- or ten-minute walks to break up instruction or when students seem particularly restless.

▸ **Setting intentions:** Instruct students to set an intention every morning, such as "I want to challenge myself today" or "I intend to make something positive out of something negative." Throughout the day, ask students to recall their intention and assess the degree to which they have been honoring it.

▸ **Three breaths:** Use this strategy when it seems that students are anxious or need a break. Ask students to take three deep breaths with their hands resting on their chests so that they can feel their lungs fill with air.

These strategies can and should be adapted for different age groups. For example, instead of talking about intentionality with younger students, a teacher could start the day by asking students about the good things they hope will happen and what they are going to do to make them happen. At the end of the day, the teacher could ask students to reflect on the day to make connections between their actions and the events that occurred.

Rachel's Challenge

A particularly powerful tool to help students experience a connection to something greater than self is the series of assemblies and workshops presented by Rachel's Challenge. These programs center around the story of Rachel Joy Scott, the first student killed in the shooting at Columbine High School in Littleton, Colorado, on April 20, 1999. The story of Rachel Scott provides compelling evidence for students' most inspirational ideals, such as the belief that one person can make a lasting impact on the world. Furthermore, the presentations themselves use Rachel's story as a vehicle to teach students directly about altruism, empathy, forgiveness, gratitude, and mindfulness.

Rachel's Story

Rachel Joy Scott was a normal junior at Columbine High School. She had two older sisters and two younger brothers. She loved to journal and was the lead in the spring play. Like other teenagers, she experienced her share of struggles and worked through the mistakes of adolescence. However, Rachel was also exceptional in many ways.

At a young age, Rachel recognized the importance of her actions and lived every day with purpose. In an essay on her personal code of ethics (Scott, n.d.), Rachel articulated that she sought to be "honest, compassionate, and [look] for the best and beauty in everyone," and this outlook informed her interactions with others. Because she was empathetic and recognized the value of kindness, she was known for her continual efforts to get to know and be kind to her peers, particularly those struggling socially. In the same essay about ethics, she also noted that while many people doubt their ability to positively impact the world, she felt differently: "My codes may seem like a fantasy that can never be reached, but test them for yourself, and see the kind of effect they have in the lives of people around you. You just may start a chain reaction." Clearly, she lived her life aware that her actions deeply affected others and intended to create a chain reaction of kindness.

Rachel always seemed aware that she would leave behind a legacy. For example, she made comments to friends and teachers that she would cause positive change in the world and once created a tracing of her hands with a statement that read, "These hands belong to Rachel Joy Scott and will someday touch millions of people's hearts." However, she also seemed to be aware that her life would end prematurely, and she discussed this premonition with her friends and wrote about it in her journal. Unfortunately, her predictions about her short life came true. Even right before her death, she reiterated to her teacher that she was going to change the world for the better. This prediction has proved to be true as well, and she left behind a legacy through Rachel's Challenge that has touched the lives of millions of people around the world.

After Rachel's death, her father, Darrell Scott, began traveling around the United States to tell her story to lawmakers, educators, and students and to advocate that education should focus more on building character and teaching principles like those Rachel valued. Over time, his speeches developed into an assembly and workshop series called Rachel's Challenge, which teaches others to follow Rachel's example by embodying the characteristics that came to define her. Since 1999, Rachel's Challenge has presented to over twenty-two million people, working in one thousand two hundred schools and businesses each year. The effects of Rachel's Challenge are notable. Teachers and administrators have reported widespread changes in the climate and culture of their schools after students heard Rachel's story. More exceptionally, Rachel's Challenge has received hundreds of letters from students who associate the assembly program with their decisions not to take their own lives.

Programs

Rachel's Challenge offers a variety of programs for schools. Each program tells the story of Rachel Scott and integrates age-appropriate lessons on social and emotional intelligence. These programs challenge students to practice altruism, empathy, forgiveness, gratitude, and mindfulness and use the inspirational ideals embodied in Rachel's story to encourage such practices. Rachel's Challenge programs are available in the formats listed in table 2.4.

Table 2.4: Rachel's Challenge Programs

Program	Recommended Grade Levels	Description
Link Up! Presentation	K–5	The forty-minute elementary Link Up! presentation introduces elementary school students to Rachel Scott and her challenge to reach out to others with deliberate acts of kindness. The presentation is a fun, energetic, interactive assembly that mixes music, video, and activities to tell her story. Students learn about a young girl named Rachel; however, they do not hear or see footage related to the Columbine tragedy or her death. Although appropriate for students in grades K–6, the presentation is most effective with K–5 students.
Kindness & Compassion Club	K–5	The Kindness & Compassion (K & C) Club is a way to involve students in fun, practical activities that keep them engaged in sustaining the culture of kindness portrayed in the Link Up! presentation. All K & C Clubs make Chains of Kindness, chains of paper links created by the students. Each time a student observes an act of kindness by another student, he or she writes that act on a strip of paper and links it to the classroom's chain. Teachers read the links weekly and acknowledge students for their efforts. At the end of the year, teachers can have a Link Up! party and read some of the links to remind students how they made their school a better place during the year.
Power of One Program	K–5	Developed by elementary school educators and counselors, Power of One is the follow-up program to Kindness & Compassion Club. It follows the same outline as its prerequisite and provides a full year of new lessons and activities. Power of One also adds a section of lessons and activities for students with special needs. There is no mention of Columbine or Rachel's death in this program. The Power of One reinforces and expands upon the same challenges for elementary students as presented in Kindness & Compassion.
Rachel's Story Presentation	5–6	This presentation introduces younger middle school students to Rachel's story and her challenge to deliberately reach out to others with kindness. Rachel's story is told through the eyes of her family. The Columbine tragedy is introduced at an intensity level appropriate for fifth and sixth graders. Her story shows the profound positive impact students can have on those around them by simply paying attention to the little things they do and say every day. Rachel's story encourages participants to consider their own behavior.
Rachel's Challenge Presentation	7–12	Conveyed through stories from Rachel's life and writings, the Rachel's Challenge presentation shows the profound positive impact we can have on those around us. It demonstrates to the listener the power of deliberately reaching out to others in word and action to start what Rachel called "a chain reaction of kindness and compassion."

Program	Recommended Grade Levels	Description
Rachel's Legacy Presentation	7–12	This sixty-minute follow-up to the Rachel's Challenge presentation program builds upon the legacy that Rachel inspired in the lives of people around her. Through a series of stories told from the perspective of those whom Rachel touched, the Rachel's Legacy presentation encourages participants to take specific steps toward making their own positive legacy a reality.
Friends of Rachel Training	5–12	The Friends of Rachel training is designed to help a select group of students (up to one hundred preassigned students) and adults (a minimum of one adult to every ten students) create a club that fosters a permanent culture of kindness and compassion in their school. The training starts with time for participants to share their feelings about Rachel's story. The bulk of the training discusses why the club is important and provides resources to plan for the club's first meeting and activity.
Chain Reaction Training	5–12	Chain Reaction is a six-hour, intensive, interactive training that consists of three parts: (1) teaching and processing segments, (2) physical activities, and (3) full- and small-group sharing. Chain Reaction includes a cross-section of a school's population represented by eighty to one hundred students and twenty to twenty-five adults. It is important to maintain a minimum ratio of one adult to four students throughout the program. The program is designed to promote personal introspection, empathy, community building, and empowerment.
Community Event	6–12, as well as community members	The Community Event introduces Rachel and her story to parents and community members using stories from her life and writings. This event is typically held in the evening. It is similar in content and intensity to the Rachel's Challenge high school program. The Community Event shows the profound positive impact we have on those around us and demonstrates the power of deliberately reaching out to others to start what Rachel called a "chain reaction of kindness and compassion."

As seen in table 2.4, Rachel's Challenge offers a variety of programs in different formats that are appropriate for a range of age levels. Visit **rachelschallenge.org** for more information.

To illustrate the power of Rachel's Challenge's programming, consider the Chain Reaction training designed for middle schoolers and high schoolers. Each Chain Reaction assembly works with around one hundred students and twenty-five adults in a school over a period of six hours. Participants move through teaching and processing segments, physical activities, and full- and small-group sharing sessions. The teaching and processing segments outline major themes of the assembly, including social labeling, appropriate affection, the power of words, isolation, shared experiences, and the ability to start chain reactions within a community. The physical activities (often in the form of cooperative activities; see page 114) forge and deepen community bonds, particularly among students who may not frequently interact in a positive way. Finally, the full- and small-group sharing sessions allow participants to reflect on the content presented during the teaching and processing segments and express their feelings in a safe environment. One particularly powerful activity that occurs during the assembly is Cross the Line, in which presenters call out prompts and ask students to step forward if they relate to what is said. Example prompts range from "I have been embarrassed at school" to "I have seriously considered ending my life." Such prompts help students recognize they are not alone in their feelings while asking students who do not cross the line to use empathy to consider others' circumstances.

Summary and Recommendations

This chapter discussed how to foster a connection to something greater than self in students. We provided strategies for the following seven topics: (1) inspirational ideals, (2) altruism, (3) empathy, (4) forgiveness, (5) gratitude, (6) mindfulness, and (7) Rachel's Challenge. Each of these topics, in some way, encourages students to think beyond themselves or to use introspection to consider and analyze their existing world views.

Although teachers can use the strategies in this chapter in a variety of ways, we recommend the following.

▶ At least once a month, present students with inspirational movie clips or videos and have them discuss the ideals they represent.

▶ Incorporate inspirational quotations into the classroom whenever possible, even if this includes providing inspirational quotations to students without comment.

▶ At least once per year, have students engage in an altruistic project.

▶ At least once a semester, use strategies related to empathy, forgiveness, gratitude, or mindfulness.

The following scenario depicts how these recommendations might manifest in the classroom.

A middle school science teacher wants to help her students experience a connection to something greater than self. When presenting new content, she provides biographical information about relevant scientists using movie clips and short reading assignments and asks students to articulate the ideals represented in them. She also posts an inspirational quote each Monday, which she calls the Quote of the Week, though she does not always directly discuss the quote with students. She tries to choose quotes that are relevant to what is occurring in class—for example, she chooses a quote on the importance of practice during a week leading up to a formal assessment. For an end-of-the-year project, the teacher decides to have students apply their knowledge to develop altruistic projects that benefit local ecosystems. Groups choose to address topics such as erosion near a local stream, damage done by off-trail hiking, and litter in a local park. The teacher serves as an advocate for students but allows them to develop and lead the projects. After the projects are completed, the teacher has students relate their projects to previously learned content and reflect on how they contributed to their communities.

CHAPTER 3
Self-Actualization

S elf-actualization involves the pursuit of personally relevant goals. In this chapter, we address the following five aspects of self-actualization: (1) an understanding of self-actualization, (2) mental dispositions, (3) the growth mindset, (4) possible selves, and (5) personal goal setting.

An Understanding of Self-Actualization

The concept of self-actualization can be intimidating to students who are unfamiliar with the term. Teachers can initially introduce students to self-actualization by providing them with clear definitions; however, definitions can and should differ based on students' ages. For example, with younger students, teachers might describe self-actualization as the act of deciding to do something and then doing it. In contrast, teachers of older students might define it as the identification and pursuit of goals that are personally beneficial and relevant to an individual. Once students become familiar with the concept, teachers can ask students to generate their own definitions. Teachers can also use specific characteristics of self-actualization to further deepen students' understanding of the concept. Here, we discuss traits of self-actualization and peak experiences.

Traits of Self-Actualization

After defining self-actualization for students, teachers can explain that people who spend a significant amount of time engaged in self-actualizing behaviors tend to develop or exhibit certain traits. Maslow (1970) identified some of these traits, listed in table 3.1 (page 30).

Table 3.1: Maslow's Traits of Self-Actualized People

Trait	Description
Clear perception of reality	The self-actualized person judges others accurately and is capable of tolerating uncertainty and ambiguity.
Acceptance of self and others	Self-actualizers accept themselves as they are and are not defensive. They have little guilt, shame, or anxiety.
Natural and spontaneous reactions	Self-actualizers are spontaneous in both thought and behavior.
Focus on problems rather than self	Self-actualizers focus on problems outside themselves.
Need privacy; tendency to be detached	Although self-actualizers enjoy others, they do not mind solitude and sometimes seek it.
Autonomy	Self-actualizers are relatively independent of their culture and environment, but they do not go against convention just for the sake of being different.
Continued freshness of appreciation	Self-actualizers are capable of fresh, spontaneous, and nonstereotyped appreciation of objects, events, and people. They appreciate the basic pleasures of life.
Social interest	Self-actualizers have feelings of identification with and sympathy and affection for others.
Interpersonal relations	Self-actualizers do on occasion get angry, but they do not bear long-lasting grudges. Their relationships with others are few but deep and meaningful.
Democratic character structure	Self-actualizers show respect for all people, regardless of race, creed, income level, and so on.
Sense of humor	Self-actualizers have a sense of humor that is both philosophical and nonhostile.
Creativeness	Self-actualizers are original, inventive, expressive, perceptive, and spontaneous in everyday life. They are able to see things in new ways.
Nonconformity	Self-actualizers fit into society, but they are independent of it and do not blindly comply with all its demands. They are open to new experiences.

Source: Adapted from Insel & Roth, 2012; Maslow, 1970.

Students can analyze the characteristics in table 3.1 and discuss how these traits may contribute to the successful pursuit of personally relevant goals. Guiding questions for such discussions might be:

▸ Why do you think self-actualized individuals manifest these traits?

▸ Which traits do you think are the most important? Which traits do you think are the least important?

▸ Choose a trait. Can you give an example of someone you know or have heard of who embodies this trait?

▸ Which of these traits do you exhibit? Which ones don't you exhibit?

Alternatively, teachers can ask students to identify such traits by thinking about the characteristics of people whom they consider to be self-actualized. Teachers can do this using the following four-step process.

1. Identify candidates for self-actualization.
2. Research candidates.
3. Identify candidates' traits.
4. Generate a class list of traits.

We discuss each step in the following sections.

Identify Candidates for Self-Actualization

In order to identify traits of self-actualization, teachers should first have students select people they believe are self-actualized (at least to some degree). As students consider individuals who frequently engage in self-actualizing behaviors, they may find that their candidates fall into categories—for example, candidates who are successful or well known in their fields, candidates who are particularly satisfied with their lives, or candidates who have accomplished extraordinary or difficult feats. These categories themselves can spark lively discussions around the outcomes of self-actualization. Teachers can also remind students that self-actualization makes us feel that we are developing into all we are capable of being. Consequently, individuals may be successful in specific areas of life but may not experience the sense of fulfillment that often accompanies self-actualization. For example, a lawyer may be successful in his profession, but this may not make him feel as though he is living up to his full potential. If the lawyer has a desire to express himself creatively, he may need to develop his skills as a writer or painter to truly experience self-actualization.

With such discussions as a backdrop, students can identify their candidates for self-actualization. Teachers can provide students with parameters for the candidates they choose, such as whether or not students should be personally acquainted with their candidates or whether candidates can be celebrities, deceased, and so on. Teachers could also provide students with example candidates, like those listed in table 3.2. Visit **marzanoresearch.com/reproducibles** for information about other candidates for self-actualization.

Table 3.2: Example Self-Actualization Candidates

Candidate	Description
Erik Weihenmayer	Despite losing his vision at age thirteen, Weihenmayer became involved in many extreme sports including paragliding, skiing, and mountain climbing. He won many awards for his accomplishments and his persistent spirit. He was the first blind man to summit Mount Everest and was one of only one hundred people in the world who has climbed the highest mountain on each continent (Adversity Advantage, n.d.).
Sandra Day O'Connor	O'Connor grew up in rural Arizona and had to leave home as a child to receive her education. She went on to attend Stanford University, where she studied economics, and then enrolled in Stanford Law. After graduating, she had difficulty finding a job because, at that time, no private firms in California were willing to hire female lawyers. She eventually started her own firm, served as a state senator, and became the first woman appointed to the U.S. Supreme Court (Oyez at IIT Chicago-Kent College of Law, 2016).

continued →

Candidate	Description
Langston Hughes	Hughes was an innovative writer and one of the first jazz poets. He fought against racism and social inequality and became one of the most well-known and prolific African American writers of the 20th century. His determination was apparent in his writing process as well. Four drafts of his poem "Ballad of Booker T." are archived in the Library of Congress; each draft is heavily annotated, and Hughes made major changes from one to the next before publishing a final draft (Wesson, 2011).
Robert Goddard	Known as the father of modern rocketry, Goddard was a physicist and inventor who built the first liquid-fueled rocket. He studied rockets extensively and, in 1919, published work that suggested that rockets could be used for space flight. This claim received a great deal of ridicule and backlash, but Goddard trusted his experiments and calculations and continued to improve rocket technology. His work directly enabled humanity's exploration of Earth's atmosphere and outer space (Garner, 2016).
Bethany Hamilton	Hamilton began surfing as a young child and dreamed of becoming a professional surfer. When she was thirteen, she was attacked by a shark and lost her left arm. Only a month after this traumatic event, she returned to surfing. She continued to compete and accomplished her goal of turning pro at the age of seventeen. As of 2014, Hamilton was a national champion surfer, as well as an author and public speaker (Soul Surfer, 2015).

Research Candidates

After identifying their candidates, students can research and write brief biographies of them in their own words. If candidates are alive and available, students might try to arrange interviews with them to get a better sense of their accomplishments. To illustrate what a biography might look like, a student who selected Eleanor Roosevelt as a candidate might write the following description.

> *Eleanor Roosevelt was born in 1884 and eventually married Franklin Delano Roosevelt, the thirty-second president of the United States. Contrary to the previous expectation that first ladies were to embody quiet elegance without much participation in politics, as first lady, Eleanor Roosevelt reimagined the role of the wife of the president. However, this was not a surprise to many who knew Eleanor growing up, as she had always been active in politics and involved in humanitarian efforts. Throughout her tenure as first lady (and after), Eleanor Roosevelt's actions showed a desire for equality by breaking down barriers that restricted women. Although traditionally women were not allowed to attend White House press conferences, Eleanor Roosevelt not only held her own press conferences but also limited her first press conference to only female reporters. Due to her husband's diagnosis of polio, she often was referred to as "the President's eyes, ears, and legs" and used this position to pursue her own agendas related to the rights of the underprivileged and underrepresented. After her husband died, Eleanor Roosevelt did not retreat from the public eye, unlike many first ladies before her. Rather, she served as chair of the Human Rights Commission in the United Nations and drafted the Universal Declaration of Human Rights, which is still in use today. After serving in the UN, she went on to fill multiple leadership roles in organizations and committees dealing in a wide range of humanitarian topics (Biography.com, n.d.; Franklin D. Roosevelt Presidential Library and Museum, n.d.).*

Students can also present their findings to small groups or to the class as a whole (once completed).

Identify Candidates' Traits

During this step, students hypothesize about various traits they believe their candidates possess. Students use previously gathered biographic information to provide evidence for their assertions about their candidates. To aid in this process, teachers may first want to provide examples to students about what appropriate traits are and how to provide evidence for them. For example, a teacher might explain that talented artists are often unconcerned with what others think of their work, as they recognize the intrinsic value of their art or find satisfaction in the process of making it. From this, the teacher could then identify nonconformity, creativity, and intrinsic satisfaction as traits related to self-actualization. To provide evidence for these traits, the teacher could explain that while he is highly appreciated now, when Claude Monet, the founder of French impressionism, first debuted his works, they were largely criticized. Despite the fact that he lived in poverty, Monet continued to paint the way he wanted, eventually experiencing success years after his impressionist debut (J. Paul Getty Museum, n.d.). After this brief lesson, teachers could ask students to identify other individuals who have shown the same traits and use evidence to back up their claims.

To further illustrate, reconsider the student who selected Eleanor Roosevelt as her candidate for self-actualization. She might hypothesize that one of the important traits possessed by Eleanor Roosevelt was her willingness to take risks for the causes she believed in. The student could use Eleanor Roosevelt's exclusive press conferences for female reporters as evidence of this trait. The student could then explain that many of Eleanor Roosevelt's actions were inherently risky because she was a pioneer for many progressive ideals and did not know how the public would respond to her actions.

Generate a Class List of Traits

After identifying specific traits and backing them with evidence, teachers can ask students to present their findings to the class. Teachers can do this through brief student presentations or class discussions about traits students have identified. Teachers should record students' findings as they are presented to compile a list of student-identified traits. Once a list is generated, small groups (or the class as a whole) can analyze its traits. Teachers should remove repeated or irrelevant traits and combine similar traits to create a composite list. In order to further narrow down the list, teachers can also discuss the relevance of traits as they pertain to self-actualization. In some cases, individual trait statements may actually contain multiple traits that can be further isolated. In the previous example of Eleanor Roosevelt's willingness to take risks for causes she believed in, students might determine that this trait would be better listed as two traits: (1) willingness to take risks and (2) passion for specific causes. A class might generate the following list of possible traits.

- Takes risks
- Fights for beliefs
- Is creative
- Works very hard
- Doesn't care when others don't believe in him or her
- Notices people who are often overlooked by others
- Is kind

‣ Cares about equality

‣ Keeps trying after failures

‣ Is humble

‣ Is grateful

‣ Is always trying to improve himself or herself

‣ Commits to pursuing a goal

Once developed, teachers can post the lists of traits in their classrooms as reminders to students and reference them when appropriate throughout the year.

Peak Experiences

Peak experiences are euphoric and joyful states derived from significant achievements or experiences that stand out in an individual's memory. These experiences occur as individuals experience self-actualization or a connection to something greater than self. When explaining self-actualization to students, it may be useful to explain peak experiences as a means of identifying self-actualizing behaviors. One powerful way to have students reflect on their peak experiences is to have them write about them.

When asking college students to write about their own peak experiences, James Polyson (1985) found:

> Every student was able to write about a peak experience that demonstrated at least a few of the characteristics of Maslow's construct—the intrinsically good feelings; the total attentiveness in the here and now; the effortless functioning; the spontaneity and harmony with the environment; and/or the freedom from blocks, fears, and doubts. Most of the peak experiences had occurred during athletic, artistic, religious, or nature experiences, or during intimate moments with a friend or family member. There were a number of peak experiences in which the student achieved an important personal or collective goal. There were also peak experiences in which the student overcame some adversity or danger or helped someone in need. (p. 212)

After asking students to evaluate their experiences with the writing assignment, Polyson found that 98 percent of students found the assignment worthwhile to some degree and that "students were . . . nearly unanimous in their approval ratings on the item 'How interesting was the assignment?'" (p. 212). While Polyson focused on college students, teachers can implement a similar writing assignment in K–12 classrooms using the following five-step process.

1. **Define peak experiences for students:** It may be helpful to provide characteristics of peak experiences (for example, a loss of sense of time, a feeling of effortlessness or a lack of inhibition, a lack of self-doubt or self-criticism, creativity, and so on) to students as well as either personal examples or accounts from self-actualized individuals.

2. **Ask students to identify their own peak experiences:** It may be difficult for some students to identify their own peak experiences, particularly for students who are younger. However, teachers can reframe this step so that students identify times in which they felt one or more of the characteristics of peak experiences. Teachers should emphasize that most individuals do

not experience all the characteristics during peak experiences; rather, peak experiences may embody just one or two of the common characteristics.

3. **Have students write a description of the event:** Teachers can provide further requirements such as a page length, word count, or more detailed topic guidelines (for example, students can explain how these experiences have continued to impact their lives or focus on the emotions associated with the experience rather than a description of the event itself). Teachers should also consider whether or not to grade the assignment, as writing about personal experiences can be a difficult task for many students.

4. **Ask students to share their experiences:** Teachers should ask students to volunteer their experiences rather than mandating it, as peak experiences are inherently personal in nature. Similarly, if teachers want to use specific students' work as examples, they should get prior permission from the students or ask if the examples can be shared with their names omitted.

5. **Facilitate a discussion about peak experiences and self-actualization:** Teachers can ask students to discuss peak experiences as a class or in small groups. Depending on previous discussions, teachers can ask students to focus on individual experiences shared in class or discuss the concept of a peak experience as a whole. Teachers may find it helpful to provide prompts that focus on particular aspects of peak experiences—for example, teachers can ask students to identify the lasting impact that peak experiences have had on their lives or discuss why they believe specific situations elicited peak experiences.

As students engage in critical analyses of their own peak experiences, teachers can ask students to reflect on why such experiences tend to be characteristic of self-actualization and discuss this relationship.

Mental Dispositions

Schools have sought to engage students in difficult tasks and expose them to complex problems as a means to help them meet the increasingly rigorous standards identified for K–12 students. The way students address these tasks, however, is a function of their existing *mental dispositions*—that is, the attitudes or actions taken during challenging situations. It is unsurprising that effective mental dispositions are necessary tools in the quest for self-actualization, as personally relevant goals often involve unexpected challenges and difficulties.

Teachers should emphasize that positive and effective mental dispositions generally run counter to natural human reactions to challenges. For example, a majority of people give up easily when they encounter problems, do not test their own limits on a regular basis, or fail to generate or adhere to personal standards of excellence. Making students aware of positive mental dispositions and providing them with opportunities to practice them increase the chances that students will develop these dispositions and use them both inside the classroom and later in life.

While many other experts have articulated desirable mental dispositions for students (for example, Costa & Kallick, 2008), our list of recommended dispositions appears in table 3.3 (page 36).

Table 3.3: Recommended List of Dispositions

Mental Disposition	Description
Staying focused when answers are not immediately apparent	We typically execute this disposition when we are trying to solve a problem. It starts by recognizing that we have become frustrated because we can't find an answer or solution and are about to give up on the task. Upon this realization, we then re-engage in the task even though we are experiencing ambiguity.
Pushing the limits of knowledge and skills	We typically execute this disposition during long-term projects. It begins by recognizing that we have set goals that are limited by our natural tendency to operate within our comfort zone. Upon this realization, we then adjust our goals such that their accomplishment will require us to acquire new knowledge and skills.
Generating and pursuing standards of excellence	We typically execute this disposition when we are working on a long-term project that culminates in a product. It starts by consciously thinking of how the product will look when it is complete and the standards by which we will judge how well we did. While considering standard conventions for the product, we might adjust them so they coincide with our personal level of development.
Seeking incremental steps	We typically execute this disposition when we are working on a long-term project. Rather than trying to address the entire project as a whole, we focus on small subsets or pieces of the overall system. With the completion of each part, we see how it fits into the whole and then move on to the next part.
Checking accuracy	We usually execute this disposition when we are learning something new. This commonly involves gathering information about a topic. It begins with an analysis of the source of the information we are receiving. If we are not completely sure of the accuracy of the source, we then consult sources we are more sure contain accurate information about the topic.
Checking clarity	We usually execute this disposition when we are trying to understand something new. It begins by asking ourselves if we have any confusion regarding the information we have processed thus far. If we do, we stop taking in new information and seek clarification from whatever resources are available.
Resisting impulsivity	We typically execute this disposition when we are making a decision or forming a conclusion. This commonly occurs when we respond to certain stimuli or form a conclusion based on new information we have processed. It begins by realizing that we have an urge to respond or form a conclusion without collecting more information. We briefly pause and allow time to think about our response or conclusion with an eye toward making revisions.
Seeking cohesion and coherence	We usually execute this disposition when we are creating something that has a number of interacting parts. Seeking cohesion means that we continually monitor the extent to which relationships between component parts are solid and stable and make adjustments if they are not. Seeking coherence means that we continually monitor whether the interaction of the parts is producing the desired effect and make adjustments if it is not.

Once students are familiar with the mental dispositions in table 3.3, teachers can lead them in examinations of their own behaviors. During self-analysis, students assess the degree to which they exhibit a specific mental disposition in a given situation. Table 3.4 provides questions to this end.

As seen in table 3.4, the eight dispositions examined in this chapter fall into five types of situations in which they are commonly employed.

1. Solving a difficult problem

2. Working on a long-term project

3. Interacting with new knowledge

4. Making a decision or forming a conclusion

5. Creating something that has interacting parts

Table 3.4: Self-Analysis Questions for Mental Dispositions

Mental Disposition	Situation	Self-Analysis Question
Staying focused when answers are not immediately apparent	Solving a difficult problem	Am I giving up because I can't find the answer right away?
Pushing the limits of knowledge and skills	Working on a long-term project	Am I stopping because I have to acquire new knowledge or skills to accomplish this?
Generating and pursuing standards of excellence	Working on a long-term project	Have I identified what the final product should look like in order for me to feel that I have done my best?
Checking incremental steps	Working on a long-term project	Am I breaking the project into smaller pieces that can be more easily accomplished?
Checking accuracy	Interacting with new knowledge	Am I doing something or asking questions to determine if this information is accurate?
Checking clarity	Interacting with new knowledge	Am I aware of when I'm getting confused, and do I stop to ask for clarification?
Resisting impulsivity	Making a decision or forming a conclusion	Am I aware of when I'm acting without thinking about my actions, and do I stop for a moment to examine my conclusions?
Seeking cohesion and coherence	Creating something that has interacting parts	Am I making sure that all the pieces fit together and work toward a common goal?

These situations provide a useful framework for creating opportunities to reinforce and analyze various dispositions in students. Here, we discuss each type of situation and provide self-rating scales to further encourage student reflection on mental dispositions.

Solving a Difficult Problem

A problem is any situation in which an individual has a goal but an obstacle or constraint prevents its accomplishment. For example, consider a person who has a goal to buy a new computer but doesn't have the funds to buy it immediately nor the means to borrow the money necessary for its purchase. In such a situation, it would be fairly easy for the individual to simply give up and stop trying to solve the problem. Self-actualized people, however, commonly cultivate the mental disposition of staying focused even when answers are not immediately apparent.

Other than simply providing anecdotes as to the importance of this mental disposition, teachers can ask students to try to solve difficult problems to help them become aware of how easily they give up when challenged. As students work through difficult problems, teachers can provide them with a self-rating scale, like the one depicted in figure 3.1 (page 38), to help them gauge the extent to which they stay focused when answers are not immediately apparent. Problems that teachers present to students should be difficult enough that students must spend a good amount of time working to find an answer but contained enough for students to execute in the classroom. There are a number of types of problems that meet these criteria, including problems of unusual thinking, never tells, and classroom mysteries.

Score 4.0	When I can't find an answer to a problem, it makes me try even harder.
Score 3.0	When I can't find an answer to a problem, I tell myself to keep trying.
Score 2.0	I try for a while when I can't find an answer to a problem, but I don't typically stay with it.
Score 1.0	I keep trying when I can't find an answer to a problem only if a teacher encourages me.
Score 0.0	When I can't find an answer to a problem, I give up right away.

Figure 3.1: Self-rating scale for staying focused when answers are not immediately apparent.

Problems of Unusual Thinking

Problems of unusual thinking are often best defined through example. As such, consider the problem in figure 3.2.

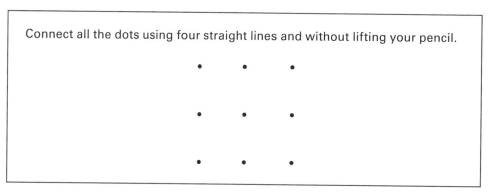

Connect all the dots using four straight lines and without lifting your pencil.

Source: Hecker, Simms, & Newcomb, 2015, p. 31.

Figure 3.2: Problem of unusual thinking.

Most individuals, when interacting with this problem for the first time, will try to draw four lines that stay within the perimeter of the square. However, the problem is impossible to solve under this assumption, as shown in figure 3.3.

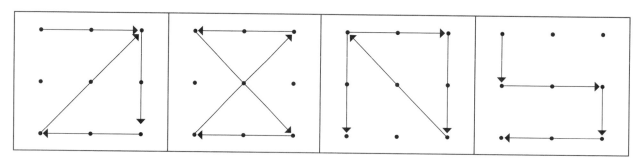

Source: Hecker et al., 2015, p. 31.

Figure 3.3: Attempted solutions based on faulty assumptions.

Rather, this puzzle necessitates that individuals try many solutions, including those that might be nontraditional—thus making it a problem of unusual thinking. As shown in figure 3.4, once an individual realizes that the four lines can be drawn outside of the perimeter of the nine dots, the problem is easily solved.

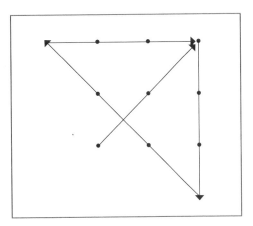

Source: Hecker et al., 2015, p. 32.

Figure 3.4: A correct solution.

Such problems are difficult to solve at first and provide good practice for the disposition of staying focused when answers are not immediately apparent. A list of additional problems of unusual thinking is available at **marzanoresearch.com/reproducibles** to help students practice this disposition. Another source for problems of unusual thinking is the game Riddle Me This in *Teaching Reasoning* by Laurel Hecker, Julia A. Simms, and Ming Lee Newcomb (2015). Additionally, there are many online resources that compile lists of logic and lateral thinking problems, which require that students stay focused when answers are not apparent.

Never Tells

Teachers can also incorporate difficult problems into their classes through the use of Never Tells. A Never Tell is a common type of inductive reasoning puzzle. Appropriate to the disposition of staying focused when answers are not immediately apparent, Never Tells gain their name from the idea that "people who know the answer should *never* just *tell* it to someone else—each person has to figure it out for himself or herself" (Hecker et al., 2015, p. 125). With Never Tells, only one person initially knows the overarching rule that informs whether other people's responses are correct; for the purposes of a classroom, this individual is usually the teacher. Other class members use questions or examples to determine what the rule is. The rules are challenging and require many examples to determine their nature; for example, a rule might relate to the number of syllables in each response or require that students make a seemingly inconsequential gesture as part of their response.

To illustrate how this manifests in the classroom, consider the Never Tell "My Aunt Likes Coffee but Not Tea." For this Never Tell, the teacher explains that his or her aunt is particular about the things she likes and does not like. As hinted by the title of the game, the rule that students must discover is that the aunt does not like anything with the letter *T* in it. The teacher then explains that students should respond using the format, "My aunt likes _____ but not _____." Before students begin guessing, the teacher might provide the following examples of correct responses: "My aunt likes dogs but not cats," "My aunt likes flowers but not plants," or "My aunt likes phones but not telephones." Students then are prompted to create their own statements about what the aunt does and doesn't like. If a student guesses an incorrect statement, such as "My aunt likes winter but not summer" or "My aunt likes tofu but not steak," the teacher notes that he or she is incorrect. A key component of Never Tells is that students get the chance to figure out the rule for themselves. Therefore, as students figure out the rule governing the game, they should be reminded to ask the teacher privately if their guesses are correct—that is, not to call out the rule or tell other students. As more students determine the rule, they can take over the role of determining whether other students' responses are correct or incorrect.

If students struggle to determine the rule, there are a number of modifications that teachers can use to make the game easier while still encouraging students to stay focused when an answer is not apparent. To this end, teachers could write down students' responses on the board as a way to visually represent the answers that have already been suggested. Teachers could also find ways to increasingly emphasize the nature of the rule as the game goes on. For example, in the case of "My Aunt Likes Coffee but Not Tea," after a certain amount of time has elapsed, the teacher might begin to emphasize the pronunciation of the letter *T* in students' responses. Finally, teachers can also give hints as needed to students, which encourage students to stay on task while still allowing them the satisfaction of discovering the answer for themselves. For "My Aunt Likes Coffee but Not Tea," the teacher might tell students to stop focusing on the thing itself or consider how the names of the things affect whether the aunt likes or dislikes them.

Another benefit of Never Tells is that they can be fairly easily incorporated into class time as a lighthearted transition between activities or as a way to start or end class. Teachers should also note that students do not need to solve Never Tells in one sitting; rather, they can be used across class periods, with students asking a few questions each day. Hecker and colleagues (2015) compiled a list of Never Tells as well as further instruction as to their implementation in the classroom.

Classroom Mysteries

Teachers can use picture mysteries, like those of Lawrence Treat (1981, 1982, 2010), to encourage students to stay focused when answers are not immediately apparent. Treat's picture mysteries always include an illustration of a crime scene, a short description of the scene, information regarding possible suspects, and a set of questions that guide the reader through solving the mystery by pointing out specific pieces of evidence. For example, figure 3.5 shows an illustration from the first book in the *Crime and Puzzlement* (1981) series. Its accompanying paragraph reads, "Pictured here is a kidnapping threat which was mailed to Iver Nutmeg, wealthy gumshoe manufacturer. From this information and an examination of the paper, can you discover who sent the extortion letter" (p. 23)?

A teacher could present the paragraph and picture to students, and then ask them to create lists of observations. Students might come up with the following observations about the image in figure 3.5.

▸ The kidnapping threat contains a lot of spelling errors.

▸ The kidnapping threat is written on paper from the Ritz-Plaza Hotel in New York.

▸ The kidnapper signed his or her name, *A Desperado*.

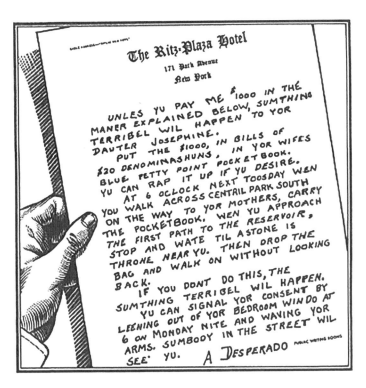

Source: From Crime and Puzzlement: 24 Solve-Them-Yourself Mysteries *by Lawrence Treat, Illustrations by Leslie Cabarga. Reprinted by permission of David R. Godine, Publisher, Inc. Copyright © 1981 by Lawrence Treat, Illustrations by Leslie Cabarga.*

Figure 3.5: "Extortion" picture mystery.

▸ The kidnapper wants Iver Nutmeg to signal consent by leaning out his window and waving his arms.

▸ Whoever wrote the kidnapping threat knows where Iver Nutmeg's mother lives.

▸ Whoever wrote the kidnapping threat knows that Iver Nutmeg's wife has a specific type of pocketbook.

Teachers can also create specific guidelines for students' observations, such as "Observations must be written in complete sentences" or "Students must come up with a minimum number of observations." Once students have generated their own observations, they can use the student organizer in figure 3.6 (page 42) to list them in the far left column. Visit **marzanoresearch.com/reproducibles** for a reproducible version of this organizer.

With observations listed, students can make inferences related to each one. For example, students might decide that the number of spelling errors in the letter implies that the kidnapper is not fluent in English. They would write this inference in the second column and their explanation for it—English learners often make spelling mistakes because they are not as familiar with the language—in the third. Students then identify qualifiers that provide evidence that is contrary to their inferences. For example, in the picture presented in figure 3.5, a qualifier might be that the kidnapper is purposefully disguising his or her identity by misspelling words in the ransom letter.

Observations (I see _____)	Inferences (Which means _____)	Explanations (I know this because _____)	Qualifiers (But still _____)

Prosecution Claim: _____

Source: Rogers & Simms, 2015, p. 183.

Figure 3.6: Student organizer for classroom mysteries.

When students struggle, teachers can prompt them to reconsider their existing observations, inferences, explanations, and qualifiers. For example, with the initial inference that the kidnapper is an English learner, a teacher could prompt students to look more closely at the language used in the letter. Students might identify the following observations in response to this prompting.

▶ Sometimes the kidnapper writes *yu*, and sometimes the kidnapper writes *you*.

▶ The kidnapper correctly spelled the words *Josephine, reservoir, signal,* and *consent* but did not correctly spell *will* or *you*.

▶ The punctuation in the letter is correct.

With these additional observations, the students might amend their initial inference about the kidnapper being an English learner and shift their focus to the qualifier—whoever wrote the note misspelled words intentionally. Once students have generated multiple inferences, they can analyze the inferences to create a final prosecution claim, which they write at the bottom of the student organizer in figure 3.6.

This game and many others are addressed in the book *Teaching Argumentation* by Katie Rogers and Julia A. Simms (2015). Picture mysteries can also be found in Treat's (1981, 1982) *Crime and Puzzlement* series, as well as in his book (2010) *You're the Detective!*, which contains nonviolent mysteries for younger students. Teachers can also use text-based mysteries to encourage students to stay focused when answers are not immediately apparent. The following resources contain text-based mysteries that teachers can use to encourage students' development of this disposition.

▶ *Two-Minute Mysteries* by Donald J. Sobol (1967)

▶ *Historical Whodunits, Kids' Whodunits: Catch the Clues!, Kids' Whodunits 2: Crack the Cases!* by Hy Conrad (2005, 2007, 2009)

- *Five-Minute Mini-Mysteries* by Stan Smith (2003)
- *Clue Mysteries: 15 Whodunits to Solve in Minutes* by Vicki Cameron (2003)

Working on a Long-Term Project

As students work on long-term projects, teachers can reinforce the following dispositions.

- Pushing the limits of knowledge and skills
- Generating and pursuing standards of excellence
- Seeking incremental steps

By definition, these dispositions must manifest over time. Consequently, teachers can introduce any type of long-term project as a means to help students practice them. While engaged in these projects, students can use the scales in figures 3.7, 3.8, and 3.9 (page 44) to assess their use of these dispositions. The personal goal-setting activities described later in this chapter (page 54) are fine vehicles to foster these dispositions in students.

Score 4.0	When working on a long-term project, I actively seek out challenges that make me acquire new knowledge and skills.
Score 3.0	When working on a long-term project, I notice when I'm not pushing myself to acquire new knowledge and skills and then try to increase my effort.
Score 2.0	When working on a long-term project, I may consider ways to push myself to acquire new knowledge and skills, but I do not typically follow through.
Score 1.0	When working on a long-term project, I may try to push myself to acquire new knowledge and skills, but only if the teacher prompts me.
Score 0.0	When working on a long-term project, even if a teacher asks me to do so, I do not push myself to acquire new knowledge and skills.

Figure 3.7: Self-rating scale for pushing the limits of knowledge and skills.

Score 4.0	At the beginning of a long-term project, I consider how I want the final project to turn out and then work hard to ensure that those standards are met.
Score 3.0	I notice if I haven't considered how I want a long-term project to turn out and then try to create and adhere to personally generated standards.
Score 2.0	When working on a long-term project, I might consider the way I want it to turn out, though I do not typically do what is necessary to meet my personally generated standards.
Score 1.0	When working on a long-term project, I only think about how I want the final project to turn out when a teacher reminds me.
Score 0.0	When working on a long-term project, I rarely consider how my final project will turn out, even if a teacher reminds me.

Figure 3.8: Self-rating scale for generating and pursuing standards of excellence.

Score 4.0	When working on a long-term project, whenever possible I break the project into smaller pieces and create deadlines for each of the smaller steps.
Score 3.0	When working on a long-term project, I break the project into smaller pieces and work on them as needed.
Score 2.0	When working on a long-term project, I may break the project into smaller pieces, but I don't typically continue this process to the end.
Score 1.0	When working on a long-term project, I only break down the project into smaller pieces if a teacher requires it.
Score 0.0	When working on a long-term project, even when a teacher reminds me, I don't break the project down into smaller pieces.

Figure 3.9: Self-rating scale for seeking incremental steps.

Interacting With New Knowledge

Interacting with new knowledge refers to how students react when they see, hear, or learn new information. Generally, self-actualized people have a tendency to cultivate the following dispositions when engaging with new knowledge.

▶   Seeking accuracy

▶   Seeking clarity

Self-rating scales for these two dispositions are presented in figures 3.10 and 3.11.

Score 4.0	When I am presented with new knowledge, I ensure the information is accurate before I accept it as true.
Score 3.0	When I am presented with new knowledge, I inquire about the accuracy of the information.
Score 2.0	When I am presented with new knowledge, I may question the accuracy of the information, but I don't typically follow through with determining its accuracy.
Score 1.0	When I am presented with new knowledge, I only check the accuracy of new information when prompted by my peers or a teacher.
Score 0.0	When I am presented with new knowledge, I do not check the accuracy of the information presented to me.

Figure 3.10: Self-rating scale for seeking accuracy.

Score 4.0	When I am presented with new knowledge, I make sure I understand the information, even if it requires additional work on my part.
Score 3.0	When I am presented with new knowledge, I ask questions to make sure I understand the information, if necessary.
Score 2.0	When I am presented with new knowledge, I might realize that I do not understand some of the information, though I don't typically try to clarify my misconceptions.
Score 1.0	When I am presented with new knowledge, I only check to make sure I understand the information when a teacher prompts me.
Score 0.0	When I am presented with new knowledge, I don't check to make sure I understand the information, even if a teacher reminds me.

Figure 3.11: Self-rating scale for seeking clarity.

Considering the nature of the classroom, teachers have many opportunities to encourage students to seek both accuracy and clarity when interacting with new knowledge. To encourage students to seek accuracy, teachers can employ accuracy checks in their classrooms, which allow students to question the accuracy of any new knowledge being offered by teachers or other students at any point in time. During an accuracy check, students consult relevant sources to confirm the accuracy of previous information and, if necessary, identify more accurate information. Teachers may also ask specific students to complete accuracy checks as homework assignments if time doesn't allow for all students to check the accuracy of information presented in class. After students complete accuracy checks at home, they can report their findings when the class reconvenes.

To cultivate the disposition of seeking clarity, teachers can use clarity checks to gauge students' understanding of new content. In such instances, teachers periodically stop lessons to have each student signal his or her level of understanding. Often, the easiest way to do this is through the use of a simple voting technique. For example, one common voting technique requires students to use one of the following hand signals to indicate their levels of understanding to the teacher: thumbs-up, meaning full understanding; thumbs-down, meaning no understanding; and thumbs-sideways, meaning partial understanding. Teachers could also use students' questions about content as opportunities to encourage students to clarify information for themselves. When students ask questions about the content being presented, teachers can ask them to consult specific resources for themselves or work in small groups to determine answers independently.

Making a Decision or Forming a Conclusion

When making a decision or forming a conclusion, self-actualized people tend to resist impulsivity. Generally, this involves considering both the importance of the decision or conclusion as well as the range of available options before taking action. A self-rating scale for this disposition is depicted in figure 3.12.

Score 4.0	When making a decision or forming a conclusion, I consider all of my possible actions and their likely outcomes and then make a thoughtful decision or conclusion based on the risk associated with the decision or conclusion.
Score 3.0	When making a decision or forming a conclusion, before taking action I consider my desired outcome and how my actions are likely to help me reach this outcome.
Score 2.0	When making a decision or forming a conclusion, I might consider how my actions relate to specific outcomes, but this doesn't typically inform my actions.
Score 1.0	When making a decision or forming a conclusion, I consider my actions and specific outcomes only when prompted by a teacher.
Score 0.0	When making a decision or forming a conclusion, I act without considering how my actions might lead to specific outcomes.

Figure 3.12: Self-rating scale for resisting impulsivity.

Central to the disposition of resisting impulsivity is the concept of *probabilistic conclusions*, which are conclusions that have probabilities attached to them, such as "I have probably studied long enough for the test" or "It doesn't seem like it will rain today." Generally, these statements include terms that denote the certainty or uncertainty of outcomes: for example, *probably, maybe, unlikely, possible,* and *not sure.* Having students assess their probabilistic conclusions is a form of risk, accuracy, and behavior analysis. As Robert J. Marzano and Tammy Heflebower (2012) noted:

> Relative to probabilistic conclusions, students should be able to discern which conclusions bear some risk if they are inaccurate. They must then strive to be as certain as possible regarding the conclusions that bear risk. If their level of certainty drops too far, then they must reconsider their conclusions and the resulting actions they will take. (p. 53)

By nature, as students consider their decisions or conclusions from a probabilistic perspective, they are resisting acting impulsively. As such, when offering choices or asking students to form conclusions, teachers can remind students of the following three questions, articulated by Marzano and Heflebower (2012), as a means to help them avoid impulsivity: "(1) Is it important that I am right about this? (2) If so, how sure am I about my prediction? and (3) If I'm not very sure, what should I do about it" (p. 53)?

The first question—Is it important that I am right about this?—asks students to consider how the outcome of the decision or conclusion may impact them. For example, a student considering whether she should walk to school or take the bus may not need to put much thought into her decision, as whichever choice she makes is unlikely to be very important in the long run. However, if the student needs to be at school before a certain time or she will not be allowed entrance into an exam, the stakes of the decision rise considerably and the student should probably put thought into her decision.

Once students determine that a decision or conclusion is important, they can ask themselves the second question: How sure am I about my prediction? For example, consider a student who generates the probabilistic conclusion that he will probably have time to study for an upcoming test, go to soccer practice after school, and see a movie with his friends in the evening. He has already recognized that the outcome of this decision is important; if he misallocates his time, he could fail the test, which might have ramifications such as being benched during his next game, getting grounded by his parents, or needing tutoring. When considering how sure he is of his initial probabilistic conclusion, he may begin to have doubts regarding his reasoning.

If students have doubts, they can consider the third question: If I'm not very sure, what should I do about it? This question requires that students reconsider the possible positive and negative outcomes of each option. The student from the previous example may prioritize studying because the negative consequences of not studying would have the largest impact on his life. The student might then consider the associated outcomes of going to soccer practice and going to the movies. If he skips soccer practice, he will likely not start in the next game. When considering the consequences of not seeing a movie with his friends, he may not be able to generate many negative outcomes that are comparable to the outcomes of not studying or skipping soccer—he can always go see the movie or hang out with his friends another time. Thus, the student might make a plan to go to soccer practice, then go home and study, and tell his friends to see the movie without him.

Creating Something That Has Interacting Parts

When creating something that has many interacting parts, self-actualized individuals continually seek cohesion and coherence. *Cohesion* refers to all parts of a system relating to one another; there are no extraneous or missing parts. *Coherence* refers to all parts of a system producing desirable results. A self-rating scale for this disposition is depicted in figure 3.13.

Score 4.0	When creating something with interacting parts, I ensure that all the parts of the project fit together and work toward a common goal as efficiently as possible.
Score 3.0	When creating something with interacting parts, I ensure that all the parts of the project fit together and work toward a common goal.
Score 2.0	When creating something with interacting parts, I might recognize that I should check to make sure all the parts of the project fit together and work toward a common goal, but I don't typically follow through.
Score 1.0	When creating something with interacting parts, I only make sure that all of the parts of the project fit together and work toward a common goal when the teacher prompts me.
Score 0.0	When creating something with interacting parts, I do not make sure that all the parts of the project fit together and work toward a common goal.

Figure 3.13: Self-rating scale for seeking cohesion and coherence.

This disposition is critical to creating systems that work effectively and efficiently. Writing compositions, computer programming, and challenge competitions all provide opportunities for students to practice creating cohesive and coherent products.

Writing Compositions

By definition, any type of written composition is a complex project with many interacting parts. As such, teachers can ask students to monitor the cohesion and coherence of their compositions.

Relative to cohesion, teachers can ask students to identify the various parts of their compositions. With multiple parts of their compositions identified, students can determine the role of each part, the relationships between parts, and if any parts are missing. For example, a teacher could ask students to take drafts of their compositions and make notes in the margins about the main idea and purpose of each paragraph as well as how the paragraphs build on one another. If students have difficulty determining the purpose of specific paragraphs, they may need to reassess how those sections fit into their larger written compositions and move, delete, or add to them to make their purpose clearer.

Relative to coherence, students can work in small groups to help assess the coherence of one another's written compositions. Because coherence relates to the production of a desired effect, students can read each other's compositions and describe what they understand to be the main idea. The authors then confirm their main ideas or explain what they were actually trying to convey. Students can then work together to identify parts of the paper that work for or against the authors' goals.

Computer Programming

By its very nature, effective computer programming requires cohesion and coherence. Increasingly, lawmakers, people in business, and educators alike have called for STEM (science, technology, engineering, and mathematics) subjects—specifically computer science—to become a larger focus in schools across the United States. This call is often accompanied by statistics related to the expansion of the technology sector and the lack of computer science graduates being produced in the United States (Kohli, 2015). In addition to its societal importance, computer programming (also known as coding) can be a particularly powerful tool to foster the disposition of seeking cohesion and coherence.

Coding requires cohesion and coherence due to the fact that, at their cores, computer programs comprise a series of commands—also known as code—that work together to create step-by-step instructions for a computer to follow. As such, even the smallest error in a line of code can compromise the integrity of the entire program. For example, the command for creating a round shape in the programming language JavaScript is `ellipse(x, y, z, h);`, where x determines the placement of the circle along the x-axis of the screen, y determines the placement of the circle along the y-axis of the screen, z identifies how wide or thin the circle is along the x-axis, and h identifies how tall or short the circle is along the y-axis. If a student wanted to begin to draw the body of a snowman using JavaScript, the student might generate the following code.

```
ellipse(200, 300, 150, 150);

ellipse(200, 175, 100, 100);

ellipse(200, 88, 75, 75);
```

Each preceding line of code creates one circle. Working as a set, the code creates three circles of different sizes stacked on top of one another, with the largest circle at the bottom and the smallest circle on top. However, if the student who wrote this code forgot to include a semicolon following any of the commands or incorrectly identified one of the parameter values, the integrity of the code would be compromised, and it would not function as desired. Thus, the need for cohesion and coherence is inherent to the process of coding, lest the code produced be inefficient or nonfunctional.

Many educators recognize the benefits of coding, yet do not feel qualified to teach it or do not have access to technology teachers who may be able to fill that role. Luckily, most schools have access to this expertise through the use of free online resources aimed at teaching students how to code, a few of which are listed here.

▸ The Beauty and Joy of Computing (http://bjc.berkeley.edu)

▸ Bootstrap (http://bootstrapworld.org)

▸ Codecademy (www.codecademy.com)

▸ CodeHS (https://codehs.com)

▸ CodeStudio (https://studio.code.org)

▸ Edhesive (https://edhesive.com)

▸ Hour of Code (https://hourofcode.com/us)

▸ Mobile CSP (http://mobile-csp.org)

▸ NMSI (https://nms.org)

▸ ScratchEd (http://scratched.gse.harvard.edu/guide)

▸ Tynker (https://tynker.com)

As an example of coding in the classroom, consider Hour of Code, which provides one-hour lessons for students on different aspects of coding. Each Hour of Code contains instructional and interactive videos called *talk-throughs* that directly explain how to write code for a specific action, such as creating a circle or shading the interior of a shape a certain color. Students can pause the videos and manipulate the code onscreen to see how commands and their outcomes are related. For example, in the first talk-through of Khan Academy's 2015 Hour of Code (Khan Academy, 2015), students learn how to make a large circle using JavaScript's ellipse function and how the parameters of the function change its shape, size, and location. The video then uses multiple ellipse functions with different parameter values to draw an open mouth and eyes on the initial circle, thus making a system of single commands that create a specific outcome (in this talk-through's case, a face drawn with circles).

Following each talk-through, students apply their knowledge in a coding challenge. During the coding challenge, students generate their own code for a specific outcome, and pop-up windows appear when the code is nonfunctioning, which reminds students to check for cohesion and coherence. Upon completing the challenge, students can move on to the next talk-through in the sequence. At the end of the hour, students combine the skills learned in previous talk-throughs in a creative project, such as drawing a colored self-portrait.

Challenge Competitions

There are a number of competitions that require students to work in teams to create products with interacting parts. Often these competitions require that students design and build devices that complete specific tasks or create intricate performances that adhere to specific guidelines. A number of such competitions are listed in table 3.5.

Table 3.5: Challenge Competitions

Program	Description
Odyssey of the Mind	Students solve problems or complete tasks that fall into one of five categories: (1) mechanical or vehicle—designing a device that performs a task or overcomes an obstacle, (2) classics—completing a task related to classic literature, art, or architecture, (3) performance—performing something that meets guidelines and relates to a theme, (4) structure—creating a structure that holds as much weight as possible, or (5) technical performance—creating a performance based on a device.
Destination Imagination	Teams of students choose one of seven challenges each year and work together without the help of adults to create a solution that best solves the requirements of the challenge. At the end of the season, teams of students from around the state, country, and world compete against one another.
InvenTeams	Students compete to win up to $10,000 based on an invention of their own design that addresses their choice of a real-world problem.
Club Invention	Students must address problems and design solutions to prompts based on a themed adventure (for example, determining a way to storm a castle in the Middle Ages or designing a shelter on a strange planet while trying to repair a spaceship).
GEAR Robotics	Students design and build a robot that accomplishes specific game objectives in a given amount of time using only materials provided.
FIRST LEGO League	Students design and build a robot that addresses a real-world issue (such as recycling or energy) out of LEGOs and competes against other robots on a playing field.
FIRST Robotics Competition	Students have six weeks to design and build a robot that completes a specific engineering challenge, and then meet at the regional and national levels to compete against one another.
Botball	Students receive a standardized kit of parts to create and program an autonomous robot designed to complete a specific objective (for example, sorting items by color or gathering specific items).
4-H Robotics	Students complete hands-on activities and projects, including designing specific devices related to robotics, rocketry, environmental science, agricultural science, biotechnology, and veterinary science.

To illustrate, consider Odyssey of the Mind. In this competition, teams of up to seven students create solutions for one of five given problems over a period of weeks or months. Each of the five problems addresses one of the following categories: mechanical or vehicle (designing a device that performs a task or overcomes an obstacle), classics (completing a task related to classic literature, art, or architecture), performance (performing something that meets guidelines and relates to a theme), structure (creating a structure that holds as much weight as possible), or technical performance (creating a performance based on a device). For example, the following prompt was previously used as a problem for the technical performance category:

> For this problem, teams will design, build, and drive a vehicle that will travel a course where a student driver attempts to complete tasks in order to pass a driver's test. The vehicle will travel using one propulsion system and then travel in reverse using a different propulsion system. The vehicle will encounter a directional signal and have a Global Positioning System (GPS) that talks to the driver. The team will create a theme for the presentation that incorporates the vehicle, a driver's test, a student, and the talking GPS.
>
> Cost limit: $145 USD. (Odyssey of the Mind, 2013)

These problem prompts are complex and allow for creativity on the part of the students. Because of their complexity, students must continually evaluate the coherence and cohesion of their solutions and determine the degree to which they effectively address a given problem.

The Growth Mindset

Another important element of self-actualization is the cultivation of the *growth mindset*. This refers to the belief that intelligence is changeable (Dweck, 2006). Specifically, individuals with a growth mindset believe that hard work can increase their intelligence and abilities. The opposite of a growth mindset is a *fixed mindset*, which involves the belief that certain abilities are innate and unchangeable—individuals either have them or they don't. These differing mindsets lead people to set different goals and respond differently to challenges. Those with fixed mindsets tend to choose activities and goals that highlight their pre-existing "innate" abilities. They also tend to give up more quickly in new and challenging situations. Individuals with growth mindsets tend to choose goals that help them learn and develop new skills (even if they might fail initially) and are often more persistent and optimistic about challenging tasks (Marzano & Pickering, 2011). Clearly, the growth mindset tends to correlate with the effective mental dispositions described previously in this chapter (page 35).

Fortunately, mindsets are not permanent—people can cultivate a growth mindset even if they originally had a fixed mindset regarding a specific ability (or vice versa; Dweck, 2006). Thus, the first step in helping students develop the growth mindset is providing information about and examples of both growth and fixed mindsets. Teachers can define each mindset and give students examples of the types of beliefs associated with each, as described in table 3.6.

Teachers can discuss the beliefs in table 3.6 with students and ask them to explain why specific statements are indicative of either the fixed or growth mindset. After students understand the differences between the growth and fixed mindsets, teachers can ask them to identify which mindset they personally tend to exhibit in different scenarios. There are a number of assessments to this end (https://www.mindsetworks.com/assess). It is also useful to note that a person might have a growth mindset for some aspects of life but a fixed mindset about others. For example, an individual could have a growth mindset about an academic or intellectual ability but a fixed mindset about athletic ability. In this case, a person might believe that academic ability can be improved through studying and hard work but that people are either athletically gifted or not.

Table 3.6: Beliefs Associated With Growth and Fixed Mindsets

Growth Mindset	Fixed Mindset
• There are some subjects in school I try harder at than others. • Failing can be okay if I learn something. • Some of my peers try harder than I do. • If I wanted to be smarter in certain subjects or better at certain activities, I could try harder. • I know I can do well at anything if I really want to.	• There are some subjects in school that I am good at and some that I am not good at. • Failing is never okay. • Some of my peers are smarter than I am. • Sometimes trying harder helps, but it doesn't really change how smart you are. • I know I can do well at the things I'm good at.

Source: Adapted from Marzano & Heflebower, 2012.

As students identify the mindset they tend to exhibit, they can begin experimenting with changing from the fixed mindset to the growth mindset in specific areas of their lives (Scott & Marzano, 2014). For example, a student who has a fixed mindset about athletic ability might consciously examine the thoughts that occur while she engages in physical activities. The student might notice certain thoughts frequently arise, such as "I'm just not good at physical things" and "Everyone is better at this than I am." The student could then relate these thoughts to the presence of a fixed mindset and try to actively alter her inner dialogue (see Thought Revision, page 67). For example, the student might try to replace thoughts related to the fixed mindset with statements indicative of a growth mindset, such as "I don't try hard enough when I'm engaged in physical challenges" or "If I want to get better, I need to keep trying."

The power of examining specific mindsets is enhanced if students are provided with information about *neuroplasticity*—the brain's ability to adapt and change—and examples of people who developed abilities that they "weren't supposed to have." Online programs like Brainology (https://www.mindsetworks.com) can be very helpful to this end. Brainology is a research-based, online program that teaches students about the growth mindset; brain structure, function, and behavior; and the brain's relationship to emotion, learning, and memory. For example, one video in the Brainology curriculum provides students with research about how the brain develops skills through repetition (for example, musicians' brains are often more developed in the area that controls finger dexterity). After watching the video, teachers could prompt students to relate this knowledge to their own academic and personal lives or to research other examples of how brain structure can change based on experience.

Once students are thoroughly familiar with growth and fixed mindsets, teachers can ask them to determine which mindset they use when they encounter challenges in class. For example, assume students need to study for an upcoming assessment. A teacher can ask students to create study guides and then discuss their content in small groups to identify gaps in their knowledge. The teacher could then bring the class together as a whole to clarify areas of confusion and ask students about their proficiency with the content using a simple voting technique (for example, "Raise your hand if you feel comfortable with the material" or "Raise your hand if you feel prepared for the assessment"). During this time, the teacher could also remind students of the difference between the fixed mindset and the growth mindset and the outcomes and characteristics of each (for example, students who already feel negatively about the assessment are probably using a fixed mindset, as there is still time to become comfortable with the material). After reiterating the control students have over their growth, the teacher could hold additional help sessions for students and encourage them to attend. If possible and with their permission, the teacher might point out students in class who regularly come to help sessions, especially if those students are known for their academic performance in class.

Possible Selves

The term *possible selves* (Markus & Nurius, 1986) refers to the range of ways a person might imagine himself or herself in the future. Possible selves can encompass potential outcomes that are both positive and negative in nature, and both are important in terms of their effects on an individual. Positive possible selves make people more open to setting and pursuing long-term goals—they are a key motivator. For example, if an individual is interested in becoming an astronaut and identifies that as a possible self, he will probably be more willing to study tirelessly in high school to ensure that he can attend a college with a good astrophysics program. On the other hand, negative possible selves often serve as deterrents for behaviors that do not serve an individual. For example, if an individual recognizes that one of her negative possible selves includes dropping out of high school, she might choose to engage in behaviors that avoid the realization of that possible self. Considering that "an individual's repertoire of possible selves can be viewed as the cognitive manifestation of enduring goals, aspirations, motives, fears, and threats" (Markus & Nurius, 1986, p. 954), individuals' possible selves directly inform their goals related to self-actualization.

While there are merits to both types of possible selves, students may be limited in the range of positive possible selves they can imagine for themselves. For example, if a student has been told throughout his life that academics are not his strength and he should focus on learning a trade, his possible selves probably would not include becoming a biologist, even if that occupation seems interesting to him. If a female student has been brought up in a culture where women are expected to be homemakers, her possible selves may not include becoming a successful businesswoman. Fortunately, limitations on students' potential selves are by no means permanent. As Shawna Lee and Daphna Oyserman (2009) noted, "Perhaps the most important message that educators can take from the research on possible selves is that possible selves are malleable and can be influenced by intervention to enhance the content of possible selves."

As such, teachers can encourage students to consider the full range of possible selves available to them, which can be expanded by learning about previously unknown possibilities. In other words, awareness of opportunities open to them or people similar to them who have gone on to achieve great things can cause students to widen their range of possible selves. Teachers can also use the following activities, adapted from *Managing the Inner World of Teaching* (Marzano & Marzano, 2015), to further cement the idea that students' possible selves are not outside the realm of possibility.

> ▸ **Accomplishment introductions:** Ask students to introduce themselves in a way that indicates something they would like to accomplish. Students might think of people who have accomplished similar goals and then incorporate these people's names into their own. For example, if a student named Jake wanted to be a star quarterback someday, he might introduce himself as Jake Manning (in recognition of Peyton Manning, former star football quarterback in the NFL) for this exercise.

- ▸ **Informational interviews:** Help students contact adults in their communities whom have accomplished similar goals. For example, a student who wants to run her own business someday might use a list of female-owned businesses to find individuals who can advise her on how to pursue her goals. A student who wants to become a nurse might reach out to a local hospital or doctor's office to ask for an interview or the opportunity to shadow a practitioner for a few hours.

- ▸ **Life images:** Ask students to find pictures of individuals doing activities that relate to their possible selves. For example, students might search in magazines or online for images of notable individuals in their desired fields, such as astronauts in orbit, scientists in research laboratories, singers in front of large crowds, or athletes holding championship trophies. Students might also collect photos of individuals engaging in activities at which they wish to become better. This activity is also useful because the collected pictures serve as powerful visual reminders for students to continue working toward their goals.

- ▸ **Possible selves research:** Ask students to find information about what is required to become their desired possible selves. For example, a student who wants to become a restaurant owner and chef might research how to operate a successful business, which culinary schools are best for their preferred type of cuisine, and how others became established in the service industry. A student who wants to become a teacher might research what jobs or volunteer opportunities are available to gain experience working with children or teens.

Teachers can use brainstorming activities to further expand the range of possible selves students imagine for themselves. In such activities, teachers identify a timeline, which can range from six months to several years, and ask students to generate possibilities of who they could become in that time. Teachers can note that while possible selves do not need to be solely positive, for the purpose of this activity, it is best if students primarily focus on what they would like to achieve. This practice, in and of itself, is a powerful tool that forces students to consider what they see for themselves in the future. Once brainstorming is complete, teachers can ask students to choose the possible selves that they find most exciting or inspiring. For example, consider a student who lists that he could become a nurse, archaeologist, athlete, writer, or car salesman in the future. In this case, the student might decide that of all these options, he would most like to become an archaeologist and identifies that as his ideal or most desirable possible self.

It is also important to note that possible selves should not just be limited to students' perceptions of themselves in terms of their careers or personal lives. Rather, having students recognize the multiplicity of possible selves related to their academic success (or failure) can also be a powerful tool in terms of motivating students in the classroom. In the beginning of the year, teachers can ask students to write letters to themselves for them to read again at the end of the year. Teachers can specify content for students to cover in the letters or allow students freedom in what they write. If teachers do want to provide parameters for this activity, they can use the following questions to prompt letters focused on academics and school itself.

- ▸ What is one goal for yourself in this class?

- ▸ What is one thing you'd like to be able to say about your growth during this school year?

- ▸ What is something you are nervous about in this upcoming year?

- ▸ What is something you want to learn in this class?

- ▶ What is one thing you think you will do well in during this class?

- ▶ Over the course of this year, what is one thing you're looking forward to?

- ▶ Over the course of this year, what is one thing you'd like to improve?

Teachers should let students know whether or not they intend to read their letters once they are turned in. If the letters will remain unread, teachers should store them in a safe place until the end of the year, at which point they can return the letters to students. If teachers decide to read students' letters, they should use the information within as a way to inform their interactions with students. For example, if a student identifies a specific academic goal for himself in his letter, a teacher could focus on praising the student on his progress toward that goal.

Once students determine their ideal possible selves, teachers can use the seven-step personal project process (page 56) to guide students through personal goal setting. Students can also coordinate the work they do related to possible selves with the work they do toward the cultivation of specific mental dispositions (page 35) or the growth mindset (page 50).

Personal Goal Setting

Asking students to set personal goals for themselves in class provides them with direct experiences of self-actualization. Goal-setting activities can also provide perfect venues for practicing the following mental dispositions, as described previously.

- ▶ Pushing the limits of knowledge and skills (page 36)

- ▶ Generating and pursuing standards of excellence (page 36)

- ▶ Seeking incremental steps (page 36)

Students' goals may be nonacademic or academic in nature. The pursuit of academic goals encourages students to take ownership of their educational experience and provides tangible practice for setting, modifying, and working toward goals in a controlled classroom setting. It also requires students to consider what they hope to get out of their education. An example of an academic goal might be achieving a specific grade by the end of a class (or, if using proficiency scales, see The Growth Mindset, page 50). Nonacademic goals, on the other hand, often require a degree of introspection in terms of who students are, what they are interested in, what they are good at, and who they would like to become (see Possible Selves, page 52). Examples of nonacademic goals might include becoming a certified lifeguard, getting into a college with a good engineering program, or running a marathon. While academic goals can overlap with nonacademic ones, academic goals generally relate directly to coursework and can be achieved over a semester or school year. In contrast, nonacademic goals involve students' thinking about their lives outside of the classroom and can be achieved over a range of timeframes.

Regardless of the nature of students' goals, the importance of goal setting derives from the central role students have in determining what their goals will be. As such, goals should relate to topics that students are actually interested in pursuing or exploring. Here, we discuss four ways to incorporate personal goal setting into the classroom: (1) SMART goal setting, (2) personal projects, (3) genius hour, and (4) TED-Ed Clubs.

SMART Goal Setting

While personal goal setting is an empowering classroom tool when successful, such activities may backfire if students do not select appropriate goals. Students' ability to set appropriate goals often varies: some students may be naturally adept at articulating goals they can effectively work toward, while others may struggle to set goals that are likely to be successful. As such, it is beneficial for students to understand the characteristics of a useful goal. To this end, teachers can introduce students to the concept of SMART goals (Conzemius & O'Neill, 2002, 2014).

As Anne E. Conzemius and Jan O'Neill (2002, 2014) said:

> SMART goals are:
>
> S = Strategic and specific
> M = Measurable
> A = Attainable
> R = Results oriented
> T = Time bound (p. 5)

Teachers can use this acronym to remind students of the characteristics of effective goals. For example, an example of a non-SMART goal is, "I will get a good grade in this class." This goal, while attainable, isn't particularly specific, measurable, rigorous, or trackable considering the personal subjectivity of the word *good*. Instead, a SMART version of the same goal might be, "I will get a final grade of at least a B in this class, and my participation grade and homework grade will be at least an A." With this latter goal, the student has a concrete and obtainable objective whose progress can be easily measured throughout the course. Once students identify their own personal SMART goals, teachers can meet with them to understand why they chose their specific goals, ensure their goals meet specific parameters, and help with revision, if necessary.

After students have set appropriate goals, they can create action plans that outline how they will achieve their goals. As defined by Loriana Romano, Lisa Papa, and Elita Saulle (n.d.), an effective action plan will "not only include a set timeline and end date, but also 'mini' goals to reach along the way." Teachers should remind students that any smaller goals in their action plans should similarly be SMART. Figure 3.14 shows a potential action plan for a student who wants to complete a short-term goal of achieving score 3.0 proficiency for a unit (for more information on proficiency scales, see The Growth Mindset, page 50).

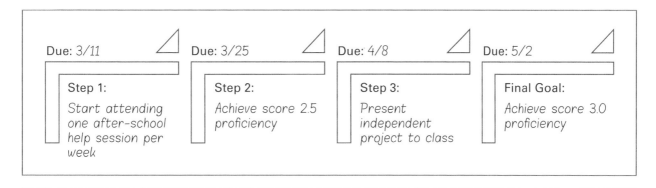

Due: 3/11

Step 1:
Start attending one after-school help session per week

Due: 3/25

Step 2:
Achieve score 2.5 proficiency

Due: 4/8

Step 3:
Present independent project to class

Due: 5/2

Final Goal:
Achieve score 3.0 proficiency

Figure 3.14: Example action plan.

To ensure that students are on the right track, teachers can occasionally check in to help them compare their action plans to their actual progress. Teachers should encourage students to modify their goals and action plans as needed and to seek out any additional help they may need. Teachers could also modify the seven-step process for personal projects as a means to guide students through the development of their own action plans. After the time outlined in their action plans elapses, teachers can ask students to reflect on the goal-setting process and their feelings about their progress.

Personal Projects

Personal projects are another means to help students engage in personal goal setting. These projects require that students consider what they would like to accomplish in the future, research what they need to do to achieve these goals, and determine a plan of action that moves them forward. A common form of the personal project is the *capstone project*, which generally occurs during students' final year of middle or high school. A capstone project often demonstrates a student's knowledge about a specific topic, requires reflection on the learning journey, and terminates in the presentation of a physical product that serves as evidence of the student's knowledge gain. Examples of final products include pictures, pamphlets, charts, lesson plans, movies, paintings, lyrics, programs, itineraries, cookbooks, and so on. Capstone projects can also include oral presentations to classmates or review boards composed of school staff and community members.

While capstone projects are generally designed for older students, teachers can implement personal projects in classrooms of all age levels. After assigning personal projects, regardless of the age of students, teachers should consider working on their own personal projects alongside students. This allows teachers to share their own progress and to model appropriate behaviors at each step. To address the issue of time, many teachers have found creative ways to incorporate personal projects into their classes. Ideas include utilizing advisory or homeroom time, dedicating one day a month to work on personal projects, capitalizing on time at the end of the quarter or semester or before breaks, or using extra time after students finish their work.

Here, we present a seven-step process—with guiding questions—to help students develop their own personal projects during class.

1. **Identify a goal:** What do I want to accomplish?
2. **Identify mentors and role models:** Who else has accomplished this goal? Who will support me?
3. **Research the necessary experiences and skills:** What skills and resources will I need to accomplish my goal?
4. **Engage in behavior analysis:** What will I have to change in order to achieve my goal?
5. **Create short-term and long-term plans:** What is my plan for achieving my goal?
6. **Take small steps:** What small steps can I take right now?
7. **Reflect on the process:** How have I been doing? What have I learned about myself?

Here, we discuss each step.

Identify a Goal

Teachers begin by asking students to identify personal goals they are passionate about pursuing. For some students, the idea of setting sizable long-term goals may be new or even frightening. One way to remove students' self-doubt or fear of failure is to remove the consequences from goal identification—that is, ask students to imagine what they would do if they knew they could not fail. Questions like this get to the core of how students imagine themselves currently or in the future. As mentioned previously, possible selves also play a large role in the goals students select for themselves, and activities to expand students' ranges of possible selves (page 52) might be employed at this time. Teachers can also discuss the benefits of self-actualizing behavior and the consequences of not pursuing personally relevant goals during this step.

Once students have an idea of the goals they might want to achieve, teachers ask students to choose one specific goal to focus on. These goals might be career oriented (for example, becoming an environmental lawyer, getting into a certain college, or playing guitar professionally) or project oriented (for example, inventing a more efficient engine, establishing a nonprofit organization, or publishing a novel). Teachers should not put limitations on the content of student-identified goals, though teachers can and should remind students to generate goals that are SMART (page 55). To illustrate, a student may decide she wants to take her creative writing more seriously. An example of a SMART goal to guide her personal project might be "I want to write and prepare a collection of short stories for submission to publishers by the end of the year." A non-SMART goal this same student might identify is "I want to be a writer," which clearly lacks the specificity of the former goal.

Identify Mentors and Role Models

The second step of the process requires that students identify role models and mentors to whom they can look for inspiration and support. Before students identify these figures, however, teachers should clearly define both terms: a *role model* is someone who has accomplished a similar goal and serves as an inspiration and reminder that a goal is possible, whereas a *mentor* provides support and advice. Role models could be dead or alive, and students may or may not know them personally. Students commonly select celebrities, athletes, historical figures, experts, and politicians as role models. Mentors, on the other hand, must be easily accessible to students, as their role dictates that they should provide advice and encouragement and connect students to necessary resources. For example, the student who wants to become a writer might identify Toni Morrison, Virginia Woolf, and Margaret Atwood as role models because they are all successful female novelists. The student's mentor, however, might be a teacher, family member, or other adult in the community with whom she has regular contact. After selecting role models and mentors, students should collect information about them including what they have achieved, the challenges they faced, the support they received, and the traits and mental dispositions they exhibited. Such research can reinforce the idea that self-actualizing behavior tends to foster specific positive characteristics. Students can also work in groups to compare notes and identify the traits of self-actualized individuals, as outlined previously in the chapter (page 30).

During this step, teachers can emphasize the importance of support from others, as few great achievements have been brought about by a single person working alone. When discussing the importance of support, teachers can describe people who required direct help from others to achieve their goals, such as political candidates, and people who relied on the emotional support of friends and family as they worked toward their goals, such as first-generation college graduates. Teachers should also ensure that students understand the following aspects of support.

▸ Support does not always come in the form of positive encouragement. Support can also come in the form of constructive criticism.

▸ Supporters are motivated by one's effort, enthusiasm, and commitment to a goal. If a person does not try very hard to reach his or her goals, his or her supporters will quickly lose incentive to help.

> ▶ Support does not mean that the supporters do all the work; the person trying to reach the goal should do the bulk of the work. In turn, if supporters offer advice, the individual can decide whether or not to follow that advice.

> ▶ Support can come from many different people who provide many different types of support.

Teachers might ask students to identify other individuals in their lives—in addition to their mentors—who can support them and the roles that these individuals could play.

Research the Necessary Experiences and Skills

The third step of personal projects requires that students research what they need to do in order to achieve their goals. This step is particularly important as it marks a discrete shift from inspirational—that is, students recognizing their goals are achievable—to practical—that is, students determining how to create their desired outcomes. To guide this research, students could first analyze the biographies of their role models to get a better idea of the paths others have taken to achieve similar goals. This research may start off broad but should eventually narrow to a list of concrete educational and experiential requirements as well as necessary mental or physical skills. For example, the student who wants to become a writer might identify graduation from college as necessary schooling and publication in writing journals as a necessary accomplishment. Teachers can remind students of the diversity of paths that people take that end in the accomplishment of similar goals and use this to further determine necessary experiences and skills.

Engage in Behavior Analysis

During the fourth step of personal projects, teachers can ask students to consider what aspects of their current behavior need to change if they are to accomplish their goals. Because students have already determined necessary experiences and skills, they can use the knowledge gained in previous steps to analyze discrepancies between where they are currently and where they would like to be. Once students have considered their current experience or skill levels, they can begin to connect their desired experiences and skills to their current behaviors. In terms of behavior analysis, teachers can ask students to determine behaviors that will help them achieve their goals and the behaviors that directly act against these goals. During this step, teachers can reiterate that success requires hard work and that rarely do people live up to their potential by accident. However, as teachers broach this topic, they should consider their tone, as behavior analysis is meant to be realistic rather than discouraging.

To illustrate the process of behavior analysis, consider a teacher asking students to identify activities that do not benefit them. If the student with the goal of becoming a writer wishes she had more time to read, the teacher could ask the student to identify activities that compose her day. The teacher could then ask the student to explain the role each of these activities plays in her life, why she engages in each of them repeatedly, and whether she would prefer to read in lieu of one of them. Depending on the student's justification for each, the teacher might suggest that she cut back on less important activities to make time for activities that work toward her goal. Teachers can take this activity one step further by asking students to consider how unproductive behaviors might affect the possibility of achieving their goals over longer periods of time. Teachers can also provide students with a worksheet like the one in figure 3.15 to facilitate this process. Visit **marzanoresearch.com/reproducibles** for a blank reproducible version of this form.

Goal: *Attend a top engineering school for college*			
Necessary experiences and skills	**Current status**	**What can I do now?**	**What will I have to do in the future?**
2100+ SAT score	*Haven't started*	*Register for the PSAT.*	*Buy SAT prep books, maybe take a class, and take practice tests.*
AP mathematics and science classes	*Taking honors geometry and biology*	*Devote extra time to studying these subjects.*	*Take honors chemistry and trigonometry.*
Engineering-related extracurricular activities	*None*	*Join the robotics club.*	*Become a student leader in robotics club and maybe join programming club.*

Figure 3.15: Behavior analysis worksheet.

Create Short-Term and Long-Term Plans

In step five, teachers ask students to create concrete and detailed plans about how they will reach their goals. An example action plan is listed in figure 3.14 (page 55). Students may want to develop deadlines for the completion of each step as well. Thus, it may be easier for students to plan backward chronologically—each student chooses a date in the future by which he or she wants to have accomplished a specific goal and works backward from that point, indicating significant milestones and when they will be completed. Some of the events on the timeline will be the accomplishments, education, and experiences that students identified previously. These timelines might also incorporate necessary behaviors, such as "I will limit my time on social media to an hour so I can read for an hour each night by this date" or "I will write an hour a day, four days per week."

Take Small Steps

One key aspect of the short-term and long-term plans students generate during the previous step is that they also serve as a kind of declaration or promise that holds students accountable. Thus, during step six, teachers can ask students to take small actions identified in their plans that help them work toward their larger goals. This also enables students to begin their work immediately—while the project is still a focus in class—even if their goals may take many years to accomplish. To further enhance accountability, teachers could have students share their plans, or at least the steps they will be immediately taking toward their goals, with small groups or the entire class. Teachers can find time to meet with students after a set period of time to assess their progress. Teachers might also find it helpful to pair students with *accountability buddies* and have these pairs meet regularly to discuss the actions they are taking.

Reflect on the Process

For the final step of personal projects, students reflect on their progress relative to their short-term and long-term goals. Teachers can guide students through general reflection using the following questions.

▸ What have I been doing well?

▸ What can I do better in the future?

▸ What have I learned about myself so far?

These questions help students think about their progress and themselves in a general way. Teachers might also ask students the following questions so they can re-evaluate their plans and timelines.

▸ "Which parts of the project have gone according to plan?"

▸ "Which parts of the project have not gone as planned? Did anything happen that I did not expect?"

▸ "Do I need to change any of my steps or deadlines? Do I need to add or delete any steps?"

▸ "Have I achieved my short-term plans or small steps? If so, do I need to modify my short-term plans?"

Teachers should also emphasize that plans frequently need adjustment and that this is not a sign of failure. Rather, teachers can note that plans frequently do not work out as anticipated and that being flexible is not only appropriate but necessary when pursuing long-term goals. Particularly, if a goal is set for the distant future, teachers can reiterate that students should repeat this step—evaluating progress, adjusting plans, and setting new short-term goals—until they achieve their long-term goals. Teachers should encourage students to learn how to evaluate themselves independently as well, as this skill will be necessary if they wish to continue working toward their goals after personal projects end in class.

Genius Hour

Genius hour involves setting aside time in the school day for students to explore their own interests. The premise of genius hour originated at Google, which allows its employees to spend 20 percent of their time working on any project they want. The company considers this time valuable to the well-being of its employees, citing that when employees work on things that interest them, their all-around productivity increases. Using that same philosophy, teachers can choose to integrate genius hours into their own classrooms. As explained by Chris Kesler (2013):

> The same genius hour principles apply in the classroom as they do in the corporate environment. The teacher provides a set amount of time for the students to work on their passion projects. Students are then challenged to explore something to do a project over that they want to learn about. They spend several weeks researching the topic before they start creating a product that will be shared with the class/school/world. Deadlines are limited and creativity is encouraged. Throughout the process the teacher facilitates the student projects to ensure that they are on task.

Depending on the teacher, guidelines for genius hour may vary. However, before they institute genius hour, teachers should consider the following questions.

▸ How much time will I allocate for genius hour? Where will I find this time during the week?

▸ What parameters will I establish related to group work? Is it acceptable? Will there be a limit on the size of a group?

▶ What is the end product students are working toward during genius hour? How will they present what they have been working on?

▶ What is my imagined timeline for genius hour? How will I get students to adhere to this timeline while still creating their own deadlines? What will I do if students do not meet set deadlines?

▶ To what degree will I be involved in students' projects? How often will I check in on their progress or make sure they are on task? To what degree will I provide assistance?

After considering these questions, it may be helpful to note that most teachers ask that students set their own goals and learn to adapt to missed deadlines independently, as one of the most powerful aspects of genius hour may be its ability to teach students how to fail. However, teachers should not just leave students to their own devices during this time. Regular check-ins are encouraged, though teachers should operate more as a resource than instructor to students.

TED-Ed Clubs

Most educators and students are familiar with TED Talks, which are experts' short presentations on interesting and culturally relevant ideas on various topics. While adults traditionally write TED Talks and aim them at adult audiences, teachers can modify the concept for classroom use and should not underestimate the power of such presentations. To introduce students to TED Talks, teachers explain what TED Talks are, if students are unfamiliar. After teachers have the class watch a few TED Talks, students can work independently or in small groups to determine their key characteristics. For example, students might identify that many of the presentations have interesting graphics or that speakers use humor to keep their audiences interested. Teachers may also find it helpful to ask students why TED Talks are so engaging, even if the topics may not be the most traditionally interesting to listeners, or how speakers connect their talks to larger themes related to the human experience. Teachers can also ask students about the effect speakers' passion for their subjects have on viewers' perception of and interest in their presentations.

After analyzing the characteristics of successful TED Talks, teachers can inform students that they will be expected to create their own presentations on topics they find interesting. These presentations should be three to five minutes in length and mimic the characteristics of an actual TED Talk. The topics students choose should be personally relevant to them and do not have to be academic in nature. Teachers should set aside time during class for students to work on their presentations. Teachers may also find it helpful to create their own TED Talks and present them first to make the assignment seem less intimidating for students. After students have had time to create their own presentations, one or two students can present each class period over the course of multiple weeks, or teachers might host all of the talks during one or two class periods. Teachers may also choose to apply to become an official TED-Ed Club, which is the school version of TED Talks. Regardless of whether teachers officially register their schools or not, the benefit of these presentations lies in students determining, researching, and creating presentations on topics of importance to them.

Summary and Recommendations

This chapter discussed ways in which teachers can address self-actualization in class. First, we provided strategies related to traits of self-actualization and peak experiences as a means to help students better understand the concept of self-actualization and its characteristics. We discussed effective mental dispositions and the scenarios in which they are deployed and provided strategies to help students practice these dispositions. We examined how to encourage students to cultivate a growth mindset and expand their range of possible selves. Finally, the chapter concluded with specific strategies to encourage successful personal goal setting to help students directly experience self-actualization in the classroom or later in life.

Although teachers can use the strategies in this chapter in a variety of ways, we recommend the following.

▶ At least once a year, provide students with opportunities to set their own goals using strategies related to personal goal setting.

▶ At least once every two weeks, reinforce effective mental dispositions in specific scenarios (for example, asking students to solve a difficult problem to encourage them to stay focused when answers are not immediately apparent).

▶ At least once a month, use strategies related to traits of self-actualization, peak experiences, the growth mindset, or possible selves.

The following scenario depicts how these recommendations might manifest in the classroom.

A third-grade teacher wants to ensure that students are exposed to experiences that encourage self-actualization. The teacher develops a long-term project related to future careers in which students choose a profession of interest, interview local community members, and identify and outline future steps they must complete if they are to join this profession. During the first step of the project, the teacher asks students to brainstorm possible selves and research the necessary knowledge, skills, and experience. The teacher also provides students with examples and activities related to the growth mindset and mental dispositions, specifically those related to working on long-term projects. To conclude the project, the teacher asks students to give oral presentations and create poster boards that summarize their long-term goals and how they plan to achieve them. In addition to this project, the teacher regularly makes connections to traits of self-actualization, effective mental dispositions, and the growth mindset whenever possible in class.

CHAPTER 4

Esteem Within a Community

Esteem relates to the way students think of themselves. It is crucial that teachers help students build esteem, especially when considering students' tendency to pull away from school if their esteem needs go continually unmet. Here, we consider five aspects of esteem within a community: (1) an understanding of esteem, (2) reflection, (3) competence, (4) significance, and (5) recognition.

An Understanding of Esteem

Helping students understand what esteem is and how it manifests is often the first step in building students' esteem. For classroom purposes, teachers can define *esteem* as "the negative or positive attitude that individuals have of themselves" (Stets & Burke, 2014, p. 1). As detailed in chapter 1 (page 6), research defining esteem and its components tends to vary greatly, though it is generally understood that the self or others can source it. Teachers can use discussions of self-concept and traits of esteem to further deepen students' understanding.

Self-Concept

Self-concept is the way individuals perceive themselves, as well as how they believe others view them. Esteem, then, could be likened to the value individuals place on their various self-concepts. Thus, students must understand how they view themselves if they wish to truly assess their esteem.

When teaching students about self-concept, it may be helpful to note that self-concept does not only address students' overarching or global constructs of themselves; rather, we can further break down self-concept into smaller categories. For example, a student might hold the self-concept that he is good at English and bad at athletics. If this student values his abilities in English class, his esteem will likely be higher in this area. If the student prioritizes athletic ability, however, some of his esteem needs will likely go unmet until his self-concept related to athletics improves or the value he places on athletics diminishes.

Teachers can ask students to assess their self-concepts by having them define some of the self-concepts they hold about themselves. Self-concept statements are useful to this end, as they articulate physical or personality traits, abilities, social roles, or abstractions with which an individual identifies. To begin this process, teachers can explain what self-concept is and provide students with examples of self-concept statements like the following.

- ▸ I am tall.
- ▸ I am a lead in the school play.
- ▸ I am an athlete.
- ▸ I am bad at mathematics.
- ▸ I am funny.
- ▸ I am an older brother.

After teachers provide students with example self-concept statements, teachers can ask students to create their own self-concept statements. This may be an appropriate time to note that while some self-concept statements may be relatively permanent (for example, "I am an older brother"), many self-concept statements relate to areas that students can improve through practice (for example, "I am bad at mathematics"). As such, when discussing self-concept and its relationship with esteem, teachers might find time to incorporate conversations about fixed and growth mindsets (page 50) to help students see that their self-concepts, and therefore esteem, can be changed.

As students identify their own self-concepts, teachers can query them about the value they place on each one. To determine areas that build students' esteem, teachers simply identify the positive self-concept statements that students noted they were proud of. For example, if a student listed that she is good at mathematics and identified it as an aspect of herself that she is proud of, a teacher could intuit that this student's mathematics skills are a source of esteem. Teachers can use the information from this exercise to guide their interactions with students.

Traits of Esteem

Much like self-actualization (page 5), there are specific traits that individuals with high esteem tend to develop over time. Similarly, individuals with low esteem tend to repeatedly engage in specific behaviors. Teachers can provide students with a list of such traits, such as those described in table 4.1, to show how esteem affects an individual's disposition.

Table 4.1: Traits Associated With High and Low Esteem

High Esteem	Low Esteem
• Believing in oneself and one's abilities • Feeling comfortable in one's own skin • Knowing and clearly expressing wants and needs • Having the ability to laugh at oneself • Accepting responsibility for actions • Expressing appreciation for and regularly praising others • Making decisions independent of others • Showing ambition and enthusiasm related to interests and goals • Being simultaneously optimistic and realistic • Accepting compliments gracefully • Trying new things and being comfortable with change • Communicating well with others • Acting independently without need for approval from others • Learning from mistakes • Respecting differences between perspectives • Recognizing one's own value • Being humble	• Excessively blaming or criticizing oneself or others • Feeling superior or inferior to others • Compulsively underachieving or overachieving • Not taking responsibility for actions • Frequently feeling victimized or jealous • Dominating others or not sticking up for oneself • Focusing on others' lives (for example, excessive gossiping) • Taking excessive risks or fearing change and risks completely • Being overly negative, or being so positive as to be unrealistic • Being extremely reactionary or lacking in emotion • Constantly comparing oneself to others • Engaging in black-or-white thinking • Having an inability to compromise or needing to always be right • Frequently bragging or lying in conversations • Being overly defensive and combative

Source: Adapted from Harrill, n.d.

After students familiarize themselves with the traits listed in table 4.1, teachers can lead students in discussions about why specific traits might be associated with high or low esteem. Teachers might also ask students about patterns they see to deepen students' understanding of how esteem affects behavior. For example, students may notice that low esteem tends to manifest on the extreme ends of a spectrum, as hyper-aggressive and hyper-passive behaviors are both traditionally symptomatic of low esteem. In relation to this pattern, students could look at where behaviors associated with high esteem fall within that same spectrum. Students might extrapolate that high esteem produces behaviors that tend to be moderate because individuals with high esteem are confident enough to stick up for themselves but not so overly confident that they become domineering. Teachers could also ask students about times they have exhibited behaviors from either list in table 4.1. As students reflect, they may find that they tend to exhibit patterns of behavior associated with low esteem. Teachers should reiterate that this is okay, and express the value of recognizing various negative behaviors as a means to work toward higher esteem.

Reflection

By definition, esteem is a product of one's thinking. As such, being able to identify and edit pessimistic or negative thoughts as they arise may be one of the most powerful tools students have to build their esteem. Here, we discuss two crucial aspects of reflection as they relate to esteem: (1) explanatory style and (2) thought revision.

Explanatory Style

The way students explain different events may be referred to as their *explanatory style*. Students' explanatory styles inform whether they view specific events optimistically or pessimistically. Teachers should note that optimism is critical to esteem, as optimistic students are less likely to let negative events hurt their esteem in a lasting way. On the other hand, pessimistic students may let negative events compound and affect their esteem over time.

Teachers can present students with examples of the effects of different explanatory styles to emphasize the power of optimism. For example, teachers might read students the following paragraph about Matt Biondi, a former Olympic swimmer.

> Matt Biondi was a famous Olympic swimmer who competed during the 1988 Seoul Olympics. After losing his first event by a slim margin, many spectators doubted his ability to rebound. Researcher Martin E. P. Seligman, however, felt fairly confident that Biondi would continue to perform competitively. Seligman, who had previously worked with Biondi, found that the swimmer was in the top quarter of optimistic athletes on his college swim team. In his experiment, in which swimmers on the team were told their racing times were slower than they actually were, Seligman found that the pessimistic swimmers' times became increasingly worse with each trial, while the optimistic swimmers met their potential, or in Biondi's case, became increasingly faster as the experiment continued. As such, Seligman was unsurprised when Matt Biondi went on to win his last five swimming events, as he knew that Biondi's initial failure would only compel the swimmer to work harder later (Seligman, 2006).

After reading this story, teachers might query students about why optimism and pessimism have these effects on performance.

Once students grasp the power of optimism, teachers can define and explain the three dimensions of explanatory style as identified by Martin E. P. Seligman (2006): (1) permanence, (2) pervasiveness, and (3) personalization. *Permanence* refers to the timescale on which an event is viewed—whether it is temporary or permanent. When people have optimistic explanatory styles, they tend to view positive events as permanent and negative events as temporary. *Pervasiveness* describes the degree to which people perceive specific events as influential on the rest of their lives. People with optimistic explanatory styles often consider positive events to be universal—that is, favorable events positively affect other aspects of their lives—and compartmentalize negative events as specific to one area of their lives. Finally, *personalization* involves the degree to which people believe they directly cause events (as opposed to external sources' influence). The beliefs that negative events occur due to something outside of someone's control and positive events occur because of one's own actions tend to be characteristic of an optimistic explanatory style.

To see how explanatory style impacts students, consider two students struggling in the same mathematics class. One student may become exasperated and declare that he will never be good at mathematics—thus showing that he considers struggling in mathematics to be permanent. The other student may also be exasperated but remind herself that after this upcoming test, the class will move on to new and potentially easier content. In other words, the optimistic student would frame the negative event—struggling in mathematics class—as temporary. If both students fail the test, the student with the negative explanatory style might believe that his performance is indicative of his academic ability as a whole. This student might also be overly critical of himself for his poor performance. These two behaviors allude to high pervasiveness and high personalization of negative events respectively, which are characteristic of a pessimistic explanatory style. The optimistic student, on the other hand, might isolate the failed test from her self-concept of her abilities in other classes and recognize that external factors may be partially responsible for her poor test score. In other words, the optimistic student might show low pervasiveness and low personalization of negative events, thereby protecting her academic esteem.

In the previous example, the event that the students attempt to justify—a failed test—is a negative event. Consider explanatory style in terms of a positive event: while high permanence may not be productive when a student encounters a negative event, it is a much more beneficial when a student encounters a positive event. Teachers and students can refer to table 4.2 as a means to understand how the dimensions of explanatory style relate to optimism and pessimism as the nature of an event changes from negative to positive.

Table 4.2: Three Dimensions of Explanatory Style

Dimension	Event Type	Optimistic	Pessimistic
Permanence	*Bad things*	**Temporary:** Temporary circumstances in my life cause the bad things that happen to me.	**Permanent:** Permanent elements of my life cause the bad things that happen to me.
	Good things	**Permanent:** Permanent elements of my life cause the good things that happen to me.	**Temporary:** Temporary circumstances in my life cause the good things that happen to me.
Pervasiveness	*Bad things*	**Specific:** When a bad thing happens in one area of my life, it doesn't negatively affect other parts of my life.	**Universal:** When a bad thing happens in one area of my life, it ruins my whole life.
	Good things	**Universal:** When a good thing happens in one area of my life, it makes my whole life better.	**Specific:** When a good thing happens in one area of my life, it doesn't positively affect other parts of my life.
Personalization	*Bad things*	**External:** A bad thing happened to me because of factors out of my control.	**Internal:** A bad thing happened to me because I didn't do something right.
	Good things	**Internal:** A good thing happened to me because I did something right.	**External:** A good thing happened to me because of factors out of my control.

Source: Marzano & Marzano, 2015, p. 70.

Once students are familiar with the three dimensions of explanatory style and how they relate to optimism and pessimism, students can consider how they have previously reacted to positive and negative events. Students can also be made aware of their personal explanatory styles by taking the short questionnaire in figure 4.1 (page 68). The questionnaire is rather easy to interpret. The first answers always indicate an optimistic explanatory style, and the second answers always indicate a pessimistic explanatory style. Questions 1 and 2 deal with permanence, questions 3 and 4 deal with pervasiveness, and questions 5 and 6 deal with personalization. Students can examine their answers after completing the questionnaire to get a sense of how they tend to explain positive and negative events.

Thought Revision

As students become aware of the power of their thinking, they can begin experimenting with thought revision. *Thought revision* involves the identification of pessimistic thoughts and their replacement with more optimistic ones. When introducing students to this concept, teachers should note to students that thought revision is not a one-time activity but instead is a powerful tool that students can use throughout their lives. Thought revision is described in two steps: (1) thought recognition and (2) thought substitution.

1. **Which of these statements do you find most accurate?**

    a) When something bad happens to me, I think it will be over pretty quickly.

    b) When something bad happens to me, I think it will probably last a long time.

2. **Which of these statements do you find most accurate?**

    a) When something good happens to me, I think it will probably last a long time.

    b) When something good happens to me, I think it will be over pretty quickly.

3. **Which of these statements do you find most accurate?**

    a) When something bad happens to me in one part of my life, it doesn't affect the other parts of my life.

    b) When something bad happens to me in one part of my life, it negatively affects other parts of my life.

4. **Which of these statements do you find most accurate?**

    a) When something good happens to me in one part of my life, everything seems to get better.

    b) When something good happens to me in one part of my life, it doesn't make the other parts of my life better.

5. **Which of these statements do you find most accurate?**

    a) The bad things that happen to me are usually not caused by me.

    b) I usually cause the bad things that happen to me.

6. **Which of these statements do you find most accurate?**

    a) I usually cause the good things that happen to me.

    b) The good things that happen to me are usually not caused by me.

Figure 4.1: Questionnaire on explanatory style.

Thought Recognition

The first step in thought revision involves students becoming aware of their thoughts about themselves or their circumstances and whether they are negative or positive. The dimensions of explanatory style in table 4.2 (page 67) and the questionnaire in figure 4.1 may be helpful to this end. If teachers have chosen not to directly teach students about explanatory style, teachers can use a list of common negative thinking patterns, described in table 4.3, to guide students through the identification of negative thoughts.

Regardless of whether students are reflecting on explanatory style or the negative thinking patterns in table 4.3, the primary goal of this step is to help students become comfortable with recognizing their own patterns of thought. It is also important to note that students should not just focus on recognizing their negative thoughts, though this is a critical skill. Instead, teachers can encourage students to identify both optimistic and pessimistic thought patterns and compare them to one another. Teachers might also ask students to examine their thinking for a twenty-four-hour period. When students return to class, they can report on their experiences through discussion or brief writing exercises. Students could also be asked to keep journals that catalog negative and positive thoughts that occur throughout the day to get a better sense of the degree to which their thoughts are generally positive or negative.

Table 4.3: Common Thinking Errors and Patterns of Negative Thinking

Error	Description
Blaming	Blaming occurs when people start holding others responsible for the negative situations they are in or when they blame themselves for things that are out of their control.
"Should" statements	When people use "should" statements, they are subtly dictating rules about how others should act. This causes anger toward people who do not meet their expectations or guilt when the people using the "should" statements violate their own self-imposed rules.
Polarized thinking	Polarized thinking distorts people's vision of reality by eliminating the middle ground. In other words, people who use polarized thinking tend to see only good or bad and failure or success without seeing improvement or progress.
Catastrophizing	Catastrophizing is a common thinking error in which people tend to expect the worst possible outcome. People who catastrophize often use "what if" statements to verbalize their negative imaginations.
Control fallacies	There are two types of control fallacies: (1) external and (2) internal. The fallacy of external control causes people to feel helpless and see themselves as victims of others or of fate. The fallacy of internal control causes people to feel responsible for the well-being of all the people around them.
Emotional reasoning	Emotional reasoning is when people assume that what they feel emotionally is what is true in reality—for example, when people *feel* useless, they must *be* useless.
Filtering	When people filter, they are unable or unwilling to see the positive aspects of their lives and amplify the negative aspects of their lives.
Entitlement fallacy	The entitlement fallacy occurs when people feel that they shouldn't have to experience discomfort that is a normal part of life (for example, illness, aging, death, loss, and so on) and find it unfair when they do.
Fallacy of fairness	The fallacy of fairness is a common thinking error in which people get upset because they believe they know what is fair, yet other people don't necessarily agree with them.
Mind reading	When people engage in mind reading, they make and act on their own assumptions about what the people around them are thinking or feeling without ever getting confirmation of the validity of those assumptions.
Overgeneralizing	People who overgeneralize conclude that single situations or events are characteristic of all other events. These overgeneralizations are often inherently negative; if something goes wrong once, it will go wrong over and over again.
Personalization	Personalization is when people believe that everything others do or say is a direct reaction to them. These people also regularly compare themselves to others as a way to figure out who's smarter, more handsome, funnier, and so on, and then use these measures as a way to judge themselves.
Fallacy of change	With the fallacy of change, people need others to change in order to be happy. These people ultimately end up pressuring others to do what they want to ensure their happiness.
Global labeling	Global labeling is the practice of generalizing one or two negative qualities into all-encompassing judgments about oneself or others.
Being right	People who fall victim to being right must always be correct and feel they must continually prove their "rightness."
Heaven's reward fallacy	This fallacy is a common thinking error in which people sacrifice for others and secretly keep score. People who do this expect that down the road, their "debts" will be paid off and feel embittered at individuals, the world, or themselves when the reward doesn't come.

Source: Adapted from McKay, Davis, & Fanning, 2011; Turk & Winter, 2006.

Thought Substitution

Once students can recognize their own thought patterns, they can begin modifying their negative thoughts to be more positive—also known as *thought substitution*. Teachers can remind students that negative thoughts are based on individuals' own interpretations. The idea that thoughts are subjective may be a difficult concept for some students to grasp initially, and, as such, teachers can provide examples to illustrate this point. Examples might relate to how students with different explanatory styles might view the same event (page 66) or reframe a belief in multiple ways. Once it seems that students understand that their thoughts are subjective and malleable to some extent, teachers can encourage them to experiment with adapting their negative thoughts to become more positive. However, teachers should also remind students that thought patterns often recur, and that if negative thoughts continue to arise, this by no means points to failure on the part of the students. Rather, teachers can emphasize that thought revision and sustained positive thinking are skills that require ongoing practice. There are a number of thought-substitution strategies that teachers can provide to students, such as those listed here.

- **Expectation checks:** In some cases, expectations (particularly those related to perfectionism) may set up individuals to experience negative thoughts, particularly if the expectations are unrealistic. As such, students can monitor their thoughts to ensure that expectations are realistic.

- **Perspective checks:** Because negative thoughts are subjective, people may lose sight of the reality of a situation. As such, with a perspective check, individuals consider how true their thoughts are and whether their thoughts rely on assumptions or exaggerations.

- **Positive affirmations:** Because patterns of thought can be practiced, students can repeat relevant positive affirmations to encourage the habit of optimistic thinking. For example, a student who repeatedly thinks that she is not liked by others might repeat, "Others like and care about me."

- **Reframing:** When a negative thought occurs, an individual can find a way to reframe it to be more positive. For example, rather than thinking, "This project is going to be a failure," a student might notice this thought and think, "I still have time to make this project a success."

- **Thought cessation:** As a student identifies a negative thought pattern, she should make an effort to stop the thought completely by acknowledging it as subjective. For example, a student who catches herself ruminating on a negative event might acknowledge that she is focusing too much on this thought and then shift her focus elsewhere.

- **Trigger identification:** Frequently, specific stimuli tend to trigger negative thinking. As such, students can analyze negative thought patterns to determine if there are specific people, places, or things that make them more prone to negative thoughts.

After a teacher explains a thought-substitution strategy to students, the teacher can provide students with personal anecdotes regarding its use. For example, a teacher might mention trigger identification as a thought-substitution strategy that has personally helped her—in this case, assume the teacher has a neighbor whose dog barks incessantly. The teacher might explain how, after reflecting on her daily thought patterns, she identified the dog barking as one of her triggers. The teacher can describe how she tends to be irritated after hearing the dog bark and explain that she understands that many of her subsequent negative thoughts are products of her frustration with the dog rather than her actual current circumstances. After providing this example, the teacher might ask students to identify their own triggers, like a specific behavior by a family member or a location that puts them on edge.

In addition to the previous thought-substitution strategies, it may be helpful to teach the process of thought revision concurrently or immediately after teaching students about explanatory style. Thus, students can practice identifying instances in which they have pessimistic explanatory styles and revising their thoughts to be optimistic. After using the questionnaire in figure 4.1 (page 68), teachers can encourage students to try to consciously change any pessimistic-thinking patterns identified by the survey. For example, consider a student who identified that he tends to have high permanence for negative events. If the student finds himself repeatedly thinking, "I'm bad at reading," he might recognize this is a fairly permanent belief—that is, it is unlikely to change. After consulting table 4.2 (page 67), which lists the dimensions of explanatory style, the student might reframe this thought as temporary, as this is the more optimistic way to view the permanence of negative events. Whenever the student catches himself thinking negative thoughts about his reading abilities, the student might actively think, "I'm not bad at reading. I'm just struggling right now, but there is always time for me to improve." Teachers may also find that the process of thought revision pairs nicely with instruction about the growth mindset (page 50).

The beauty of thought revision is that it is useful both inside and outside the classroom. As such, examples should not just be limited to academics. Instead, teachers can provide examples of thought revision being used in extracurricular or social settings to reinforce the idea that thought revision is a transferrable skill that students can use to increase esteem in all aspects of their lives.

Competence

A fairly obvious component of esteem is an individual's sense of *competence*, the capacity to do something well or with skill. One could safely say that a primary goal of education is to build students' competence with specific knowledge or skills. However, while education programs tend to focus on enhancing students' performance on academic tasks, such efforts often fail to recognize the importance of encouraging students' sense of competence as they engage in this learning. For instance, research has shown that students' beliefs about their competence directly affect their performance, motivation, and perception of the value of specific tasks (Ghazvini, 2011; Jacobs, Lanza, Osgood, Eccles, & Wigfield, 2002). Conversely, if students feel incompetent in the classroom, they are more likely to disengage from academic tasks completely as a means to protect their esteem. To avoid these negative outcomes, we recommend teachers emphasize academic growth in their classrooms and consider their responses to struggling students.

Emphasis on Academic Growth

Ultimately, individuals feel competent when they see themselves getting better at something. In a classroom, teachers can design assessments that allow students to observe and track their own progress, thus building their sense of competence and esteem. This approach stands in stark contrast to more traditional grading systems that focus primarily on students' final grades and do not acknowledge student growth. The following five steps can help teachers emphasize academic growth in their classrooms.

1. Create a proficiency scale.

2. Administer a pretest.

3. Use multiple methods of assessment.

4. Have students track their progress.

5. Interact with students about their progress.

Here, we further discuss each step.

Create a Proficiency Scale

Proficiency scales have been used for years (see Marzano, 2000, 2006, 2009, 2010; Marzano & Kendall, 1996; Marzano & Yanoski, 2015; Marzano, Yanoski, Hoegh, & Simms, 2013) to emphasize academic growth. They commonly take the form presented in figure 4.2.

Score 4.0	More complex learning goal	
	Score 3.5	*In addition to score 3.0 performance, partial success at score 4.0 content*
Score 3.0	Target learning goal	
	Score 2.5	*No major errors or omissions regarding score 2.0 content, and partial success at score 3.0 content*
Score 2.0	Simpler learning goal	
	Score 1.5	*Partial success at score 2.0 content, and major errors or omissions regarding score 3.0 content*
Score 1.0	With help, partial success at score 2.0 content and score 3.0 content	
	Score 0.5	*With help, partial success at score 2.0 content but not at score 3.0 content*
Score 0.0	Even with help, no success	

Source: Adapted from Marzano, 2009, p. 67.

Figure 4.2: Generic form of a proficiency scale.

Using the format in figure 4.2, teachers can create proficiency scales that articulate learning goals for each unit of instruction. When creating a proficiency scale, it is often easiest to start with the score 3.0 content, also called the target learning goal. Score 3.0 content represents the content teachers want students to understand by the end of a unit. To illustrate, consider a high school science class learning about stars. The overall goal for the unit might be articulated as follows.

▶ Explain how stars produce energy and elements throughout their life cycles.

This goal would be considered the score 3.0 content or the target learning goal.

Score 2.0 content, the simpler learning goal, would include information or skills that are directly taught and essential for students to know in order to meet the target learning goal. Score 2.0 content typically includes basic terms, details, and processes. In this case, the score 2.0 content might include the following simpler learning goals.

▶ Describe the stages of a star's life cycle.

▶ Explain the differences between types of stars.

After identifying the score 2.0 content, the teacher could then identify the score 4.0 content, or a more complex learning goal. Score 4.0 content involves information and applications that go beyond score 3.0 content.

In this case, the more complex learning goal contains a generic statement that reads as follows.

▸ Make in-depth inferences and applications that go beyond what was taught in class.

This statement can remain generic, which implies that score 4.0 performance is at the discretion of the teacher, or it can contain specific learning targets that identify more advanced content related to the unit. Figure 4.3 depicts how these learning goals would be arranged within a completed proficiency scale.

Score 4.0	The student will: • Make in-depth inferences and applications that go beyond what was taught in class.	
	Score 3.5	*In addition to score 3.0 performance, partial success at score 4.0 content*
Score 3.0	The student will: • Explain how stars produce energy and elements throughout their life cycles.	
	Score 2.5	*No major errors or omissions regarding score 2.0 content, and partial success at score 3.0 content*
Score 2.0	The student will: • Describe the stages of a star's life cycle. • Explain the differences between types of stars.	
	Score 1.5	*Partial success at score 2.0 content, and major errors or omissions regarding score 3.0 content*
Score 1.0	With help, partial success at score 2.0 content and score 3.0 content	
	Score 0.5	*With help, partial success at score 2.0 content but not at score 3.0 content*
Score 0.0	Even with help, no success	

Figure 4.3: Proficiency scale for a high school unit on stars.

While score 2.0 and 3.0 (and in some cases 4.0) content of a proficiency scale is specific to the unit, as shown in figure 4.3, the meaning of some scores remains consistent across all proficiency scales, regardless of their content. Score 0.0 indicates that even with the teacher's help, the student does not understand the content. Score 0.5 indicates that with the teacher's help, the student partially understands the score 2.0 content but not the score 3.0 content. Score 1.0 indicates that with the teacher's help, the student can correctly answer some questions related to both the score 2.0 and score 3.0 content. Score 1.5 indicates that the student independently understands parts of the score 2.0 content but harbors large misconceptions about the score 3.0 content. Score 2.5 indicates that the student understands the score 2.0 content but only partially comprehends the score 3.0 content. Finally, score 3.5 indicates that the student has met the score 3.0 learning target and has partial success with the more complex content at score 4.0.

Administer a Pretest

Once developed, teachers can use proficiency scales as templates to design pretests. Specifically, pretests should have items for the score 2.0, 3.0, and 4.0 content of a proficiency scale. A pretest based on the proficiency scale in figure 4.3 is presented in figure 4.4 (page 74).

Section I:

1. Chronologically arrange the following stages in a star's life cycle from earliest to latest: red giant, protostar, main-sequence star, white dwarf, nebula

2. Explain two differences between main-sequence stars and massive stars.

Section II:

1. Explain how nuclear fusion produces energy at an atomic level.

2. Explain how the stage in a star's life cycle determines the elements the star produces.

Section III:

Choose a star or star system of your choice, and briefly compare and contrast it to the sun.

Figure 4.4: Pretest for unit on stars.

In the pretest in figure 4.4, section I assesses students' knowledge of the score 2.0 content—the simpler learning goal—with questions about types of stars and their life cycles. Section II assesses students' knowledge of the score 3.0 content or the target learning goal. As such, it asks about how stars produce energy and elements over their lifetimes. Finally, section III tests students on content that goes above and beyond the score 3.0 content—in other words, the more complex learning goal. Once a teacher administers the pretest in figure 4.4 to the students in a class, the teacher scores the test to determine the starting level of proficiency for each student. Pretests can be scored using the point method or the response-pattern method.

With the point method, each item on an assessment has a specific number of points that students can possibly earn. For example, in the pretest in figure 4.4, section I might be worth seven points, as students could receive a point for each life cycle stage they correctly order and for each difference they identify between main-sequence and massive stars. Each of the prompts in section II might be worth five points for a total of ten points. Finally, the prompt in section III might be worth eight points, meaning the entire assessment would be worth a total of twenty-five points. Figure 4.5 shows a student's scoring pattern on the pretest shown in figure 4.4, as determined by the point method.

Section	Item Number	Possible Points	Points Earned	Section Percentage
I (Score 2.0)	1	5	5	6/7 = 86 percent
	2	2	1	
II (Score 3.0)	1	5	2	5/10 = 50 percent
	2	5	3	
III (Score 4.0)	1	8	2	2/8 = 25 percent

Figure 4.5: The point method of scoring assessments.

When looking at the scoring pattern presented in figure 4.5, a teacher first examines the responses in the score 2.0 section. The student received six of the seven total points available in section I so the teacher determines that the student is mostly proficient with this content and has earned at least a score of 2.0 on the pretest. In the next section, the teacher determines that the student is not fully proficient with the score 3.0 content because only half of the possible points available in that section were earned. Based on this scoring pattern, the teacher determines that the student has earned a score 2.5—no major errors or omissions regarding score 2.0 content, and partial success at score 3.0 content—as this seems like the most apt description of the student's proficiency. After determining this score, the teacher stops grading the pretest and does not factor in scores from the third section on score 4.0 content.

With the response-pattern method, rather than assigning points to each assessment item, teachers code each response as *correct*, *partially correct*, or *incorrect*. Figure 4.6 shows a student's scoring pattern on the assessment shown in figure 4.4 as determined by the response-pattern method.

Section	Item Number	Correct, Partially Correct, or Incorrect	Section Pattern
I (Score 2.0)	1	C	Correct
	2	C	
II (Score 3.0)	1	C	Partially correct
	2	PC	
III (Score 4.0)	1	I	Incorrect

Figure 4.6: The response-pattern method of scoring assessments.

As shown in figure 4.6, the teacher determined that the student is proficient with all the content in the first section, and, thus, earned at least a score of 2.0. In the second section (on score 3.0 content), the student receives a partially correct score. The teacher can then determine the student is at score 2.5 proficiency because of the student's full proficiency with score 2.0 content and partial proficiency with score 3.0 content.

Use Multiple Methods of Assessment

After an initial pretest, teachers can use multiple methods of assessment to monitor and measure students' progress toward a target learning goal. The following list contains a number of such assessments.

> ▸ **Observations:** With observations, teachers watch and monitor individual student behaviors without directly interacting with the students. Observations are unobtrusive and particularly applicable when teachers want to evaluate students' competence with skills or processes.

> ▸ **Probing discussions:** Probing discussions are verbal interactions between teachers and students. In probing discussions, teachers ask questions of students to gauge their familiarity with specific content.

> ▸ **Student-generated assessments:** With student-generated assessments, students determine ways to provide evidence of their competence with specific content. Students design projects or assessments that they believe show their proficiency at a certain level of a proficiency scale, and teachers determine the degree to which the student-generated assessments address the content correctly.

> ▸ **Traditional tests:** Traditional tests are written assessments. They are similar in nature to the pretest depicted in figure 4.4. They often consist of series of closed-response questions (such as multiple choice questions) and open-response questions (such as essay prompts).

It is important to note that not all students will need the same number of assessments to arrive at their final scores for a unit. For example, a teacher might have a probing discussion with one student during a particular class period and record an assessment score for that student but not for any other students on that day. Furthermore, teachers may need to additionally assess some students, particularly students with half-point scores, to confirm their proficiency status. In contrast, other students may be clearly proficient at a specific level of a scale after only a few assessments.

Have Students Track Their Progress

As assessments are administered, students can and should keep track of their own progress and personal growth as it occurs. This can be done quite easily by teaching students to plot their assessment scores using simple bar or line graphs. Figures 4.7 and 4.8 depict an example of each type.

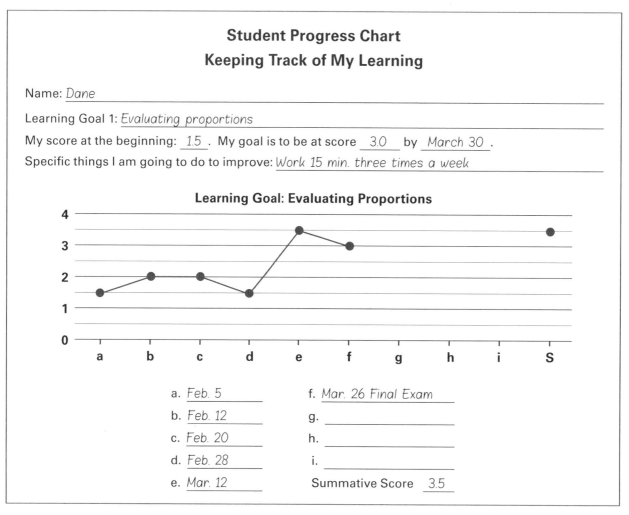

Source: Marzano, 2010, p. 82.

Figure 4.7: Line graph of student progress.

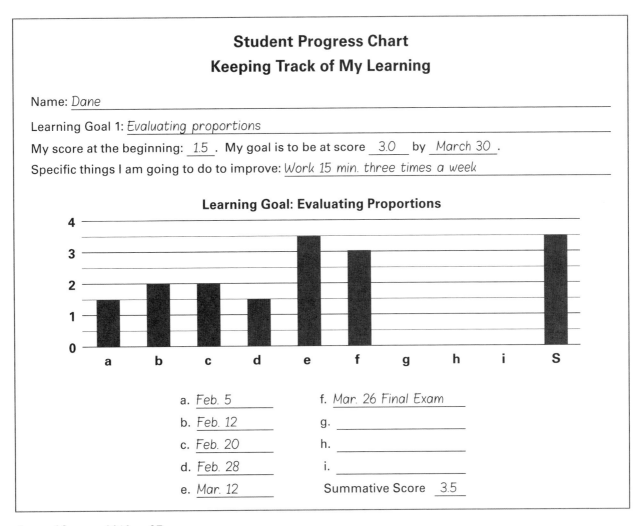

Student Progress Chart
Keeping Track of My Learning

Name: *Dane*

Learning Goal 1: *Evaluating proportions*

My score at the beginning: _*1.5*_ . My goal is to be at score _*3.0*_ by _*March 30*_ .

Specific things I am going to do to improve: *Work 15 min. three times a week*

Learning Goal: Evaluating Proportions

a. *Feb. 5*   f. *Mar. 26 Final Exam*
b. *Feb. 12*   g. _____
c. *Feb. 20*   h. _____
d. *Feb. 28*   i. _____
e. *Mar. 12*   Summative Score *3.5*

Source: Marzano, 2010, p. 87.

Figure 4.8: Bar graph of student progress.

As seen in figures 4.7 and 4.8, both bar graphs and line graphs are appropriate for tracking progress toward a target learning goal in a proficiency scale. With both types of graphs, students plot their scores for the pretest in the first column to represent their initial proficiency with the content. Students continue to plot their scores for assessments as they receive them and mark their dates in the appropriate spaces below the graph. At the end of a unit, students record their summative score in the rightmost column, which represents their final proficiency level with the content. Teachers can then use the summative scores to determine students' *growth scores*—the difference between students' initial scores on a pretest and their current status or, if a unit has come to an end, summative scores. The student whose growth is depicted in figures 4.7 and 4.8 has a growth score of at least 2.0, as the student went from a score of 1.5 on the pretest to a summative score of 3.5.

Interact With Students About Their Progress

As students track their progress, teachers should interact with them about their growth and the factors contributing to or inhibiting it. Teachers might choose to do this in a variety of ways. For more formal interactions, teachers might set aside time during class to meet with students individually to talk about their growth. During these meetings, teachers can also question students about the relevance of the content to their lives, their learning styles and preferences, and other information that can be used to personalize instruction. Alternatively, teachers could periodically engage the class in discussions about the progress of the class as a whole. These discussions provide the perfect vehicle to discuss the growth mindset (page 50) and the importance of effort, as well as to identify and clarify content with which students may be struggling. Teachers might also query students about things they have learned or how it feels to become increasingly familiar and competent with specific content. Teachers should also be aware that they can casually interact with students about their growth by simply writing them short notes or having brief conversations with them in passing or when convenient.

Using proficiency scales and multiple assessments keyed to those proficiency scales also enables recognition and celebration of both current status and growth over time. However, such celebrations, particularly class-wide celebrations, should focus on the progress that has occurred rather than the individual scores of students at the end of a unit. Additionally, teachers could return or ask students to retake their initial pretests to further highlight their growth since the unit began. When academic growth occurs and is tracked and celebrated by teachers, students will start to recognize how their competence increases over time. In turn, recognition of competence is likely to build students' esteem within the classroom.

Response to Struggling Students

Though teachers may emphasize academic growth and progress to build students' sense of competence, inevitably some students will struggle with content presented in class. If such difficulties continue unaddressed, they may negatively affect students' esteem as it pertains to education in a lasting way. There are a variety of strategies teachers can use to aid struggling students before their unmet needs compound into maladaptive behaviors. Here, we address three responses to struggling students: (1) nonjudgmental opportunities for help, (2) failure insulators, and (3) leniency.

Nonjudgmental Opportunities for Help

Struggling students often engage in behaviors that help them avoid embarrassment and protect their esteem. This sometimes manifests as students not seeking academic help, even when this may be the very intervention they need. Fortunately, research has shown that "when students perceive teachers to be . . . less inclined to embarrass them, students are less likely to report that they avoid seeking help, disrupt class, or use projective coping strategies" (Friedel, Marachi, & Midgley, 2002, p. 3). In other words, if opportunities for students to seek help seem nonjudgmental, it is more likely that students will utilize them.

To create nonjudgmental opportunities for help, teachers should consider how they interact with struggling students and the opportunities they offer those students. Teachers should avoid directly identifying specific students who attend mandatory help sessions and be discreet when addressing meetings with those students. Teachers can also offer additional help sessions to all students in a class so that struggling students do not feel singled out. For example, a teacher might create a schedule for open help sessions during lunch periods or before or after school so that students can drop in at times that are convenient for them, regardless of their proficiency with the content. Before an assessment, the teacher might remind the class of extra-help sessions and encourage all students' attendance. Some teachers have also found success in requiring all students to attend at least one extra-help session per semester, incorporating review sessions into class time, or asking students to articulate their questions about content for homework. If students with low academic self-concepts see students they perceive as academically competent asking questions or holding misconceptions about the content, they may feel less embarrassed about needing help. Teachers could also consider using the following strategies to create nonjudgmental opportunities for help.

▶ **Acknowledging content as challenging:** One reason students do not seek help is that they are afraid to admit that they are struggling in the first place. Teachers can mention instances when they have struggled to learn content or acknowledge how and why certain content is confusing. Teachers can also use affirmations like "Good question!" to show that students' questions are legitimate and necessary.

▶ **Establishing a place with extra resources:** Some students may always be avoidant of meeting with teachers when they are struggling. If teachers recognize that some of their students have this quality, teachers can create resources (such as review sheets of relevant information) and place them in a specific location so that students can independently clarify their questions about content. It may also be beneficial to create a check-out system to keep tabs on which students are using the provided resources.

▶ **Establishing an anonymous question box:** Teachers can establish anonymous question boxes in their classrooms so that students can ask questions about content without drawing attention to themselves. Once established, teachers should check the boxes frequently and respond to any questions in front of the entire class. Teachers should also emphasize that all questions are legitimate and that students shouldn't be embarrassed by the questions they may have. Teachers can require that all students submit questions to these boxes as an assignment to further protect struggling students' sense of competence.

▶ **Incentivizing help sessions:** Help sessions should not feel like a punishment, as students will be less inclined to continue attending them. Instead, teachers should try to make help sessions fun and lighthearted by always being cheerful and positive during these meetings. Teachers might also consider providing snacks or candy to students during help sessions.

▶ **Meeting with every student to identify challenges:** Rather than just meeting with struggling students, teachers can take time to meet individually with all members of a class to talk about their growth and challenges. This not only prevents struggling students from feeling singled out but also allows teachers to better understand every student's unique learning challenges.

▶ **Sending letters or notes to students:** Teachers can formally write letters to students or their parents or attach notes to assignments that ask students to meet with them privately. By communicating nonverbally, teachers are less likely to draw attention to students, thereby avoiding their embarrassment. However, teachers should consider their tone when writing such letters to ensure that it is friendly and welcoming rather than overly critical or negative.

▶ **Using independent seatwork time to meet with struggling students:** Teachers can use independent seatwork time to meet with specific students who may be struggling. Teachers provide the rest of the class with a specific activity or assignment, such as a worksheet or problem. While the rest of the class works, teachers individually meet with struggling students to clear up any existing misconceptions or talk about students' previous work.

Ideally, as these strategies or others are employed, struggling students will feel less embarrassment about seeking academic help and their competency will ultimately increase as a result.

Failure Insulators

When students anticipate their own poor performance, their expectations can become self-fulfilling prophecies. Particularly at the beginning of the year, teachers should remind students who have previously struggled that they can be successful in an academic setting. Merrill Harmin (2006) suggested the use of *failure insulators* to this end, which provide "many successful test-taking experiences at the start of the school year" (p. 385) to students who may not feel competent due to previous negative experiences in school. The following suggestions are adapted from Harmin (2006).

▸ **Don't grade every test:** Give a number of assessments that will not be scored. Instead, simply respond with a general comment such as "You seem to understand" or "You may need to study more." This is especially useful at the elementary school level.

▸ **Give easier tests early:** Adjust the difficulty of tests early in the year so all students experience high achievement, build confidence, and reduce their test-taking anxiety. If teachers use proficiency scales, this simply means focusing on the score 2.0 content first.

▸ **Use *A, B, Needs Improvement*:** If teachers must give grades, they can restrict them to *A*, *B*, or *Needs Improvement*, if allowed by the school. When students receive a *Needs Improvement* grade, it is especially useful to offer specific suggestions for how students can improve or, if possible, make tutoring or extra help available. Proficiency scales avoid this issue, as letter grades are not assigned to assessments.

As we will discuss later, expectation levels (see Academic Equity, page 125) can drastically affect student performance, as students tend to live up to what is expected of them—that is, if a teacher has low expectations for a student, the student is likely to meet those expectations. However, this does not only apply to teachers' expectations for students. Rather, students' negative expectations for themselves can also negatively impact their performance. Failure insulators mitigate students' own low expectations for themselves by allowing them to experience academic success (or at least avoid academic failure) throughout the school year, thereby also guarding their sense of competence.

Leniency

Another important aspect of addressing struggling students is recognizing students' commitments outside of school and being lenient when appropriate. As mentioned previously, students' esteem is not just composed of their academic self-concepts (or self-concepts related to abilities with a specific subject) but also their self-concepts as family members, friends, volunteers, athletes, artists, and so on. As such, teachers may have to readjust their own expectations in order to ensure students fulfill their responsibilities in all aspects of their lives. Examples of teachers showing leniency might include the following.

▸ Recognizing that a student has to travel for an extracurricular activity and extending a deadline for work due the following day

> ► Recognizing that many students have a major assessment in another class at the end of the week and shifting deadlines for assignments to allow students time to study

> ► Recognizing that a student takes care of his or her siblings after school and arranging time during or before school hours for the student to make up a test

While providing leniency may seem inconvenient at times, such actions build positive relationships with students and let them know that teachers care about them as individuals. Furthermore, leniency prevents students' esteem needs from going unmet for prolonged periods of time due to anxiety around completing necessary work. When readjusting expectations for students, teachers should consider previous instances in which students received leniency. Conversations may be warranted with students who often ask for deadline extensions or appear overwhelmed. The following list includes various strategies for providing leniency to students.

> ► **Allowing for assignment revision:** Teachers commonly provide leniency through assignment revision. If students do poorly on an assessment, teachers can let them correct their own work to make up partial or full credit for the assignment. Such opportunities allow for leniency while still maintaining a rigorous academic environment focused on learning.

> ► **Allowing independent projects:** For some students, time constraints will always be an issue. This may mean that they will not be able to fully participate in group projects. Rather than inconveniencing other group members, teachers can assign particularly busy students independent projects to avoid the difficulties of coordinating meeting times.

> ► **Collaborating with other teachers to avoid scheduling conflicts:** As previously mentioned, students often juggle assignments in multiple subject areas. Teachers of various subjects can make an effort to coordinate their major assignments and assessments so that they fall on different weeks. With such practices in place, students are more likely to succeed in multiple subject areas and will not be forced to compromise their performance in one subject area for success in another.

> ► **Communicating with students:** In order to be lenient with students, teachers should be aware of the events occurring in students' lives and around school. Teachers should encourage students to tell them about things that could affect their academic performance, citing that they would prefer to know rather than have students struggling in class without discernable causes. Teachers can also make an effort to stay informed about upcoming events and plan accordingly.

> ► **Modifying assignments:** If students have many extracurricular obligations, teachers can modify assignments to suit their time constraints. For example, if a student has a game after school, a teacher may ask the student to complete only one of the homework questions rather than five or to watch a related educational YouTube video rather than read an entire chapter in a textbook.

> ► **Providing alternative assessments with less stringent deadlines:** If students know that they will not be in class for an assessment, students can design their own student-generated assessments to prove their proficiency with the content. This strategy is particularly useful

for students who may be absent for a prolonged period of time due to family emergencies or illness.

▸ **Scaffolding deadlines to be more manageable:** Many students struggle with deadlines, particularly deadlines that are in the distant future. Teachers can break up long-term assignments into more manageable sections and monitor students' progress. If students are struggling to meet smaller deadlines, teachers can modify timelines or further break up assignments to encourage success.

Showing leniency is a critical tool in meeting students' esteem needs, as leniency not only protects students' sense of academic competence but also accounts for students' esteem outside of school.

Significance

A sense of *significance*, the belief that individuals impact the people and environment around them, also directly contributes to esteem. Teachers can make students feel significant by creating opportunities for input, choice, and responsibility within the classroom.

Input

Teachers can make students feel significant by asking them for their input, as this shows that teachers value their opinions and feedback and want them to have a say in their learning. Opportunities for student input abound in the classroom, and teachers can use student responses to inform future content, activities, and interactions. For example, after completing a unit, a teacher might ask students to use a simple voting technique to indicate how much they enjoyed the unit and whether it should be taught next year to other students. The teacher might then query students about activities that they particularly enjoyed or disliked and suggestions for improvement. Even though this action is fairly minimal on the part of the teacher and does not need to take more than five or ten minutes of class time, it can make students feel as though they are impacting the learning of future students and that the teacher cares that their experiences in the classroom are positive. Additional opportunities to ask for student input are listed here.

▸ **Classroom parking lots:** Classroom parking lots allow teachers to gather student input related to a day's lessons. A poster or part of the board (the "parking lot") is divided into sections that prompt students for different types of input, such as questions, suggestions, things they learned, or things they are still confused about. Teachers give students a few sticky notes at the end of class and ask them to provide input based on the sections of the parking lot. Students write their answers, then "park" their responses in the appropriate section of the poster or board as they leave the classroom.

▸ **Discussions:** Another way to ask students for input is through class discussion. Students share their thoughts or opinions about a specific topic, and other students respond accordingly. Teachers should monitor the amount that various students speak during` discussions to avoid some students monopolizing the conversation. Teachers may also want to recap conclusions drawn from a specific discussion to ensure they correctly interpreted students' comments.

- ▸ **Exit slips:** Exit slips are written responses to prompts that are assigned and turned in at the end of class. Traditionally, exit slips check students' understanding or ask students to reflect on what they learned during the day. However, teachers can modify exit slip prompts to provide space for students to register concerns or give feedback about aspects of a lesson. For more about exit slips, see page 109.

- ▸ **Interactive notebooks:** A powerful way to help students reinforce their learning is through the use of academic notebooks. Interactive notebooks take this idea one step further, as teachers prompt students to write entries about their academic experiences or suggestions for the classroom. Teachers then correspond with students in their notebooks to show that they hear and consider their students' input.

- ▸ **Suggestion boxes:** With suggestion boxes, teachers establish a space where students can anonymously write their comments related to class. Suggestions could be limited to a specific topic or open for students to voice their thoughts as needed throughout the year. Periodically, teachers review the notes within suggestion boxes either privately or with the class.

- ▸ **Voting:** Incorporating voting into the classroom is an easy way to ask students for input. Voting can be formal or informal. Formal voting requires students to write their preferences on ballots, whereas informal voting allows teachers to quickly survey student opinion on a certain topic through a show of hands or other signals.

These strategies represent a few ways to solicit input from students. However, teachers should not feel limited by this list. Rather, teachers can take advantage of any opportunity for students to provide their thoughts or feedback as a means to make students feel significant. For example, classroom meetings (page 108) are another way to solicit student input while simultaneously building a sense of belonging among students.

Choice

While often talked about in conjunction with input, offering students *choice* in the classroom refers to opportunities for students to select the actions they engage in based on their own wants and needs. Teachers can use the following four guidelines to inform how they incorporate choice into their classrooms.

1. **Start small:** Teachers might find it easier to start small as they incorporate choice into their classrooms. Teachers can restrict the number of choices available to students (for example, the option between two types of assessments versus any type of assessment) or offer choices with limited impact (for example, the choice of homework assignment versus the choice of final assessment). This allows both students and teachers to get a better feel for the process of making and accepting choices appropriately.

2. **Choose wisely:** Because of the importance of following through with choices offered, teachers should consider the potential outcomes of the options they offer students when designing opportunities for choice. In other words, teachers should not offer choices to students if they are not comfortable enacting subsequent suggestions.

3. **Follow through:** To make students feel significant, teachers must follow through on the choices they offer students. If a teacher offers a choice but does not follow through, it may hurt teacher-student relationships and make students feel undervalued.

4. **Be transparent:** If follow-through becomes unlikely or impossible, teachers should let students know the reasons why their suggestions are not being followed. In such instances, when possible, it may behoove teachers to provide students with alternative choices or forums to determine the next course of action. If students make inappropriate choices, teachers should clearly explain why the students' suggested course of action is not plausible and offer an alternative choice.

After considering these guidelines, teachers can incorporate choice into the classroom by offering options in terms of: (1) tasks, (2) reporting formats, (3) learning goals, (4) behaviors, and (5) environment.

Tasks

Think of tasks as the short-term activities that students complete as a means to gain competence during a unit. Tasks also serve as perfect low-stakes vehicles for integrating choice into a lesson. For example, a teacher might provide students with a few prompts to guide a written homework assignment and ask students to write about the one they find most interesting. To create a larger choice, the teacher might have students construct their own prompts for the assignment and use these prompts to guide their writing. While both are legitimate ways of providing students with choice of task, the benefit of having students generate their own tasks is that they will most likely generate prompts of personal interest to them, which, as discussed previously, contributes to motivation. When providing open-ended tasks, teachers can use the following questions to guide students' selections:

- Relative to the topic we are studying, is there an important decision you want to examine?

- Relative to the topic we are studying, is there an important problem that you want to solve?

- Relative to the topic we are studying, is there an important hypothesis you would like to test?

- Relative to the topic we are studying, is there an important concept, past event, or hypothetical or future event you want to study? (Marzano & Pickering, 2011, pp. 101–102)

Reporting Formats

When offering a choice of reporting formats, teachers can ask students to choose between multiple assessment formats or ask students to design their own assessments. Offering students multiple choices in terms of reporting format is fairly straightforward—teachers identify which types of format they find acceptable for the particular assessment and allow students to choose between them. As articulated by Robert J. Marzano and Debra J. Pickering (2011), teachers may provide any number of the following reporting format options to students:

- A written report
- An oral report
- A dramatic presentation
- A debate

- A videotaped report
- A demonstration or simulation (p. 103)

However, teachers should not feel limited by this list when offering choice of reporting format—rather, based on the needs of the assignment, teachers can expand offerings to students to include whatever they feel is appropriate. Once teachers determine the options, they can present the choices to students and allow them to select among them. If teachers prefer that all students complete the same type of assignment, students can vote on the reporting format offered. For example, for a summative assessment, a teacher might ask students if they would prefer a written test or an oral examination and have students vote, with the majority of students determining the nature of the assessment for the class as a whole.

As students become more proficient in making choices, teachers may decide to use student-generated assessments. Student-generated assessments are assessments that students develop independently to show their competence with specific content. Before allowing students to create their own assessments, however, it may be beneficial for teachers to clearly articulate expectations and check in with students as they design their assessments to ensure they meet the grading standards.

Learning Goals

Learning goals articulate the content that students will learn over the course of a unit. Providing students with choice of learning goal, then, allows students to identify areas of personal interest and explore those interests in class. This is a particularly powerful method of incorporating choice into the classroom because students have agency in what they study. Teachers should not interpret this type of choice as the abandonment of teacher-identified learning goals; rather, students can simultaneously pursue student-identified and teacher-identified learning goals. In such a scenario, the progress students make toward both types of goals should contribute to their final grades in a unit. Teachers may also find it helpful to introduce students to SMART goal setting (page 56), particularly if students are pursuing goals independently or if student-generated assessments will be used to show proficiency.

To illustrate how a choice of learning goals might manifest in a classroom, consider a second-grade class learning about geography. The teacher-identified learning goal might be to learn how to correctly read a map and to identify the major landmasses and oceans on Earth. As the students work toward this goal, the teacher might ask students to identify their own learning goals related to a more specific aspect of geography. For example, students might decide to learn more about the geography of a specific country, study the formation of a type of landmass, or research how maps have changed over time. As students work toward their student-identified goals, the teacher might ask them to make connections between their goals and the teacher-identified learning goal. For example, if a student chose to study the geography of Brazil as her student-identified goal, the teacher might ask the student to create a map of Brazil and neighboring countries to assess her proficiency with map reading as well.

Behaviors

Behavior refers to the actions and demeanor students take in the classroom. Teachers can easily provide students with choices in this regard by allowing them to determine the behavior expectations that ultimately govern their behavior in the classroom. However, as students are given choices about behavior expectations, teachers should ensure the expectations create a safe environment that supports learning (see Order, page 118).

The Marzano Compendium of Instructional Strategies (Marzano Research, 2016e) articulated the following six-step process to generate classroom rules and procedures with students.

1. Facilitate a whole-class discussion about the characteristics of a class that facilitates learning.

2. Assemble small groups of students and ask them to create initial lists of suggestions for rules. Provide examples of previous classes' rules if necessary.

3. Combine the rule suggestions from all the small groups into one list and post it somewhere in the classroom.

4. Facilitate another whole-class discussion about the aggregated list of rules. Groups who suggested a rule can explain why they think it is important, and students can discuss the benefits of each one.

5. Have the class vote on each rule and add the rules that obtain a majority (or consensus, depending on the teacher's preferences) to the class's final list of rules.

6. Facilitate a whole-class discussion about the final list of rules and address students' questions or concerns. Students might design procedures for rules that need further clarification. (p. 10)

Teachers can also ask students to monitor and modify classroom behavior expectations throughout the year to further enforce the idea that they have control over the behaviors they can and cannot express in the classroom.

Environment

Choice of environment refers to providing students with options related to the space in which they learn. Choice of environment may not seem to have as large an impact on student learning as other choices related to academics or classroom management, but such decisions can go a long way in making students feel significant. Like other types of choices, teachers can also provide students with pre-established or open-ended choices. For example, a choice between various options might include a teacher offering students a break immediately or in half an hour, whereas an open-ended choice might include having students bring in their own decorations for the classroom or allowing them to choose their own partners for an activity. Common environmental choices teachers offer include the following.

▶ Seating or desk arrangement

▶ Decorations

▶ Opportunity to play music before or after class

▶ Timing of breaks

▶ Selection of partners or group members

Teachers can continue to offer choices to students related to their classroom environment above and beyond the previous list. As with choices related to behavior, teachers may need to limit students' choices if they do not support a safe environment as described in chapter 6.

Responsibility

Significance is directly tied to the perception that an individual fulfills a specific role that others need and are affected by. In other words, significance derives from a sense of responsibility. While school generally fosters a sense of individual responsibility in most students through class- and homework, teachers can further emphasize responsibility using strategies that help create interdependence among students. Here, we discuss two such strategies: (1) jigsaw activities and (2) classroom jobs.

Jigsaw Activities

Teachers can enhance students' sense of responsibility by utilizing jigsaw activities in class. These activities derive their name from the fact that each student in a group is responsible for a unique part of a project or assignment, and eventually the group comes together to assemble the pieces of their "jigsaw puzzle." Besides contributing to students' sense of responsibility, research has shown that this model

> can revive that hardwired cooperation and help children put themselves into other children's shoes.... Kids who had jigsaw classrooms in fifth grade... were more cooperative, more empathic and less prejudiced [three years later] than children who had never experienced a jigsaw classroom. (Clay, 2006)

Elliot Aronson (n.d.) developed ten steps to execute a jigsaw activity in class, which are adapted in the following list.

1. **Divide students into small groups:** Teachers should try to make the groups as diverse as possible in terms of gender, ethnicity, race, and ability.

2. **Appoint one student as the leader:** When choosing leaders, teachers should select the most mature student in each group.

3. **Divide the lesson into smaller parts:** Teachers should try to make these parts as equal as possible in terms of content covered.

4. **Assign each student one of the lesson parts:** Teachers should assign each student in the group his or her own unique part of the lesson, and content between parts should not overlap.

5. **Give students time to familiarize themselves with the content:** Depending on the content, give students time to research or read.

6. **Create expert groups where students assigned to the same lesson parts from different groups convene:** These students collaborate to rehearse their presentations, correct misconceptions, and discuss the main point and importance of their part.

7. **Reconvene the original jigsaw groups:** After the expert groups converse with one another, ask students to arrange themselves back into their original jigsaw groups.

8. **Have each student present his or her part to the group:** Encourage other students to ask questions of the presenting student.

9. **Observe jigsaw groups throughout the process:** Teachers should float between groups, intervening as necessary, though it is best if group leaders try to handle this task initially.

10. **Administer an assessment on the material:** Assess all students on their own lesson part and the content they learned from their peers.

Teachers do not need to follow this exact process to employ jigsaw activities. Rather, teachers can simply use the idea of each student being responsible for a unique part of a project to guide how work is divided for certain assignments or activities. Teachers can then directly discuss the concept of responsibility with students and how students are not only responsible for their own learning but the learning of their peers.

Classroom Jobs

Teachers can assign students specific jobs or roles to give them responsibilities in the classroom outside of their academic obligations. To create classroom jobs, teachers should first consider the roles they need filled in their classrooms and then design jobs around these tasks. For example, a teacher may notice that the classroom library is frequently in a state of disarray or that students are disorganized when returning their assignments. As such, the teacher might develop the jobs of librarian—responsible for ensuring the classroom library is orderly at the end of the day—and assignment organizer—responsible for collecting students' assignments and stacking them neatly before turning them in. Other common classroom jobs include the following.

- ▸ **Attendance taker:** This student records attendance at the beginning of class.
- ▸ **Board eraser:** This student erases the board as needed.
- ▸ **Class notetaker:** This student is responsible for taking notes for students who are absent. If this student is absent, the teacher might assign a substitute for the day or always have a back-up notetaker assigned.
- ▸ **Cleanliness monitor:** This student takes note of messes around the classroom and ensures that each student does his or her part in cleaning up.
- ▸ **Errand runner:** This student runs errands for the teacher as needed.
- ▸ **Line leader and line ender:** These students are responsible for taking the first and last spots in line when the class moves between locations.
- ▸ **Materials collector:** After students complete work that needs to be turned in, this student quickly and efficiently collects it and returns it to the teacher.
- ▸ **Materials distributor:** When materials such as worksheets or assessments need to be handed out, this student quickly and efficiently passes them out to the rest of the class.
- ▸ **Messenger:** This student is responsible for delivering attendance reports and taking messages to other faculty and staff when necessary.
- ▸ **Pet caretaker:** This student makes sure that the classroom pet is fed and has adequate water.
- ▸ **Peer mediator:** This student is trained to help other students independently resolve conflicts. (For further information about creating a peer mediation program, see page 105.)
- ▸ **Photocopier:** This student makes photocopies for the teacher as needed.
- ▸ **Technology supervisor:** This student makes sure that students use classroom computers appropriately and turns computers on and off at the start and end of the day.

As teachers determine the jobs they will have in their classrooms, they should decide how they will assign jobs, how long students will hold certain jobs, and how many students will have jobs at any given time. Teachers can have students rotate in and out of jobs in a specific order or assign jobs as rewards for good behavior. When using classroom jobs as a reward, teachers may want to consider giving jobs to students who may struggle academically to boost their esteem and make them feel significant. Teachers should also consider how long students will hold their jobs. For example, some teachers rotate classroom jobs on a weekly basis, whereas others choose to assign one job, like class notetaker, to one student for a longer period of time (like a month or semester). Finally, teachers should decide if all students will always have a specific responsibility to fill or whether only a handful of jobs will be established. Traditionally, teachers of younger students tend to assign each student a specific job whereas teachers of older students often only create classroom jobs that are particularly relevant or necessary. If a teacher wants to assign each student a job but does not have enough roles to assign, the teacher can designate students without jobs as "on vacation." Teachers should also post job listings somewhere in the classroom and issue verbal reminders to further develop students' sense of responsibility.

Recognition

One of the easiest ways to build students' esteem is to recognize individual students, their abilities, and their achievements. In a classroom setting, students' esteem derived from others has two sources: (1) peers and (2) teachers. As such, teachers can find ways to reward and recognize students when appropriate while also encouraging active appreciation for their classmates.

Peer Recognition

Students' esteem from others is directly tied to how they believe their peers perceive them. Unfortunately, many students may be too embarrassed to express affection or admiration for other students and their accomplishments, abilities, or traits. To combat this tendency, teachers can use specific strategies that require students to recognize their peers and the value they add to the classroom. Here, we provide two strategies that encourage students to articulate their appreciation for their classmates: (1) student interviews and (2) compliments.

Student Interviews

One aspect of recognition relates to having other people recognize an individual's complexities or uniqueness. To help students understand their classmates as individuals with unique interests and accomplishments, teachers can ask students to briefly interview one another. For example, a teacher might choose to start each class period by having students spend five minutes interviewing one another about their interests, hobbies, and accomplishments. The teacher would continue this activity throughout the year until each student in class has interviewed all of his or her classmates. As students interview their classmates, the teacher might prompt them to identify one unexpected thing they learned or something they found to be notable about their partner. This can be a particularly powerful activity in the beginning of the year to help students get to know one another and to create a sense of belonging (page 95).

Alternatively, teachers might assign partners—preferably two students who rarely interact—and ask the pairs to conduct more in-depth interviews of one another. With this activity, students may spend anywhere from fifteen to thirty minutes learning about their partners' backgrounds, families, interests, achievements, beliefs, and other unique characteristics. After both partners have interviewed each other, students can share their findings with the class. To guide these presentations, teachers can provide students with the following questions.

▶ What is one thing you learned about your partner that you found surprising?

▶ What is one strength of your partner? Why?

▶ What is one notable thing that you learned about your partner?

▶ If you had to describe your partner in three adjectives, what would they be?

▶ What are your partner's interests? How does that affect who he or she is as a person?

Teachers should remind students that the reports should be positive and are designed to help the class get to know its members. As such, students should also provide background knowledge about their partners that may be relevant. After a student is finished presenting, the rest of the class asks the student questions about his or her partner. If a presenting student does not know the answer to a question, their partner directly answers it. The anticipation of other classmates' questions also encourages students to engage in more in-depth interviews.

Compliments

Compliments are an easy way for students to boost one another's esteem, as compliments are direct statements that acknowledge positive aspects of their recipients. There are a number of ways to build compliment giving into class. However, teachers may also want to review with students how to give and receive compliments appropriately. Once it seems that students have a firm understanding of the etiquette surrounding compliments, teachers can encourage compliment giving in a number of ways, such as the following.

▶ **Brag boards:** Brag boards provide a public space via a designated bulletin board for students to thank and compliment their classmates using written notes. It may be helpful to provide premade forms to guide students' brag-board posts. These forms often request the names of the students giving and receiving the compliments, the compliment itself, and the date.

▶ **Compliment boxes:** Students anonymously write compliments or thank-you notes for other students and place them in a pre-established box or jar. Teachers can read one or two submissions out loud to start or end class. Teachers may also want to keep track of students who receive compliments, as this strategy may backfire if one or two students consistently do not receive compliments from other members of the class.

▶ **Compliment cards:** Teachers ask students to write their names at the top of a piece of paper or index card. Students pass the papers around and, each time they receive a card, write one compliment for the person whose name is at the top. Students continue to pass the cards around until they have written a compliment for each of their classmates, at which point the cards are returned to their owners. For an abbreviated version of this activity, teachers can have students write compliments for three to five of their classmates before asking that cards be returned to their owners.

▸ **Compliment discussion:** To start a compliment discussion, teachers ask students to sit in a circle and go around the circle in one direction complimenting the student next to them. After every student in the circle has received a compliment, teachers can lead students in discussions about how they felt giving and receiving compliments. Alternatively, teachers could designate specific times for students to publicly thank or compliment their peers.

In addition to these strategies, teachers can model the behavior by complimenting students when appropriate, which can also positively affect students' sense of esteem.

Teacher Recognition

Through recognition, teachers can bolster students' esteem. While such recognition is frequently academic in nature, teachers should not feel as though they can only recognize students for their academic successes. Rather, it can be very powerful when teachers find ways to actively recognize students who may struggle academically, as these students are often the least likely to have received praise in a school setting. Teachers can use the following four strategies to recognize students: (1) student examples, (2) specific feedback, (3) students of the week, and (4) awards.

Student Examples

A particularly easy way for teachers to directly impact students' esteem is to publicly recognize their actions or work. This can be done fairly easily by using students' work as models for well-done assignments. Depending on the nature of student examples, teachers may want to confirm that students are comfortable with their work being shared with the rest of the class, as some students may be shy about being publicly recognized.

There are a number of ways to bring attention to notable student examples. One way is to directly discuss one student's work with the whole class. For example, a teacher might provide copies of a student's essay to a class and use it to explain the characteristics of a high-scoring essay. If the student doesn't want to be identified, the teacher could remove the name of the student or save the essay to be shown to future classes. Teachers can also have students demonstrate specific skills or processes. For example, if a teacher sees that a student is particularly good at showing her work for a problem on a previous night's mathematics homework, the teacher could have the student work through the problem in front of the class. The teacher should note that the student is being called on because of her exemplary work and allow the student to consult her homework as she demonstrates. Finally, teachers should not dismiss the power of mentioning students who particularly excel on specific assignments. To this end, a teacher might refer to one or two students who have a strong grasp on a concept or process and tell the class to ask them for help if needed.

Teachers should monitor which students they often recognize in class. If a teacher repeatedly chooses examples from the same students, it may be disheartening for students whose work the teacher has not yet chosen. Rather, teachers should seek out ways to honor students whose work may not be traditionally chosen as examples. Teachers can do this by drawing attention to specific students' positive actions or contributions. For example, teachers can call attention to students who always come prepared to class, who offer assistance without prompting, or who model good listening or speaking skills as examples of positive behavior.

Specific Feedback

Another way for teachers to recognize students is to provide them with individualized feedback. This is not to say that all feedback should be positive—rather, when providing feedback, teachers should make an effort to find a few things that emphasize the value of the student, even if the student's grade could use improvement. When providing comments to students about an assignment, teachers can note specific things that show growth or competence and use evidence from the assignment to back up their claims. For example, consider the following example of specific feedback regarding a student's essay.

> *Keely, this essay shows so much growth since the beginning of the year! Your thesis was complex and unique, and you supported it well. When compared with your previous essay on* The Catcher in the Rye, *you've gotten a much better feel for organizing essays and adding only relevant details. I also thought that the quotes and textual evidence that you chose to support your argument really worked. You are still making some grammatical mistakes, though these are increasingly minor, and I think could be eliminated with a quick chat about commas (please find time to come and see me). However, even with those small mistakes, you should feel proud of yourself! It's been wonderful watching you grow over the past few months, and the hard work you are doing is not going unnoticed!*

This feedback is specific to the assignment but also recognizes the growth the student has made over a period of months. The comment also compliments the student and includes a direct statement of recognition. Finally, the teacher still notes areas in which the student could improve. However, the criticism is sandwiched in between positive comments and includes a concrete step toward resolving the problem.

Students of the Week

Teachers can establish long-term programs that honor specific students each week. With a student-of-the-week program, teachers select one student each week who receives special recognition and privileges. Such recognition systems are also a good way for students to learn about their classmates, much like student interviews (page 89). Teachers can create a schedule that designates a specific honor or activity for the student of the week each day. For example, a teacher might create the following schedule.

Monday: The student of the week gives a short presentation about himself or herself. The student might also bring in a special item to show to the class. The teacher takes the student's picture and posts it on the student-of-the-week bulletin board.

Tuesday: Students each write a compliment to the student of the week; the teacher reads them out loud and then posts them on the student-of-the-week bulletin board.

Wednesday: The teacher invites the student of the week's parents to visit the class for lunch. The student might choose to have a sibling, grandparent, or other important individual come visit instead. If no one is available, the teacher can arrange a special lunch with the student's favorite dessert.

Thursday: The student of the week gets to choose the music played at the beginning of class. That student also gets to guide discussion and choose between options for tasks in class.

Friday: Students play a trivia game that uses previously learned information about the student of the week. At the end of the class period, the student of the week is presented with a personalized letter from the teacher thanking him or her for contributions to the class.

The activities listed represent only a few possibilities for daily recognition activities. Teachers can create their own student-of-the-week schedules to fit the needs of their particular classrooms.

Awards

Teachers commonly recognize their students through personalized awards given at the end of the year. When determining the awards to be given to students, teachers can independently draft awards and choose recipients, create a master list of potential awards and ask students for nominations, or ask students to develop awards and nominate one another. Regardless of how teachers decide on awards and their recipients, teachers should ensure that each student in class gets an award and that each award is unique and positive.

When creating awards, teachers may want to avoid traditional superlatives; rather, teachers should generate personalized awards that lend themselves to noncompetitiveness. For example, instead of using the terms *best* or *greatest*, which may hurt the esteem of other students, a teacher might create awards like Aspiring Astronaut for a student who excelled in a unit on outer space, Typing Whiz for a student who can type very fast, or Never Late for a student who is particularly prompt to class. Teachers may also find value in awards that take the format of "Most likely to _____." This format lends itself to comical results, such as "Most likely to wrestle an alligator" or "Most likely to create a time machine." Not only are such awards funny in their own right, but the personalized humor often eliminates competition that might surround awards like Most Adventurous or Best at Science.

Summary and Recommendations

In this chapter, we discussed ways in which teachers can address the esteem needs of their students. First, we discussed how to define and describe esteem using self-concepts and traits of esteem. We described explanatory style and thought revision as ways to encourage students to reflect on their thinking and its effect on esteem. We also provided a number of strategies designed to enhance students' sense of competence, significance, and recognition to bolster their esteem as a whole.

Although teachers can use the strategies in this chapter in a variety of ways, we recommend the following.

- ▶ At the beginning and end of the year, ask students to assess their own esteem by examining the various self-concepts they hold about themselves as well as the traits of esteem they tend to exhibit.

- ▶ At least once a semester, ask students to reflect on their thoughts and consider how they may contribute to their esteem.

- ▶ Focus on students' academic growth and incorporate responses to struggling students that protect students' esteem into classroom practice whenever possible.

- ▶ At least once a month, use strategies that make students feel significant and recognized by their teachers and peers.

The following scenario depicts how these recommendations might manifest in the classroom.

In a high school English class composed primarily of students who have previously struggled academically, the teacher decides that he will focus on meeting students' esteem needs throughout the year. With the use of proficiency scales, the teacher shifts his grading to focus on growth rather than solely on final outcomes. He also builds failure insulators into his curriculum design—for example, he begins testing more frequently on easier score 2.0 content and does not grade every test. He decides to end Friday afternoon classes with compliment discussions as a means to build students' relationships with one another and tries to offer students opportunities for input or choice at least once every two weeks. Throughout the semester, the teacher uses surveys to assess students' esteem. After a few months of these changes, he compares survey data to monitor the effects the use of such strategies has had on students' esteem.

CHAPTER 5
Belonging

Belonging is a foundational need for students that teachers can directly address by considering the relationships that exist in the classroom. Such interactions should contribute to a sense of community if they are to fulfill students' belonging needs. In this chapter, we address four topics related to belonging: (1) inclusion, (2) respect, (3) affection, and (4) cooperation. Rachel's Challenge assembly programs (page 26) can also contribute to a sense of belonging, as such programs encourage positive relationships among students.

Inclusion

Inclusion involves the sense that others actively welcome someone into a community. Considering its definition, it should not be surprising that inclusion underlies a sense of belonging. Here, we consider four topics that affect an inclusive environment: (1) invitational education, (2) similarities, (3) interventions, and (4) bullying.

Invitational Education

To ensure students feel welcome at school, teachers should consider how elements of the classroom work toward or against a sense of inclusion. Teachers can use the invitational education framework (Purkey, 1991; Purkey & Novak, 1988, 1996) to identify these aspects and to assess whether the various elements of the classroom work together to meet students' belonging needs.

The invitational education framework has two dimensions: (1) invitation and (2) intention. *Invitation* refers to the degree to which an aspect of a classroom contributes to or takes away from a sense of inclusion. *Intention* refers to the degree to which the teacher actively creates and reflects on these aspects. Stated differently, a teacher can assess a classroom by considering whether it is inviting or disinviting to students and whether its level of invitation is intentional or unintentional. Thus, teachers can assess their classrooms using the following four levels of functioning.

1. **Intentionally disinviting:** Things that are intentionally disinviting "are deliberately designed to demean, dissuade, discourage, defeat and destroy" (Purkey, 1991, p. 4). Examples of intentionally disinviting practices include insulting students, using policies that actively discriminate against subsets of the student population, or maintaining environments that are noticeably unpleasant yet left unaddressed.

2. **Unintentionally disinviting:** Things that are unintentionally disinviting are not a function of policies or design, yet they demean students or make them feel unwelcome. Policies at this level of functioning might be well intentioned but interpreted negatively by students, such as rules against getting water or going to the restroom during class. Teacher actions that are unintentionally disinviting may convey apathy, condescension, or hostility, even if the teacher does not mean to. For example, a teacher who frequently uses "but" statements, such as "This assignment was well done, but _____," may come off as insincere, as the criticism may negate the initial praise.

3. **Unintentionally inviting:** As William W. Purkey (1991) stated, "Educators who usually function at the unintentionally inviting level [have] stumbled serendipitously into ways of functioning that are often effective. However, they have difficulty when asked to explain <u>why</u> they are successful" (p. 5). For example, teachers might be popular with students but not able to explain why. When unintentionally inviting practices break down, teachers often struggle to correct them, as the nature of their previous success is unknown.

4. **Intentionally inviting:** At the intentionally inviting level of function, elements work together so that students feel welcome and comfortable during class. To accomplish this, teachers regularly reflect on how they contribute to and ensure an inviting atmosphere. When necessary, they make corrections to ensure that students' belonging needs are met throughout the school day.

With these four levels of functioning in mind, teachers can directly ask students about whether they find class to be inviting or disinviting. It may be easier to ask younger students about these elements using simpler language, such as asking them to identify things they like and dislike about their classes, teachers, or classrooms. Teachers should emphasize that students' opinions will not be held against them and that the purpose of such activities is to ensure that all students feel included and comfortable during class. Alternatively, teachers can offer students the option to write down their thoughts and submit them anonymously. Table 5.1 provides a few examples of inviting and disinviting classroom elements.

Table 5.1: Inviting and Disinviting Classroom Elements

Inviting	Disinviting
• Talking about the weekend at the start of class on Monday • Students being able to select partners for some assignments • The teacher bringing in treats as a surprise • The teacher asking students what they thought about a unit and ways it could be improved	• The teacher chewing gum while students can't • Students not being allowed into the classroom until the first bell rings • The teacher taking a long time to give feedback on assignments to students • Not having decorations in the classroom

Teachers can reflect on the classroom elements identified by students to determine the degree to which each practice is intentional or unintentional. This often highlights how teachers can accidentally engage in behaviors that make students feel uncomfortable or unwelcome. For example, in terms of the classroom elements listed in table 5.1, the teacher might have been unaware of her tendency to chew gum during class—making it an unintentionally disinviting practice. With this newfound awareness, the teacher could be more cognizant of this habit and stop it completely. By periodically checking in with students, teachers can remain aware of how they are perceived and modify their actions to create intentionally inviting spaces that foster a sense of belonging.

Similarities

Students who do not believe they have anything in common with their peers may struggle to feel included. To address this, teachers can highlight similarities between students, particularly among those who rarely interact. This enables students to recognize that they have more in common than they might have thought and creates a foundation on which to build an inclusive environment. There are a number of strategies that let students see similarities between themselves and their classmates. For example, consider the following list of strategies adapted from Larry Ferlazzo (2012) and TeachThought (2013).

▶ **Four Squares:** Each student folds a piece of paper into quarters and writes a teacher-identified topic at the top of each. Example topics might include "Family," "What I like about school," "My favorite movie and why," "My biggest accomplishment," "Personal challenges," and so on. Teachers give students time to write about each topic, then students pair up four times, each time with a different partner, to share their responses.

▶ **"I Am" Project:** Students create projects that describe who they are in a format of their choice, such as a poster, movie, slideshow, or essay. To begin, teachers provide students with sentence stems, such as "I love _____ because _____," "I hope to _____," or "I am happy when _____." Students can then use this information when developing their projects. Teachers can ask the class to identify similarities between its members after all the students in class have presented their projects.

▶ **Inside-Outside Circle:** Students form two concentric circles, with students finding a partner in the opposite circle and standing face-to-face with them. Teachers announce a topic and give students a few minutes to share their thoughts with their partners. After time has elapsed, the inside circle shifts to the left or right, and the new student pairs discuss a different topic.

▸ **Introducing Me (or Three Objects):** Students choose three objects to represent themselves and share them with the class. Teachers might first model this strategy by bringing in their own objects, explaining the importance of each one, and fielding questions from the class after their presentations. Teachers can then ask students to bring in their own sets of objects and explain their significance. Prompts to help younger students with this strategy include "Why is the item you picked important to you?" or "What does this item tell us about you?"

▸ **Me Too!:** Students stand in a circle, and one student steps forward and says a fact about himself or herself. Example statements might include "I play basketball," "I have three siblings," or "Green is my favorite color." If this fact is true for other students, they step forward and announce, "Me too!" The activity continues until each student has said a personal fact. To add movement to this activity, teachers can ask students to physically switch places with other students who step forward. Students can also play a variation of this activity by announcing things they've never done.

▸ **Personal Characteristics Scavenger Hunt:** Teachers give out lists of personal characteristics, and students find classmates who fit each description. Example characteristics might include "Has been to the ocean," "Whose favorite book is written by a woman," "Has broken a bone," "Has more than three pets," and so on. After the scavenger hunt, the class convenes to share their responses, and teachers follow up with individual students about the personal characteristics identified by their classmates.

▸ **Stranger Than Fiction:** Students write down one strange but true fact about themselves on a strip of paper or index card. Teachers collect the facts and read one to the class. Students then discuss the fact and try to guess which of their peers wrote the statement. Teachers might choose to read all the facts in one or two sittings or read a few per class over a longer period of time.

▸ **Two Truths and a Lie:** Students think of three statements about themselves—two that are true and one that is false. Students share their sets of statements in pairs, small groups, or as a class. Other students work together to try to identify which of the three statements is false. Students should choose unusual facts about themselves for the two truths to make identification of the false statement more difficult.

Clearly, similarity strategies focus on students getting to know one another in ways that may not typically arise in class. Teachers can also use follow-up activities that require students to make connections about how they are similar to one another or identify specific things they learned about their classmates as a means to further facilitate a sense of inclusion.

Interventions

Even with the use of specific inclusion strategies, some students may still feel isolated in the classroom. Teachers can use specific interventions designed to identify and address these students before their unmet belonging needs have lasting negative consequences. Here, we discuss five of these interventions: (1) student surveys, (2) staff surveys, (3) shadowing students, and (4) ten-and-two-minute interventions.

Student Surveys

To monitor whether students have an in-school support system, teachers can give students index cards and ask them to write their own names on one side and the names of one peer and one adult in school whom they trust on the other. Teachers collect and review the index cards, making sure each card has two names on the back. When using this intervention, teachers should recognize that this activity is designed to ensure students feel personal connections with at least one other student and one adult in the building. Teachers should speak with students who cannot identify an adult or peer that they trust and should design further intervention as needed. Teachers should also build positive relationships with these students to let them know that there are people in school who are actively looking out for them.

Staff Surveys

Teachers should not wait to take an interest in students until after they have obvious unmet belonging needs. To preemptively identify such students, teachers can collectively reflect on the nature of their relationships with students in the school. During staff meetings, teachers can post lists of students and read each name aloud. If a teacher knows something about a student personally, the teacher puts a line through the student's name. At the end of this exercise, teachers read the names of students who are not crossed out, and they discuss ways to build positive relationships with these students. Teachers can also modify this strategy for their classrooms by periodically reviewing their attendance lists to ensure they know something extra about each student.

Shadowing Students

To consider how the larger practices of a school affect students' sense of belonging, teachers can coordinate with administrators and other staff to shadow specific students during a school day. Teachers select random or targeted students and follow them from class to class, considering how the students' interactions and experiences throughout the day contribute to or take away from a sense of inclusion. Depending on time availability, teachers could shadow students for one or two class periods or for the entire day. Teachers should notify students of the proposed date and the purpose of the exercise in advance and get their approval before shadowing them. After the shadowing period, teachers can have short conversations with shadowed students to share notes and ask them about their own personal experiences at school. This debriefing period also provides time for teachers to ask students about any sort of negative experiences the teachers observed and discuss how the school could better meet students' various needs.

Ten-and-Two-Minute Interventions

The ten-and-two-minute intervention involves teachers meeting with specific students for at least two minutes each day over the course of ten days. Teachers identify students in need of intervention and agree to touch base with them consistently over this timeframe. During these interactions, teachers may find it helpful to use observational statements rather than judgmental statements, such as "I noticed that you're always smiling" or "I noticed that you wear a lot of Denver Broncos gear." Observational statements avoid putting students on the defensive and open the door for further elaboration by students. After ten days have passed, teachers evaluate the effectiveness of the intervention and decide whether to commit to ten more days if necessary.

Check-Ins

With a check-in program, students meet with a selected teacher at given times during the day. Commonly, these meetings occur at the beginning or end of the school day (and in some cases, both) and are used to discuss notable events that occur at home or during school. Such programs show students that teachers want to know about their lives and feel accountable for their well-being. Teachers may find the following five-step process helpful when developing a check-in program.

1. Identify students who could benefit from a check-in routine.

2. Introduce the program to parents, and get their permission for student participation in daily check-ins.

3. Explain to students the purpose of the check-in program.

4. Begin the check-in program.

5. Monitor the program's progress and how it affects relationships with students.

As teachers implement check-in programs, teachers can track informal individual student data simply by keeping notes about their interactions with and observations of students. As teachers gather this information, they can modify their interactions with students as needed. If the program is schoolwide, teachers involved in the program may want to meet periodically as well to discuss their experiences, successes, and challenges.

Bullying

Bullying can be defined as repeated aggressive behaviors that create imbalances in power between students. Therefore, it should not be surprising that these behaviors have devastating effects on students' sense of belonging and actively work against a sense of inclusion. Thus, it is critical that teachers address bullying before it has lasting negative effects on students. This can be accomplished by regularly monitoring students' interactions with one another and confronting any problems directly.

To identify and prevent bullying, teachers should have a firm understanding of the behaviors and roles associated with bullying. Bullying can involve a variety of behaviors, though most commonly these behaviors fall into three categories: (1) verbal, (2) social, and (3) physical (StopBullying, n.d.a). *Verbal bullying* involves using written or spoken words to put down others; *social bullying* involves actions that negatively affect others' relationships; and *physical bullying* involves harm done to another's body or their belongings. Table 5.2 provides examples of each. However, students engaged in bullying behavior might not limit their actions to these behaviors. Furthermore, some bullying behaviors are subtle or done when teachers are less likely to notice them, so teachers should be proactive about identifying bullying behaviors.

Once teachers can identify instances of bullying in their classrooms, they can begin to identify the roles of various students involved. There are generally three roles in bullying behavior: (1) those engaged in bullying, (2) those bullied by others, and (3) witnesses to bullying. Students can be involved in more than one role. For example, a student who bullies her classmates could be a victim of bullying at home and a bystander to bullying that occurs on the bus. To ensure prompt identification of students involved in bullying, it is helpful to note that some students are more likely to engage in bullying behaviors.

Table 5.2: Bullying Behaviors

Type of Bullying	Behaviors
Verbal bullying	• Teasing • Name calling • Inappropriate sexual comments • Taunting • Threatening to cause harm
Social bullying	• Purposefully excluding someone • Telling others not to be friends with someone • Spreading rumors about someone • Embarrassing someone in public
Physical bullying	• Hitting, kicking, or pinching • Spitting • Tripping or pushing • Taking or breaking someone's things • Making mean or rude gestures

Source: StopBullying, n.d.a.

StopBullying (n.d.b) identified two types of students who are most likely to engage in bullying behaviors.

- Some are well-connected to their peers, have social power, are overly concerned about their popularity, and like to dominate or be in charge of others.

- Others are more isolated from their peers and may be depressed or anxious, have low self esteem, be less involved in school, be easily pressured by peers, or not identify with the emotions or feelings of others.

As teachers monitor students' interactions, they may want to pay particular attention to these students to ensure that their interactions with others are kind and contribute to an inclusive classroom environment.

If it becomes apparent that students are bullying one another, a pro-kindness approach is often most effective in stopping bullying behavior. That is, teachers should view bullying behaviors as symptoms of unmet needs and use empathy to inform how they address students who bully others. Teachers can meet with students and ask about their bullying behaviors, why they engage in them, and if they have considered how their actions affect others. Teachers can also use the following seven guidelines, adapted from Darrell Scott and Robert J. Marzano (2014), to ensure pro-kindness interactions with these students.

1. Differentiate between students and their behavior. They may engage in bullying, but it is not who they are. Additionally, avoid labeling students as victims, as this may become part of their identity.

2. Accept—unconditionally—students who demonstrate bullying behavior. Acceptance cannot be faked; teachers must make a conscious choice to accept and care about these students.

3. Focus on positive aspects of the students doing the bullying. While this may be difficult, it is an essential step in the pro-kindness movement.

4. Help the person displaying bullying behavior want to change. For example, a teacher might say, "Madalyn, I admire you as a person, and the way I see you treating Frances isn't a reflection of who you really are." Teaching empathy (page 17) can be especially useful during this step.

5. Reinforce positive behavior, however small, from students demonstrating bullying behavior. Even slight changes should be recognized and acknowledged.

6. Model the desired behavior. Positive modeling is key, as individuals tend to learn by watching others.

7. Diminish the perceived differences between students bullying and students being bullied; help them see their similarities (page 100).

Following these guidelines changes teachers' responses to bullying from punishment—which often fails to create long-term results—to a more profound, student-improvement approach. The overall message is that bullying is a *behavior* that does not need to define a person. This mentality avoids ostracizing students who demonstrate bullying behavior, which may worsen their behavior. Rather, a pro-kindness approach helps modify students' behaviors by modeling the desired inclusive attitudes and actions and inviting students to be a positive part of the community.

While the previous guidelines addressed how to interact with students who engage in bullying behaviors, there are also strategies that directly address students who are either bullied or witnesses to bullying. Students who are regularly bullied may benefit from targeted interventions (page 98). Students who regularly witness bullying can be taught about the importance of intervening and how they play an indirect role in bullying. Strategies related to empathy (page 17) may also be helpful to this end. Rachel's Challenge assembly programs (page 26) can benefit all students by creating a more inclusive school and classroom where students' belonging needs are met, regardless of the roles related to bullying they tend to take.

Respect

Respect involves taking other people's thoughts, feelings, and ideas seriously. However, there is a common tendency to confuse respect with maintaining a "courteous, decorous, civil, or deferential attitude" (Cohen, Cardillo, & Pickeral, 2011). Instead, such attitudes could be considered an outcome of respect, as considerate behaviors tend to develop as a response to feeling legitimized in a community. When establishing a respectful classroom atmosphere, teachers should recognize the importance of mutual respect—that is, students feel respected by their teachers, and teachers feel respected by their students. To foster mutual respect, teachers can consider interactions between teachers and students, interactions among students, and the climate of the classroom.

Interactions Between Teachers and Students

Respectful interactions between teachers and students set the climate for the entire class. Classrooms in which interactions are not mutually respectful are unlikely to be particularly comfortable for instructors or students. As such, teachers should monitor whether their actions and words convey that they take the wants and needs of their students seriously. Here, we discuss the tone of their interaction with students, as well as how to address concerns.

Tone of Interaction

Teachers should frequently reflect on how their demeanor and classroom behaviors show or imply respect for their students. Teachers can use the following questions to determine whether the tone of their interactions tends to be respectful.

- ▶ What actions or behaviors do I use to let students know that they are being heard? How do I acknowledge my students?

- ▶ Do I understand what students are trying to say? If not, do I use questions to ensure I fully understand them?

- ▶ What emotions do I feel as I interact with students? How do these emotions affect my interactions?

- ▶ When difficulties arise in the classroom, how do I address them? Do I correct students without making them feel as though I do not take them seriously?

- ▶ What do I do to let students know that they can trust me? Are my actions consistent with what I say and consistent with all students?

- ▶ When students offer their thoughts or opinions, how do I react? Do I take them into consideration and use them to inform classroom instruction or management?

Such questions ask teachers to reflect on the degree of respect inherent in their interactions with students.

Concerns

Teachers must, by law, accommodate students with learning disabilities, poor vision, and so forth. However, teachers should also address students' academic, extracurricular, or personal concerns to show them respect. Academic concerns might involve poor time management, anxiety about upcoming assessments, or difficulty mastering content. Extracurricular concerns could involve upcoming events or pressures associated with involvement in a club or team. Finally, personal concerns often involve struggles related to family, friends, or personal well-being.

If specific students seem preoccupied, nervous, or overwhelmed, teachers can reach out to them to discuss possible actions to alleviate their stress. For example, if a student is spending increasingly more time at field hockey practice after school and seems to be avoiding going home, the teacher might meet with the student to get a better idea of her specific needs. Teachers can also encourage students to come to them with their problems and emphasize that they are there as a resource. Teachers should also note that some students may struggle in more than one capacity—that is, have concerns that are simultaneously academic, extracurricular, or personal. For example, students who are new to a school may have concerns that cross multiple dimensions as they adjust to their new environment.

As teachers identify students' concerns, they must take those concerns seriously. Inadequately addressing students' concerns, no matter how inconsequential they may seem, can deter students from disclosing larger issues that arise in their lives. Teachers can tailor reactions to students' concerns to the unique needs of each student. For example, if a student says that she feels overwhelmed before a big game, a teacher might meet with the coach of her team, offer the student an extension for a specific assignment until after the game, arrange to meet with the student during school hours to work on academics, or just acknowledge that the student's situation is difficult and offer her reassurance. Teachers can also work with students to determine what they believe is the best course of action and use this to inform how they address their concerns. If students' concerns are academic in nature, there are a number of responses to struggling students (page 78) that teachers can use to address them.

Interactions Among Students

Not surprisingly, students' relationships with each other also contribute to the sense of respect in a classroom. If teachers see that students repeatedly struggle with respectful behaviors, they can design standard operating procedures (page 112) or specific behavior expectations (page 118) that outline what respectful behavior looks like in that situation. If students' interactions with one another are continually disrespectful, teachers can reflect on whether they fall into patterns of bullying behavior (page 100) and address them as such. Most commonly, disrespectful interactions among students occur during disagreements or conflicts. While some situations require teacher intervention, it is often beneficial for teachers to provide students with tools to resolve their conflicts with one another independently. Here, we address three strategies that help students respectfully resolve their interpersonal conflicts: (1) conflict analysis, (2) "I" statements, and (3) peer mediation.

Conflict Analysis

When conflicts arise, teachers can ask students to consider how they played a role in the events leading up to the conflict. Figure 5.1 provides a questionnaire that can help students through this reflection process. Visit **marzanoresearch.com/reproducibles** for a reproducible version of this worksheet. Teachers can have students fill out the questionnaire and follow up with them about their responses to make sure they recognize that their actions are choices that lead to specific outcomes. If similar conflicts arise repeatedly, teachers can reference previous questionnaires to highlight students' tendencies toward specific behaviors. Teachers can also use the questionnaire in figure 5.1 to get a better sense of the nature of the conflicts that arise in their classrooms. If teachers find discrepancies in students' accounts or find that students focus on different issues in the survey, they can arrange meetings between students to better understand what occurred.

"I" Statements

Students, particularly younger ones, can have a tendency to place blame solely on others or fail to realize that their emotions play a role in their interpretations of specific situations. *"I" statements*, developed by Thomas Gordon in 1970, shift explanations of conflicts away from placing blame, making judgments, or name calling (such as, "He started it" or "She's being mean to me"). Instead, they require that students articulate how others' actions affected them through the use of an explicitly defined format. The format is as follows.

I feel [**feeling**] when you [**behavior**] because [**concrete effect or consequence**].

"I" statements are particularly useful in helping students see the relationship between their behaviors and their effect on others. Teachers can acquaint students with this model at the beginning of the school year and ask them to use the format when discussing personal conflicts. Teachers can further expand "I" statements to include the following statement.

I want [**desired behavior**], and I do not want [**undesired behavior**].

Conflict-Analysis Worksheet

Name: _____   Date: _____

Who was involved in this conflict?

Explain in your own words the events leading up to the conflict:

Explain in your own words the results of the conflict:

What did you want to have happen?

How did your actions contribute to the problem or make it get worse?

Identify a few ways that you could have lessened, solved, or prevented the conflict:

What can you do in the future to avoid similar situations?

Figure 5.1: Conflict-analysis questionnaire.

This final statement teaches students to be assertive with their wants and needs, but in a way that is respectful and considers the feelings of all parties involved.

Peer Mediation

Peer mediation involves student mediators who are trained in conflict resolution helping their peers resolve their disputes respectfully and independently of teachers. Peer mediators should not force decisions, advice, or judgments onto their peers but, instead, serve as an impartial resource. School counselors often run programs to train students as peer mediators. However, if schoolwide peer mediation programs do not exist, teachers can create them for their own classrooms. There are a number of conflict-resolution frameworks that can be taught to students to this end. Table 5.3 (page 106) outlines an example of one conflict resolution procedure developed by David W. Johnson and Roger T. Johnson (1987, 1991).

Table 5.3: Peacemakers Program's Negotiation and Conflict Mediation Procedure

Step	Procedure
Introduction	1. The peer mediator introduces himself or herself, and explains the guidelines of peer mediation. • "Mediation is voluntary. My role is to help you find a solution to your conflict that is acceptable to both of you." • "I am neutral. I will not take sides or attempt to decide who is right or wrong. I will help you decide how to solve the conflict." • "Each person will have the chance to state his or her view of the conflict without interruption." 2. The mediator asks students if they want to solve the problem and does not proceed until both answer, "Yes." 3. The peer mediator explains the rules for negotiation. • Solve the problem. • Do not resort to name calling. • Do not interrupt. • Be as honest as you can. • If you agree to a solution, you must do what you have agreed to do. • Anything said in mediation is confidential. 4. The mediator asks students if they agree to these rules and does not proceed until both answer, "Yes." 5. Students enter the negotiation phase.
Negotiation	1. State what you want: "I want to use the book now." 2. State how you feel: "I'm frustrated." 3. State the reasons for your wants and feelings: "You have been using the book for the past hour. If I don't get to use the book soon, my report will not be done on time. It's frustrating to have to wait so long." 4. Summarize your understanding of what the other person wants, how the other person feels, and the reasons underlying both. 5. Invent three optional plans to resolve the conflict. 6. Choose one plan and shake hands.

Source: Adapted from Johnson, Johnson, Dudley, & Burnett, 1992.

Teachers would first explain a peer mediation process, like the one outlined in table 5.3, to their students by describing each step, situations in which peer mediation is and is not appropriate, and rules and procedures related to the process. At this time, students could ask clarifying questions to ensure their understanding. After students are familiar with the process, teachers can have them practice peer mediation through roleplaying. As students become proficient with this process, teachers can ask a few students to volunteer as classroom peer mediators. Teachers can assign specific students to this role for an extended period of time, or all students in a class can rotate through the role of peer mediator. Regardless of who is serving as a peer mediator, teachers should review the peer mediation process with their classes periodically to ensure all students understand the characteristics of respectful conflict resolution.

Climate

A classroom's climate refers to how the various aspects of the class combine to create an overall mood or tone. Teacher-student interactions as well as interactions among students are critical components of a classroom's climate. However, in addition to previous strategies related to interactions that might occur throughout the school day, teachers can provide opportunities for all stakeholders in a classroom to openly express their thoughts, feelings, and wants. Here, we discuss bills of rights and classroom meetings, though teachers can also use strategies for input (page 82) and choice (page 83) as a means to foster a respectful classroom climate. When using such strategies, teachers can model respect by taking all comments seriously and acting upon them as such.

Bills of Rights

One way to establish a respectful climate is to ask students to articulate their nonnegotiables—things they need to feel comfortable and respected. Bills of rights are documents that clearly define such needs. A bill of rights might include items such as, "All students and teachers have the right to be treated with respect" and "I have the right to feel safe." An example bill of rights that might be used in a classroom is presented in figure 5.2.

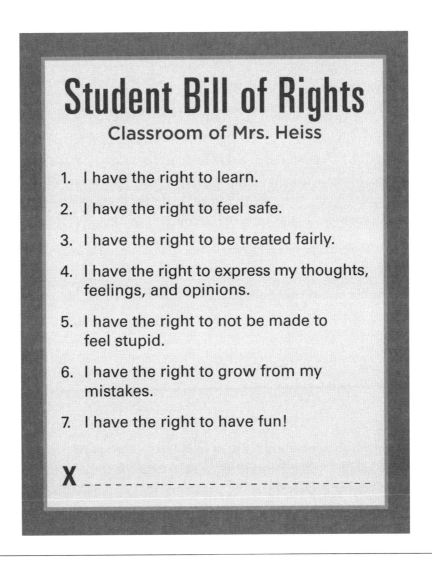

Figure 5.2: Example classroom bill of rights.

While similar to behavior expectations (page 118) in some capacities, a bill of rights tends to focus on establishing a tone for interactions within a classroom rather than defining specific student behaviors. For example, a bill of rights might note, "Students have the right to be listened to," whereas a set of classroom rules might include, "Students should be quiet when others are speaking." Bills of rights help articulate what students want and need without explicitly creating limitations on their behavior, which can be particularly empowering for students who do not feel as though they belong in the classroom community.

When creating a bill of rights, teachers can first lead discussions about what rights are and how they relate to the concepts of respect and belonging. As students' understanding of these concepts solidify, teachers can ask them to identify two or three items that make them feel respected during class. Teachers can also ask students to brainstorm nonnegotiables by identifying characteristics of a respectful classroom or actions that make them feel disrespected. Students can reword these into rights using the sentence stem, "I have the right to _____." For example, if a student notes that he or she has felt stupid for asking questions in previous classes, this could manifest as "I have the right to ask questions" or "I have the right not to be made to feel stupid." After students have independently generated their own rights, teachers can bring the class together to create a classwide bill of rights. Students can discuss and edit items as needed to create a final list on which all students in the class agree. Once created, teachers can post these lists in their classrooms and refer to them throughout the year. Teachers can also ask students to sign one classroom copy of the document to signal their understanding of the rights it articulates.

Classroom Meetings

Classroom meetings provide a respectful space for all members of a classroom to share their thoughts, feelings, concerns, or questions. They also are powerful tools to develop students' responsibility and strengthen a sense of community (Glasser, 1969, 1986, 1990). Barbara McEwan, Paul Gathercoal, and Virginia Nimmo (1997) identified the following steps as important to class meetings.

▶ Determine who can call a class meeting and when it should be held according to standards of appropriate time and place.

▶ Seat students and teachers so that they can see the faces of all other class members.

▶ Establish the expectation that names will not be used in a class meeting because the purpose of class meetings is to address issues, not people.

▶ Establish the ground rule that the meeting will stay on topic.

▶ Establish the ground rule that students have the right not to participate in class meetings.

▶ Encourage or require students to use journals in conjunction with the class meetings.

Classroom meetings might occur on a regular basis or in reaction to specific events. To illustrate how a classroom meeting might manifest, consider a fourth-grade class that has been struggling with teasing. Before starting the meeting, the teacher might explain the purpose of the classroom meeting and the rules under which the meeting will operate (such as one student speaking at a time, no using names of specific students, and so on). The teacher can then open the discussion about the topic at hand to students or, if no students volunteer, share his or her thoughts on the situation. After all students have gotten a chance to share, the teacher could ask students to write journal entries about the discussion that occurred. The teacher might read the journal entries privately to get a better sense of how teasing in the classroom is affecting students and to guide further action to ensure a climate of respect.

Affection

A simple way to increase students' sense of belonging is through affection. To help students show affection for one another, teachers can have students practice giving compliments to one another (page 90). For teachers, showing affection involves finding appropriate ways to express genuine care for students. Affectionate gestures do not have to be grandiose. Rather, small expressions of affection go a long way in reminding students that teachers are personally invested in them. Teachers can easily do this with the use of personal information, simple courtesies, humor, and affectionate physical behaviors. Affection can also be used as a subtle and indirect way to let students know that teachers can separate them from their behavior. For example, if a teacher sends a student to the office for disruptive behavior, showing affection for that student the next day can send the message that the teacher is not holding a grudge.

Personal Information

Teachers can incorporate personal information into their interactions with students to show affection for them. This demonstrates that teachers have taken an interest in knowing their students personally and that they want their students to feel comfortable with them. From the beginning of the school year, teachers can consciously get to know their students as quickly as possible and continue to gather information about them as the year progresses.

Teachers can use interest surveys to gather information about students' interests, aspirations, backgrounds, families, and hobbies. Teachers can also incorporate items on these surveys about their academic preferences, such as favorite subjects, learning styles, frustrations, and previous experiences in school. They can also add personal questions to exit slips to gather academic and personal information about students simultaneously. Figure 5.3 contains an example exit slip with academic and personal questions.

One thing I understand really well	
One question I still have	
One thing I'm excited to learn more about	
What I'm most looking forward to this weekend	

Figure 5.3: Example exit slip.

Informal conferences are another common way to gather personal information about students without the pressures that may be characteristic of more formal meetings. With informal conferences, teachers have an opportunity to compliment students, ask for their input (page 82), and better understand their backgrounds. The beauty of informal conferences is their flexibility—they can occur while students work independently, in between classes, before or after school, or during free periods. Teachers should also recognize that informal conferences do not need to focus on mining data about students. Instead, the goal of such meetings should be to show students that teachers are interested in their lives. As such, informal conferences can directly address students' interests and activities or inquire about their opinions on classroom topics, pop culture, or news events.

Teachers should not limit how they gather information about students to the strategies described in this section. Rather, there is a variety of ways that teachers can stay up to date with students' lives. For example, teachers can read local or school newspapers, talk with other school staff, or use parent-teacher conferences (page 133) to learn about their students. As personal information is gleaned from various sources, teachers can casually mention such information to students or incorporate the information into later conversations. Such actions go a long way in showing students that teachers care about them.

Simple Courtesies

Simple courtesies—small gestures and behaviors that may not be necessary but are done voluntarily—may be one of the easiest ways for teachers to show affection for their students. For example, a teacher might go out of his way to learn each student's name quickly at the beginning of the year or greet students by the classroom door at the beginning of class. Each of these actions could be considered a simple courtesy because they are actions the teacher does not necessarily need to do, yet does anyway to show he wants to build positive relationships with students. Here, we provide a list of simple courtesies that teachers can use throughout the year.

- ▶ Acknowledge students when encountering them outside of school.
- ▶ Congratulate or thank students after they turn in an assessment.
- ▶ Give students full attention when they are speaking.
- ▶ Greet students as they enter class.
- ▶ Inquire how students are doing or how their weekends were.
- ▶ Make eye contact with students when speaking with them.
- ▶ Make positive comments or give compliments to students when appropriate.
- ▶ Remark on changes to students' appearance or behavior.
- ▶ Say goodbye to students as they leave class.
- ▶ Smile at students.
- ▶ Stand close to students.
- ▶ Thank students for their help (such as holding the door or passing out papers).
- ▶ Use students' names when calling on them.

Teachers should also note that the preceding list is by no means comprehensive and that there are a multitude of other actions that can be used to show affection for students. Because simple courtesies only require that teachers go out of their way to treat students kindly, such behaviors often come quite naturally or can be easily adopted by teachers if they are not already in use. When using affectionate behaviors, teachers should keep in mind the personality and cultural background of students. For example, some students may not be comfortable returning eye contact or find that a teacher standing too close violates their personal space. Teachers should monitor students' reactions to simple courtesies to ensure that they are having a positive effect.

Humor

Teachers can use humor to verbally show students affection, as humor typically implies a comfort around others and can be easily integrated into lessons, presentations, and day-to-day interactions. The following list, articulated in the Marzano Compendium of Instructional Strategies (Marzano Research, 2016g), provides a few ways to incorporate humor into the classroom.

- ▸ **Jokes:** Teachers can tell jokes to students at any point in a lesson or during one-on-one interactions. Jokes can be content related, though teachers can use jokes unrelated to content as well. Alternatively, teachers can ask students to bring in their own jokes to share, though they should be screened for appropriateness before being shared with the class.

- ▸ **Playful banter:** Teachers and students can exchange playful banter in which both parties engage in lighthearted teasing. Teachers should be aware of when playful banter has gone on for too long and monitor the tone of the banter to ensure it remains appropriate.

- ▸ **Puns and plays on words:** Puns and plays on words are fun ways to manipulate language in humorous ways and can be incorporated into one-on-one interactions with students or into a lesson itself. However, puns and plays on words will not be successful if students do not understand them. Teachers should consider age level and difficulty before sharing puns or plays on words.

- ▸ **Self-directed humor:** Teachers can use self-directed humor by pointing out when they do something silly or when they make a mistake. This strategy is particularly powerful for perfectionist students, as it models that people do not need to take themselves seriously all of the time.

While humor can be a powerful way to show affection for students, teachers should also keep in mind that humor can backfire if it crosses the line from lighthearted to mean-spirited. To avoid miscommunication, teachers can consider how their attempts at humor could be interpreted by students, particularly those who may doubt that the humor is affectionate. For example, a teacher might gently tease one student who shows the traits of high esteem (see table 4.1, page 65) but not a different student who tends to be unsure of herself. With the latter student, the teacher can express affection in other ways, such as through simple courtesies or use of personal information.

Physical Behaviors

Physical behaviors refer to physical contact and gestures that teachers use to let students know they are cared about. The following list, articulated in the Marzano Compendium of Instructional Strategies (Marzano Research, 2016g), contains several appropriate physical behaviors that teachers can use to show affection for students.

- ▸ Applauding
- ▸ Making eye contact

- ▸ Nodding the head

- ▸ Giving high-fives

- ▸ Leaning forward while sitting

- ▸ Giving pats on the back

- ▸ Shaking hands

- ▸ Smiling

- ▸ Standing close to students

- ▸ Waving

In addition to these behaviors, teachers can think about how their body language may be interpreted by others. For example, a teacher might be intentional about using open body language after he notices his own unintentional tendency to cross his arms when interacting with students. Regardless of the physical behavior, teachers should make sure to use these strategies appropriately and with attention to individual students' age, gender, and cultural background to ensure they actually contribute to students' sense of belonging (Marzano & Pickering, 2011).

Cooperation

One way to foster a sense of belonging among students is to provide them with opportunities to cooperate with one another—that is, to work together toward a common goal. Cooperation not only contributes to a sense of belonging among students but also has benefits spanning students' educational and personal lives. As John Shindler (2010) explained:

> There are many reasons to decide that cooperative learning is worth the effort. First, it has been shown to have a positive effect on student learning when compared to individual or competitive conditions. . . . Second, cooperative learning has the potential to meet more learning style needs more of the time than individualized direct instruction. . . . Third, the interpersonal and collaboration skills that can be learned in a cooperative learning activity teach skills that are critical for later personal and professional success. Fourth, it has the potential to produce a level of engagement that other forms of learning cannot. . . . Fifth, it can be a powerful tool toward several transformative goals including building communal bonds, learning conflict resolution skills, learning to consider others' needs, and learning to be an effective team member. (pp. 227–228)

Clearly, there are many benefits to asking students to cooperate with each other throughout the year. Teachers can establish standard operating procedures and use cooperative activities in addition to jigsaw activities (page 87) to encourage cooperation.

Standard Operating Procedures

To ensure students successfully cooperate with one another, teachers can establish standard operating procedures that are conducive to these behaviors. *Standard operating procedures* (SOPs) create consistent behaviors among students by providing specific directions. SOPs are most successful with skills that can be defined, exemplified, and practiced. In terms of creating an environment conducive to cooperation, teachers can create SOPs that address participation, discussion, division of work, or conflict resolution.

SOPs generally are articulated in two common forms: (1) procedural lists and (2) flowcharts. Procedural lists directly outline the steps needed for a specific behavior in the order that they occur. For example, consider the following seven-step procedural list for respectful discussion.

1. Take a moment to consider your thoughts about the topic of discussion.

2. Listen to other students when they are speaking.

3. Think about the comments that were just said before speaking yourself.

4. Mentally generate your own comment.

5. Think about what you have to add in relation to what was just said by your peers. Ask yourself if what you are going to say is kind, relevant, and necessary. If yes, proceed to step 6. If no, repeat the process from the beginning.

6. Raise your hand.

7. When called on, say your comment.

SOPs can also take the form of flowcharts, an example of which is shown in figure 5.4.

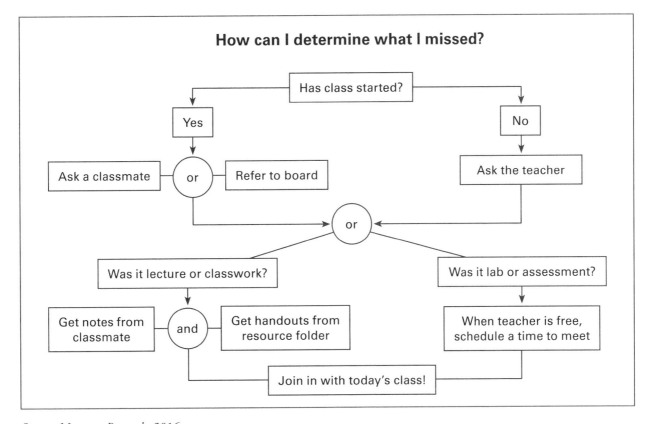

Source: Marzano Research, 2016e.

Figure 5.4: SOP flowchart for addressing missed work.

Regardless of which type of SOPs are in use, teachers should explain SOPs to students before they are expected to use them independently. When teaching an SOP, teachers should make sure that students do not have any questions about the procedure before it is practiced in class. Teachers might also find it helpful to display SOPs in the classroom and remind students of them before or as they engage in cooperative activities or group projects.

Cooperative Activities

Once students have an understanding of the prerequisite behaviors that enable successful cooperation as outlined by standard operating procedures (page 112), teachers can integrate cooperative activities into their classrooms. It may be relevant to discuss the difference between the effects of cooperative and competitive activities. While competitive games focus on individuals or groups of students competing against one another, cooperative activities encourage all students to work together toward a common goal, thus contributing to their sense of belonging and deepening their relationships. This is not to say that competitive games do not have a place in the classroom. Rather, competitive games can increase individual students' esteem (page 63), though teachers may want to regularly change team structures so that all students experience winning and losing.

Cooperative activities can be particularly helpful at the beginning of the year to help students get to know one another. A number of cooperative activities adapted from Adam Fletcher and Kari Kunst (2006) are listed here.

- **Blind Partner Walk:** Blindfold students and have them navigate obstacle courses using verbal guidance from students who are not blindfolded. For the purposes of this activity, the majority of the class could guide one or two blindfolded students or the majority of the class could be blindfolded with one or two seeing students guiding them.

- **Bloop:** Give groups of four to six students a balloon and ask the members of the group to hold hands. Tell students to keep their balloon off the floor for as long as possible without letting go or using their hands to touch the balloon.

- **Duo Sit or Group Sit:** Have students pair up and link arms while back-to-back. From standing, have students sit down and stand back up without unlinking arms. Once students become familiar with this activity in pairs, ask students to do the same activity in increasingly larger groups.

- **Human Knot:** Have students get in a circle and hold right hands with someone across the circle. Repeat this process with students' left hands. Ask students to unravel the knot they have created without letting go of each other's hands (for this activity to work, students must be allowed to adjust their hand grips).

- **Impulse:** Have the class hold hands and send "pulses" around the circle. To do this, students squeeze the hand of the person next to them, squeezing only after they feel the person on their other side tighten their grip. Ask the class to do this multiple times to see if they can get increasingly faster times sending the pulse around the circle.

- **Lap Sit:** Have students stand in a circle and arrange themselves so that someone of approximately similar size is to their left and right. Students take one step closer toward the center, then each turn to their right. Have students put their hands on the shoulders of the person in front of them and slowly sit in the lap of the person behind them (a trial run of this activity may be required in which students briefly sit on the knees of the person behind them to ensure correct spacing). Once students have formed a sitting circle, have students clap their hands simultaneously. If a teacher chooses to use this activity, he or she should implement it appropriately in the classroom by considering the age and maturity of students as well as the level of comfort of students with being touched.

▸ **Line Ups:** Have students line up based on a specific criterion, such as by height, birthday, or alphabetically by last name. To make this game more difficult, create parameters by which students must abide, such as lining up without talking or with blindfolds on.

After a cooperative activity, teachers can ask students to reflect on their experiences to highlight the importance of cooperation and strengthen the sense of community in the classroom. To this end, teachers can prompt students to discuss their experiences using the following questions:

- What did you enjoy most about this activity?
- What was your first impulse when given the challenge?
- How did you feel when . . . ?
- What was the biggest challenge?
- What were some of the questions that came up?
- Did you consider more than one solution?
- How did you go about including everyone?
- What do you think about some of the other ideas that were tried?
- If you were to try this again what might you do differently?
- What did you learn about your group? About yourself?
- How could you apply what you've learned to other areas of your life? (Trent, 2005)

Teachers can have students answer these questions in small groups or as a class. If students work in small groups, it is often beneficial to bring the entire class together to share.

Summary and Recommendations

This chapter addressed ways in which teachers can ensure students' belonging needs are met while at school. The chapter first addressed inclusion through strategies related to invitational education, similarities, interventions, and addressing bullying. We also provided strategies that ensure that a classroom's climate, as well as interactions between teachers and students and interactions among students, are respectful. We concluded the chapter with strategies related to affection and cooperation to further support students' sense of belonging.

Although teachers can use the strategies in this chapter in a variety of ways, we recommend the following.

▸ At least once a semester, use the invitational education framework to identify aspects of the classroom that are inviting and disinviting and address disinviting aspects of the classroom as needed.

‣ At least once a semester, assess the need for interventions for specific students and whether bullying is occurring in the classroom.

‣ At least once a week, use strategies that contribute to a respectful learning environment.

‣ At least once every two weeks, use strategies related to affection or cooperation.

The following scenario depicts how these recommendations might manifest in the classroom.

In the beginning of the year, a middle school social studies teacher determines the degree to which her class is inviting or disinviting to students. The teacher begins to greet students as they enter class to show affection for them. Each month, she considers specific students who may be in need of intervention and schedules regular check-ins to get to know them better and to ensure that they don't slip through the cracks. The teacher also creates a peer mediation program to address conflicts and, when larger issues arise, calls classroom meetings to allow all students a chance to voice their thoughts and feelings. When the teacher notices that specific students repeatedly engage in bullying behavior, she directly addresses them to determine the motivation of the behavior. As students seem to become more comfortable with one another, she uses similarity activities and cooperative activities to strengthen the relationships among students.

CHAPTER 6

Safety

When considering safety, teachers can examine how they support both the actual and perceived safety of students. Despite tragic and widely publicized violent incidents (such as those at Columbine High School in 1999 and Sandy Hook Elementary School in 2012), statistically speaking, schools tend to succeed at creating environments free of genuine danger. Nevertheless, teachers can ensure students *feel* safe by addressing various aspects of perceived safety in addition to securing the actual safety of their classrooms. In this chapter, we address four aspects of safety: (1) actual safety, (2) order, (3) fairness, and (4) consistency.

Actual Safety

Strategies for meeting the actual safety needs of students are often implicit in K–12 schools. For example, while some classes may be more predisposed to potentially dangerous situations (for example, science laboratories), state and school requirements often mandate the development of standard operating and emergency procedures as well as the presence of specific safeguards to ensure students' actual safety. Additionally, many schools have security guards, metal detectors, and support from local law enforcement as a means to further bolster their actual safety. This being stated, teachers can still take specific actions to support actual safety throughout the year.

Teachers should familiarize themselves with various emergency procedures at the beginning of the year as well as necessary teacher and student behaviors for each. Schools commonly test fire and lockdown drills, and an understanding of the protocols and procedures for both supports their success. While most schools issue reminders before emergency drills, it is beneficial for teachers to have an idea of how to proceed in various emergency scenarios without the prompting of administrators. As such, teachers can consider how they might react in the following emergency situations and whether they have access to necessary resources to ensure students' safety.

- **Emergency weather situations:** Tornadoes, earthquakes, blizzards, tropical storms, and so on (depending on climate)

- **Fire:** Within the classroom, elsewhere in the school, during passing periods, and so on

- **Medical emergencies:** Choking, bleeding, fainting, allergic reactions, asthma attacks, panic or anxiety attacks, and so on

- **Security emergencies:** Intruders on school property, missing students, fights between students, extreme student behavior, and so on

For each category, teachers should consider what their immediate response would be for themselves and for students. For example, in the event that a student has a severe allergic reaction, a teacher might consider whether to call the school nurse or other emergency services, the degree of medical assistance he or she is qualified to offer, and how to manage the class while attending to the student. If teachers have questions about appropriate responses to certain emergencies, administrators or senior staff can confirm school policies and procedures. Furthermore, in preparation for medical emergencies, teachers can take first aid or CPR certification classes (if they are not already a mandatory requisite for educators in their state).

While teachers should review their schools' emergency procedures independently, they should also directly explain such procedures to students to ensure that responses to emergency situations proceed smoothly. To this end, teachers should outline both required student actions in a given emergency scenario, such as the path to the nearest exit during a fire, and general attitudes that make emergency procedures successful, such as remaining calm and quiet. For example, a teacher might explain the individual steps required of students during a lockdown and what to expect during a lockdown drill. The teacher could then note how certain behaviors, such as staying away from doors and windows, are necessary for the actual safety of themselves and others.

After explaining an emergency procedure, teachers might emphasize the rarity of such scenarios to alleviate students' worries and note that preparedness can only contribute to the actual safety of the classroom. Teachers may also want to consider the age and maturity of students when determining the amount of information to disclose about various safety risks and whether to let students know in advance that an emergency procedure will be tested.

Order

Students feel safe when they sense that there is order in their classrooms—that is, they feel that the teacher has command of the class and the space. Teachers can be intentional about the design and enforcement of behavior expectations and reflect on how the classroom design lends itself to a feeling of order. Such considerations not only ensure the actual safety of a classroom but also contribute to students' sense of perceived safety.

Behavior Expectations

Behavior expectations explicitly define desired student behaviors and establish an orderly environment in which teaching and learning can successfully occur. To ensure their effectiveness, teachers can consider how the development and enforcement of classroom behavior expectations contribute to a sense of order. Here, we discuss the following five items regarding order and behavior expectations: (1) developing behavior expectations, (2) teaching behavior expectations, (3) reinforcing positive behaviors, (4) correcting negative behaviors, and (5) being proactive.

Developing Behavior Expectations

As mentioned previously, students can be involved in creating behavior expectations as a vehicle to provide choice to students (page 83). However, to create effective behavior expectations that support a sense of order, teachers can consider the following guidelines (Harlacher, 2015).

▶ **Create three to five behavior expectations:** Having fewer than three behavior expectations often fails to cover the breadth of desired classroom behavior, and more than five may be difficult for students to remember and implement correctly.

▶ **State expectations in positive terms:** Rather than limiting students' behaviors with rules such as "Do not be rude," teachers can phrase their behavior expectations positively, such as "Be considerate of others."

▶ **Keep the expectations brief and simple:** Create expectations that describe broad actions concisely and in the simplest language possible. This makes students more likely to remember them and allows for flexibility when applying them in various situations.

▶ **Make sure expectations can easily translate to concrete behaviors:** Similar to keeping expectations brief and simple, teachers can use actionable language when designing behavior expectations to ensure that students can easily understand how specific behaviors align or don't align with the expectations.

To see how these guidelines might translate to behavior expectations, consider table 6.1 (page 120) which shows examples and nonexamples of each.

In addition to the guidelines in table 6.1, teachers can consider existing schoolwide behavior expectations and design their individual classroom behavior expectations to support them. For example, if schoolwide behavior expectations focus on the concepts of respect, responsibility, and safety, teachers and students could define what each means in terms of desirable and undesirable behaviors exhibited in class.

As general behavior expectations are developed, they can be used to define more specific rules and procedures for various classroom situations. Rules and procedures could address any of the following classroom scenarios:

- Beginning and ending the period or school day
- Transitions and potential interruptions
- Group work
- Seat work and teacher-led activities
- Use of common materials, supplies, and equipment (Marzano, 2012, p. 97)

For example, if a teacher creates a behavior expectation that mandates student responsibility, the teacher could ask students to consider how this concept manifests during whole-class, small-group, and independent work, as well as how being responsible affects the use of common materials, supplies, and equipment.

Table 6.1: Guidelines, Examples, and Nonexamples for Behavior Expectations

Guidelines	Examples	Nonexamples
Limit a list of expectations to between three and five.	Be prepared. Demonstrate integrity. Show empathy.	Have fun. Be safe. Make friends. Take care of things. Mind your business. Be sincere. Be respectful.
State expectations in positive terms.	Be safe. Be respectful. Be responsible.	Don't fight. Don't bring drugs or weapons on school property. Don't be mean.
Keep the expectations brief and simple.	Be there and be ready.	Be fully prepared and on time when you arrive at your location.
Make sure expectations can easily translate to concrete behaviors.	Follow directions. Accept responsibility. Respect ourselves and others.	Be eager, diverse, and steadfast.

Source: Harlacher, 2015, p. 20.

Teachers should be cognizant that the need for specific rules and procedures may change throughout the year. Thus, teachers can reflect on the effectiveness of rules and procedures and the degree to which they support a safe and orderly classroom. Teachers can revisit and modify rules and procedures that do not seem to be working. For example, in the beginning of the year, a teacher might establish the behavior expectation of respect and translate it into a rule for discussion that requires that students raise their hands before speaking. As students become adept at raising their hands, the teacher might find that the rule actually hinders fluid conversation and decide it is no longer necessary. Instead, the teacher might develop new rules related to students waiting their turn to speak, not speaking over one another, and not monopolizing discussion to ensure conversation remains orderly as students navigate discussion without mandatory hand raising.

Once teachers articulate behavior expectations, rules, and procedures, they can find ways to display and refer to them throughout the year. Teachers may also want to consider the placement of such displays so that they support order. For example, teachers may want to put more general behavior expectations where they can be easily viewed from all quadrants of the classroom, whereas procedures related to borrowing books or using computers might be best displayed near libraries or technology centers respectively.

Teaching Behavior Expectations

Before expecting students to adhere to specific behavior expectations, teachers must directly teach and model the desired behaviors as well as provide students opportunities to practice them. Without explicit instruction, students may fail to correctly use the behaviors and feel unfairly punished if they are reprimanded. From a more practical standpoint, teaching behavior expectations directly facilitates the use of desired behaviors and contributes to a classroom's sense of order.

When teaching a behavior expectation, teachers can explain its purpose, how it contributes to safety and order, and what the expectation looks like when executed correctly and incorrectly. During this time, teachers can clarify any misunderstandings students may hold about the behavior. Once taught, teachers can create opportunities for practice in a low-stakes environment. For example, rather than teaching students a protocol for discussion and expecting them to implement it without error, a teacher could ask students to model the behavior or roleplay in small groups to get a sense of what the behavior looks like. If one group models the behavior particularly well, the teacher might call the entire class together to watch the group demonstrate and then ask the class to identify the behavior's characteristics.

Teachers should revisit behavior expectations frequently once they have been taught to support continued understanding by students, particularly as behavior expectations are applied to different scenarios. For example, in a classroom with a behavior expectation to be prepared, the teacher might discuss what being prepared looks like before testing, during a field trip, or for group presentations as these situations arise throughout the year. As negative patterns in student behavior emerge, teachers can remind students of behavior expectations to encourage more desirable alternative behaviors. For example, if a teacher finds that students are failing to turn in their homework in a timely manner, he or she could begin class by explaining why homework is important and how the behavior expectation to be prepared applies to the successful completion of homework. By actively and frequently teaching behavior expectations, teachers can reinforce in students' minds what positive and negative behaviors in the classroom look like.

Reinforcing Positive Behaviors

Underpinning successful classroom management is the reinforcement of desired student behaviors as they occur. Emphasis on students' positive behaviors can avoid unnecessary punishment and, in many cases, curtail negative behaviors before they become established—students may recognize that outcomes tend to be better when they display appropriate behavior. Teachers can use the following reinforcement strategies, listed in the Marzano Compendium of Instructional Strategies (Marzano Research, 2016a), to this end.

> ▸ **Certificates:** Certificates are awarded to students when they go above and beyond the actions mandated by classroom behavior expectations. Teachers may want to keep track of which students receive certificates to ensure that they are evenly awarded. Teachers might also present certificates privately to students to further support belonging.

> ▸ **Phone calls, emails, and notes:** Teachers can use phone calls, emails, or notes to inform parents of positive student behaviors exhibited in class. In such messages, teachers can explain how students helped the classroom function effectively and efficiently. This strategy can also go a long way in forming solid partnerships with parents.

> ▸ **Nonverbal affirmations:** Nonverbal affirmations encompass a range of physical gestures that let students know they are behaving appropriately. For example, a teacher might high-five students who quietly and calmly enter the classroom. Teachers can also pair nonverbal affirmations with verbal affirmations to target and reinforce specific student behaviors.

> ▸ **Tangible recognition:** Tangible recognition involves rewarding students' good behavior with specific privileges, activities, or items. However, in consideration of students' sense of belonging (page 95), teachers should avoid using tangible recognition if it will repeatedly exclude certain students. As such, this strategy may be best used when the class as a whole

does something well. For example, after a class quietly engages in independent seatwork, a teacher might teach the remainder of the period outside as a reward for the entire class.

- ▶ **Verbal affirmations:** Verbal affirmations let students know when they do something correctly. For example, a teacher might note that a student is sitting quietly in his seat and then thank him for this behavior.

When using these strategies, teachers should establish connections between the reinforcement and the desired behavior that lead to it. For example, saying, "Thank you for pushing in your chair when you got up" is more effective in reinforcing students' positive behavior than saying, "Thank you" alone.

Correcting Negative Behaviors

While teachers should use reinforcement as often as possible, inevitably they will need to correct students when they are disruptive or behaving inappropriately. Here, we list a few common methods of correction adapted from Jason E. Harlacher (2015) and the Marzano Compendium of Instructional Strategies (Marzano Research, 2016b).

- ▶ **Error correction:** Error correction involves identifying an undesirable behavior, modeling the correct one, and asking students to try again using the correct behavior. After students correctly perform replacement behaviors, teachers thank students for their cooperation or reward them with a desired result.

- ▶ **Extinction:** Extinction involves withholding reinforcement of an undesirable behavior as a means to stop the behavior entirely. For example, if a student continually calls out during class, a teacher would ignore the student until he or she used a desired behavior, such as raising his or her hand, at which point the teacher would call on the student. Over time, extinction helps students habitually engage in desired behaviors as they learn that disruptive behaviors do not achieve the outcomes they want.

- ▶ **Pregnant pause:** Pregnant pauses involve stopping instruction when students engage in undesirable behaviors. With this strategy, the uncomfortable silence that follows often draws attention to misbehaving students and mitigates their behavior. Before using this strategy, teachers should consider the motivations for students' misbehavior, as this strategy is likely to backfire if students are seeking attention.

- ▶ **Verbal cues:** Verbal cues involve teachers quietly bringing attention to students' undesirable behavior. Teachers might also cite specific behavior expectations as a means to help students understand why they are being cued to stop or use questions such as "Is what you are doing appropriate?"

When using the previous strategies, it benefits teachers to be aware of the "golden ratio" of using at least five reinforcements for each correction (Flora, 2000). This ratio maintains a positive classroom environment, as it ensures that teachers focus on reinforcing desired behaviors rather than correcting undesirable ones. Furthermore, when making corrections, teachers should try to lead with positive comments when possible before addressing negative behaviors.

When reacting to students' undesirable behavior, it may also benefit teachers to use a series of graduated actions, which create multiple opportunities for students to correct their behaviors. To see how graduated actions might be used, consider two students who are having a side conversation during class. If the teacher decides to use a series of graduated actions, the teacher would first make eye contact with the students to let them know he is aware that they are not paying attention. If this action does not stop their side conversation, the teacher might physically move closer to the pair, thus making it harder for the students to ignore him. If the undesired behavior continues, the teacher could use nonverbal and then verbal cues to ask the students to refocus. In the event that the side conversation continues, the teacher could offer students a choice between a more direct consequence and an appropriate behavior.

Being Proactive

Successful classroom management requires that teachers be *proactive*. This means that they are aware of what is happening in every part of the classroom at any given moment and take steps against undesirable situations. Not surprisingly, inherent to being proactive is reinforcing students' positive behaviors as they occur (page 121) and correcting negative behaviors (page 122) before they begin. However, being proactive can also manifest in a multitude of other ways. Proactive teachers regularly monitor the classroom for potential problems, such as whispering or giggling among students, and investigate their causes to prevent them from compounding into full-blown disruptions. Eye contact and movement around a classroom can show awareness of the physical space. Other examples of being proactive include the creation of contingency plans for various behavior scenarios, establishment of hand cues that signal inappropriate behavior, or discussion of specific incidents that might affect students' behavior. In short, being proactive encompasses actions that prove to students that their teachers are aware and in control.

Proactivity relies on an understanding of students, their tendencies, and triggers for undesired behaviors. Thus, the first step in being proactive requires that teachers know their students personally. To this end, teachers can determine whether any of their students might be classified into one of the five types of behavioral categories of potentially disruptive students listed in table 6.2.

Table 6.2: Proactive Behaviors for Types of Potentially Disruptive Students

Type of Student	Indicators	Proactive Teacher Behaviors
Passive	Avoidant of social interactions for fear of having a negative interaction or being dominated by others; afraid of criticism, ridicule, or rejection	Create a safe and inclusive classroom environment; encourage assertiveness and positive self-talk; reward and celebrate even the smallest of successes; withhold criticisms
Aggressive	Interrupts during class; lashes out; intimidates other students physically or verbally; rude or disrespectful to teacher; experiences relatively few successes	Describe student's behavior; reward or apply consequences consistently when behavior is or is not appropriate; encourage extracurricular involvement; give student additional responsibilities so that he or she can experience success
Perfectionist	Holds him- or herself to unnecessarily high standards; motivated by fear of embarrassment rather than intellectual curiosity; unwilling to participate if there is a chance of failure	Talk with student about expectations and try to help student create realistic expectations; encourage student to make mistakes; show acceptance; have student tutor other students; create time limits for the amount of time the student can spend on an assignment

continued →

Type of Student	Indicators	Proactive Teacher Behaviors
Socially inept	Has few or no friends; seems unaware of how his or her actions affect others; seems unaware of subtle social cues or struggles to keep up natural conversations; appears anxious when interacting with others; considers him- or herself a loner	Talk to student about social cues and ways in which he or she may miss them; make suggestions regarding hygiene, dress, mannerisms, and posture; spend time interacting with student modeling appropriate behavior and showing that he or she is a valuable member of class
Attention difficulties	Inattentive; distracted easily by unusual events; difficult to re-engage or get on task; late or incomplete work; difficulty with organization, remembering, or listening	Talk with necessary individuals about getting student tested or creating an individualized learning plan; create signals to let student know when he or she is being disruptive or needs to refocus; teach basic concentration, study, and thinking skills; assign a peer tutor

Source: Marzano Research, 2016d, p. 6.

If students fall into one of the five categories of potentially disruptive students, interactions with them can be informed by the proactive teacher behaviors listed in table 6.2.

Classroom Design

Classrooms are generally safe, and teachers can reach out to maintenance staff or administrators to correct any problems that might arise. However, teachers can organize their classrooms to further support students' perception of safety by ensuring classrooms are orderly. For example, when determining how to arrange their classrooms, teachers can consider the following questions.

▸ Does the classroom have clear traffic patterns?

▸ Are students visible from all areas of the classroom at all times?

▸ Can students see the teacher and any necessary displays (such as boards and projectors) from their seats?

▸ Are frequently used materials easily accessible?

▸ Does the classroom design minimize distraction or encourage it?

▸ Does the way that students' desks are arranged support order and safety?

In addition to these questions, teachers should also consider whether the classroom itself is comfortable, as students will be less likely to remain orderly and engaged if they are uncomfortable during class.

To complete an analysis of the physical space, teachers can examine their classrooms from a sensory perspective using the following list (Scott & Marzano, 2014).

▸ **Sight:** Teachers can consider the décor (such as the use of wall space and the age and relevance of posted work and decorations), organization (such as the degree to which student, teacher, and shared spaces are cluttered or organized), and lines of sight (such as whether students can see the front of the room from their seats and whether the teacher can see all students from various locations).

▸ **Hearing:** Teachers can consider sources of unintentional sound (such as from other classes, hallways, or heating or air conditioning units) and intentional sound (such as music played before or after class and the volume levels of the teacher and the class).

▸ **Smell:** Teachers can consider if there are any odors (positive or negative) that are prevalent in the classroom.

▸ **Touch:** Teachers can consider the physical layout of the classroom (such as the ease of movement and traffic patterns in the classroom) as well as opportunities for movement (such as stretching breaks).

▸ **Taste:** Teachers can consider the availability of sustenance (such as healthy snacks and water as well as the timing of breaks and lunch).

Once discerned, teachers should eliminate negative sensory elements from the classroom when possible. For example, decorations can improve a plain room, and lamps or natural lighting can create a more comfortable environment than harsh fluorescent lights. Teachers can use curtains, wall hangings, or foam masked by fabric to dampen irritating sounds, and music can create an actively positive aural environment. To cover disagreeable odors, teachers can use cleaning products, air fresheners, essential oils, or natural scents (such as flowers). Teachers might also incorporate stretching breaks or movement into their lessons if students seem disengaged and re-evaluate policies related to food and drink periodically to further ensure students' comfort.

Fairness

Fairness is a critical component of students' sense of perceived safety and requires that teachers consider whether their treatment of students is fair and contributes to an equitable classroom. Teachers should note that equity is not isolated to one aspect of their interactions with students, such as grading tendencies or behavior management. Rather, teachers should consider the academic and behavioral equity of all their interactions with students.

Academic Equity

Academic equity involves ensuring that all students have the opportunity to experience success with their classwork. This involves identifying low-expectancy students and taking specific actions to help them succeed. Teachers can ensure that they encourage academic equity by using the following four-step process.

1. Identify expectation levels.

2. Identify differential treatment.

3. Interact positively with low-expectancy students.

4. Question low-expectancy students.

Here, we discuss each step.

Identify Expectation Levels

The first step toward academic equity involves teachers identifying their expectation level for each student. Specifically, teachers classify their expectations for each student as high, medium, or low. Unfortunately, as fallible human beings, teachers are prone to develop expectations about students' chances of doing well academically. This happens unwittingly and quite naturally. While it is difficult for teachers to become aware of their expectations as they form, it is relatively straightforward to identify them once they are established. Figure 6.1 contains a survey to guide teachers through this process. Visit **marzanoresearch .com/reproducibles** for a reproducible version of this worksheet.

Student	Expectation	Cause
Harmon	Low	I think this because Harmon often fails to turn in homework and struggles during questioning sequences.
Emma	High	I think this because Emma has met with me outside of class when she doesn't understand the material, which shows she cares about her success.
Imani	Medium	I think this because Imani rarely speaks up in class unless called upon, though the quality of her written work is good.
Marquis	High	I think this because Marquis always turns in his homework and makes eye contact throughout class.

Figure 6.1: Academic expectations worksheet.

The columns in figure 6.1 allow teachers to examine and reconsider the logic underlying their expectations. For example, in figure 6.1, the teacher identified that one student struggles to regularly turn in his homework. Apparently, this is the reason the teacher has low expectations for the student. Upon reflection, the teacher might realize that the student has begun turning in his homework with increasing regularity and that he engages in this behavior at similar rates to other students who the teacher views more positively. Teachers can also consider whether they hold generalized low expectations for certain groups of students. For example, teachers can analyze expectations for students based on ethnicity, appearance, gender, patterns of speech, or socioeconomic status. If they notice they hold low expectations for certain groups of students, they should consider why they might have internalized these biases and actively work to correct them.

Regardless of the nature of expectations, once teachers form impressions, they are often difficult to change. As Robert J. Marzano (2007) noted:

> It is difficult, if not impossible, for a person to change his or her thinking about students. Yet it is entirely possible to change behavior toward students so that all students—regardless of the teacher's level of expectation for them—receive the same behavior in terms of affective tone and quality of interactions. (pp. 167–168)

As teachers engage in this work, they may realize the potential negative consequences of their expectations. As such, once articulated, teachers must be willing to be wrong about their low expectations in order to create a more equitable classroom.

Identify Differential Treatment

Once teachers identify expectation levels for students, they can reflect on how expectations contribute to the differential treatment of specific students. This is the most serious consequence of forming low expectations about students; teachers tend to treat low-expectancy students in ways that send subtle messages that they are not expected to do well. Unfortunately, many students live up to these low expectations. Table 6.3 can be useful when identifying differential treatment of low-expectancy students.

Table 6.3: Example Behaviors Associated With Affective Tone and Interaction

	Affective Tones	Quality of Interactions
Positive	Friendly tone of voice Close proximity Friendly and open body language Frequent eye contact Smiling Playful dialogue Physical contact Range of questioning	Positive or thoughtful feedback Probing for more complex information Coaching for an answer Calling on student High level of questions Low or average level of response required for a reward (verbal or otherwise)
Negative	Monotone or harsh tone of voice Distant proximity Closed-off body language Avoidant of eye contact Frowning or unexpressive facial expression Infrequent or oppositional dialogue Infrequent physical contact Infrequent or quick questioning	Vague or negative feedback Quick interactions without depth Not staying with student Not calling on student Low level of questions High level of response required for a reward (verbal or otherwise)

Source: Adapted from Marzano Research, 2016c.

Using table 6.3, teachers can consider the frequency with which they use positive and negative affective tones throughout a class period as well as the quality of their interactions with students. For example, a teacher might realize that he is more prone to take a harsh tone of voice and avoid smiling at students for whom he has low expectations. Furthermore, in terms of quality of interaction, the teacher might recognize that he generally assumes these students' answers will be incorrect and avoids spending the time necessary to coach them toward correct answers. In contrast, the teacher might note that he takes more positive tones with other students and designs his questions to help them answer correctly.

Interact Positively With Low-Expectancy Students

Once teachers identify differential treatment, teachers should confront their biased patterns of thought and strive to transform negative interactions into positive ones. For example, consider a teacher who catches himself holding lower expectations for certain students. He might remind himself of reasons why these expectations are unfair and how they contribute to differential treatment in the classroom. As he makes behavioral changes, they should gradually become more natural and habitual.

Another way for teachers to address differential treatment in their classrooms is to actively build positive relationships with low-expectancy students. The getting-to-know-you process not only demonstrates interest in and value for students but also provides teachers with an opportunity to gather data that can inform later interactions with students. For example, a teacher might try to learn more about low-expectancy students' personal goals or interests and use this knowledge to make connections to content or to better understand students' specific needs. There are also a number of strategies teachers can use to show affection (page 109) for low-expectancy students which can further build positive relationships with them. As teachers build these relationships, they can monitor how these changes affect their perceptions of these students.

Question Low-Expectancy Students

Effective questioning is always a difficult task and becomes even more so when it involves low-expectancy students. Even when intentionally trying to question students equitably, teachers often fail to call on low-expectancy students with the same frequency as they do other students. This may be due to the fact that it is easier to choose volunteers who are likely to provide correct answers, rather than engaging low-expectancy students in long and potentially embarrassing or uncomfortable questioning sequences. However, teachers should avoid this mentality, as it only reinforces the expectation that certain students will fail to answer questions correctly. When teachers ask questions of low-expectancy students, students may not be given the time needed to think through their answers and prove their competence with the material. Teachers should stay with low-expectancy students and spend as much time with their incorrect or incomplete answers as they would with other students. This approach requires that teachers listen carefully and intently in order to determine what students do and do not understand. Additionally, teachers can use the following strategies when questioning low-expectancy students.

- Demonstrate gratitude for the response.
- Do not allow negative comments from other members of the class.
- Take time to identify what is correct and what is incorrect about an answer.
- Restate the question in a different way.
- Provide ways to let students off the hook temporarily.

Finally, teachers can implement specific strategies that provide a safe environment for students who might be reluctant to volunteer answers to difficult questions. Robert J. Marzano and Julia A. Simms (2014) offered the following list of strategies.

- **Class voting:** Teachers pose a question, and students respond as a class. This prevents low-expectancy students from being put on the spot while still allowing teachers to get an idea of students' understanding of the content. There are various ways that teachers can use this technique in the classroom. For example, a teacher might have students raise their hands or move to different corners of the room to signal their answers. If a teacher sees that a low-expectancy student correctly answered during class voting, the teacher might call on the student to explain his or her answer using specific evidence for support.

- **Paired or small-group response:** Teachers ask a question to the class, and then organize students into pairs or small groups to discuss. Teachers may want to create groups that allow low-expectancy students to work with students who have a firmer grasp on the content. Thus, teachers can preassign partners or create seating charts that easily break down into groups in which low-expectancy and high-expectancy students are represented equally. Once organized, teachers give students time to discuss the question and develop an answer. When gathering responses, teachers can call on low-expectancy students directly or ask each member of a group to contribute.

▸ **Random names:** Teachers randomly determine which students to call on. For example, a teacher might assign each student a number and use a die or random-number generator to call on students. Another common random-name strategy involves writing students' names on ice pop sticks and drawing names randomly when answers are needed. After students answer, teachers replace the sticks into the jars, indicating that the same students could be called on again at any time.

▸ **Short written responses:** Short written responses allow teachers to check in with each student and assess his or her understanding of the content privately. This can be done using exit slips, entries in academic notebooks, or brief notes on index cards or sticky notes. After students write down their answers, teachers can collect and review their responses to inform instruction and clarify common misunderstandings. When prompting students for short written responses, teachers can explain that responses will not affect their grades, but rather are used to identify the level of proficiency of the class as a whole.

▸ **Speaking props:** Another popular semi-random name generator involves the use of a ball or other prop to indicate when it is a student's turn to speak. Teachers throw the speaking prop to a student and ask him or her a question. After a student correctly answers a question, he or she throws the prop to another student, who is asked a new question. Teachers can have students stand up at the beginning of this activity and have them sit down after they correctly respond. Teachers can ask that the speaking prop be thrown to standing students only.

With the use of these strategies and the four-step process to identify and address the differential treatment of low-expectancy students, teachers can create more equitable classrooms that students perceive as fair.

Behavioral Equity

When students repeatedly misbehave, it is easy to become frustrated. It is also common for teachers to make assumptions about the intentions behind certain behaviors, such as believing that students are actively being confrontational or challenging their authority. For example, students who are known as "troublemakers" often have reputations that precede them. To some extent, a student's reputation might be deserved—he or she might act out more often than the average student and require more behavior management. However, these reputations may also unintentionally create biased feedback cycles in which teachers are more sensitive to specific students' negative behaviors and more likely to punish them than they would be others. Obviously, these sentiments are unlikely to lead to a positive classroom environment or contribute to students' sense of fairness. Teachers can guard against behavioral inequity by developing an overall disciplinary plan. Table 6.4 (page XX) presents sample considerations that might be detailed in such a plan.

Table 6.4: Overall Disciplinary Plan Considerations

Developing Relationships With Students	Being Proactive	Articulating Positive and Negative Consequences for Behavior	Dealing With High-Intensity Situations
Seek to improve relationships with all students, especially those who tend to be disruptive in class.	List typical responses to student misbehavior. Analyze the list and determine which responses are effective and which are not.	Make sure that students can describe appropriate and inappropriate behavior. Meet with students to point out specific behaviors that need to be curtailed. Help students develop explicit plans to curtail inappropriate behavior and refine the plan as needed. Isolate offending students from the class until they make a commitment to appropriate behavior.	Develop an action plan for responding to high-intensity situations. Know when to involve administrators to help avoid or deal with high-intensity situations.

Source: Marzano Research, 2016b, p. 20.

As shown in table 6.4, teachers can be intentional about how they choose to develop relationships with students, be proactive, articulate consequences for behavior, and deal with high-intensity situations. We have previously discussed strategies for developing positive relationships with students (for example, see strategies related to respect, page 102, affection, page 109, and being proactive, page 123). Here, we consider the importance of articulating consequences for behavior and dealing with high-intensity situations to ensure behavioral equity.

Articulating Consequences for Behavior

Previously in the chapter, we discussed the importance of establishing behavior expectations for students. This is foundational to establishing a perception of order. Articulating the ramifications of not following behavior expectations is foundational to developing a sense of fairness. When students understand the consequences of their negative behaviors, they can connect their actions to specific outcomes, thus countering the idea that consequences are the product of a vindictive or spiteful teacher. That is, if teachers articulate the consequences for undesirable behaviors before any negative behavior occurs, students can recognize that the consequences they receive are dictated by a clearly laid-out plan that is applied to all students.

In the event that some students repeatedly engage in undesirable behaviors and the universal consequences become ineffective, teachers should meet with students individually to develop specific behavior intervention plans that outline which behaviors are unacceptable, why such behaviors are undesirable, and the consequences of continued misbehavior. During these conversations, teachers should consider how their tone may be interpreted by students. Rather than being accusatory or overly critical, teachers may find that students are more cooperative if the intention of these meetings is to understand why students engage in disruptive behaviors in the first place. To further support a sense of fairness, teachers should have students commit to the behavioral plans or at least signal their understanding of future consequences if their behavior continues.

Teachers can later reference these plans to remind students that they understood and previously agreed to the consequences of their continued misbehavior.

Dealing With High-Intensity Situations

In some cases, students' behaviors may escalate to the point that they are out of control. While this may not happen regularly, it is likely that most teachers will face this scenario at least once. To make certain that teachers react in a way that ensures the safety of all members of the classroom as well as avoids reactionary and unfair responses, teachers can consider the following seven recommendations (Marzano & Marzano, 2015).

1. **Know students' tendencies:** Teachers can use previous instances of negative behavior as indicators of future negative behavior. However, as mentioned previously, there is little benefit in labeling students as troublemakers (see Behavioral Equity, page 129). Instead, to prevent future outbursts, teachers should pay particular attention to students who have previously displayed aggressive behavior and plan for positive interactions on a systematic basis.

2. **Recognize that the student is out of control:** Students react differently when they have reached their breaking points. For example, some students may become increasingly uncontrollable whereas others may be quiet before erupting. Students also have different triggers that may result in a high-intensity situation. As such, it is particularly important for teachers to be aware of the signs and triggers of students before they are out of control.

3. **Avoid escalating the threat of the situation:** If students seem like they may act out physically, teachers should consider the safety of both themselves and their students. Teachers should give aggressive students space so that they do not feel threatened, and use physical and verbal behaviors that do not escalate the situation. If it seems like students might harm their classmates, teachers can place themselves between out-of-control students and the rest of the class.

4. **Be calm:** When a student is out of control, it can be easy to act impulsively to stop the situation. However, this often backfires and may escalate the situation unnecessarily. Instead, teachers should talk to students calmly and positively and remind themselves that the students' behaviors are not a personal attack on them.

5. **Listen attentively:** To show respect for students who are acting out, teachers should use active listening skills to let them know they are being heard. This can be done with the use of frequent eye contact and paraphrasing. Teachers should let students vent for as long as they need. Teachers can ask questions such as "What else is bothering you?" to ensure students feel that all of their thoughts were heard.

6. **Remove the student:** As a high-intensity situation de-escalates, teachers can politely ask students to leave the class. For example, a teacher might calmly repeat, "Billy, I'd like you to go with me out to the hallway to get things back to normal. Will you please do that with me now?" until the request is followed.

7. **Set up a plan to avoid future outbursts:** After incidents occur, teachers should set up meetings with the students involved. Teachers should use these meetings to emphasize that no grudges are held and that teachers want to re-establish positive relationships. During these meetings, teachers discuss what occurred and why, and develop action plans to prevent future incidents.

Clearly, dealing with high-intensity situations necessitates that teachers act in a calm and respectful manner to avoid further escalation. When teachers are reactionary, they may act regrettably, thus combating both the actual safety of the classroom and students' perception of fairness.

Consistency

Consistency means that students can predict what will occur during their day-to-day experiences. The more that students perceive class as a consistently positive environment, the safer they feel. Teachers can consider how classroom structure and interactions with parents contribute to students' sense of consistency.

Classroom Structure

As defined by Harlacher (2015), "*Structure* refers to the amount of predictability within the classroom, including established procedures for specific activities" (p. 37). This includes schedules, procedures, and classroom design that support a sense of consistency. Classroom design was discussed previously in the chapter (page 124), as was the development of behavior expectations (page 119) and how they can be applied to create specific rules and procedures. Here, we discuss how to develop a consistent schedule that supports students' sense of perceived safety.

A predictable schedule is critical when creating a consistent learning environment. Schools generally have a daily schedule that defines when students are supposed to be in class. However, teachers can use schedules to create internal consistency between class periods. Harlacher (2015) identified the following guidelines for creating an effective daily classroom schedule:

- Schedule less desirable tasks before highly desirable tasks—for example, independent work before group work, or difficult academic tasks prior to a relaxing activity or recess.
- Balance the energy level between tasks—for example, follow a high-energy task with a lower-energy task to moderate students' energy levels.
- Try to break longer instructional periods into smaller, more manageable segments.
- Visually display the schedule and call attention to it as a way to help students manage their time.
- Alert students to any changes in the schedule well before the change occurs—for example, tell students at the beginning of the day if there are changes to the afternoon schedule. (pp. 39–40)

While a consistent schedule supports students' sense of perceived safety, this is not to imply that teachers should wholly avoid changes to scheduling. Rather, changes to daily schedules—such as surprise activities like holding class outside or planned events like field trips or service days—can be very beneficial for students. Instead, a consistent daily schedule refers to the idea that most schools days should operate with relative predictability and that advance notice should be given to students if the schedule is to change.

Interactions With Parents

When considering consistency, teachers may also want to reflect on how their interactions with parents ensure that students receive similar messages both in school and at home. Teachers should regularly update parents on the events happening and the content being covered in class. There are a myriad of ways to communicate this to parents: newsletters, class websites, school newspapers, regular email blasts, class calendars, and so on. Because many parents like to be involved in their children's lives at school, teachers (when possible) can find ways to allow them to participate. Teachers commonly do this by asking parents to serve as chaperones for school trips or dances, assist in or visit the classroom, or get involved in school organizations or boards.

Teachers should aim to establish positive relationships with parents from the beginning of the year, and parent-teacher conferences often are the first interactions that occur between teachers and parents. Table 6.5 (page 134) contains procedures for specific teacher actions for before, during, and after parent-teacher conferences to encourage their success. In addition to parent-teacher conferences, teachers can regularly reach out to parents to keep them aware of how their students are doing academically and socially. Teachers should not just contact parents when students misbehave, however. Unfortunately, many parents only receive negative communications from teachers—that is, teachers only reach out when students exhibit undesirable behaviors in class. To combat this tendency, teachers should frequently communicate with parents and keep them updated on students' successes and challenges. As behavioral issues occur in the classroom, positive relationships with parents can go a long way in creating consistent expectations for students in school and at home.

Summary and Recommendations

This chapter discussed how actual and perceived safety affect students' safety needs. The chapter began by addressing actual safety, specifically through teachers' and students' familiarity with emergency procedures. In terms of perceived safety, the chapter provided strategies related to order, fairness, and consistency. We discussed how behavior expectations and classroom design support students' sense of order as well as how the equitable treatment of students—both academically and behaviorally—create a sense of fairness within a class. Finally, we examined how to create consistency within the classroom and between messages received at home and school.

Although teachers can use the strategies in this chapter in a variety of ways, we recommend the following.

- At the beginning of the year, reach out to parents to ensure consistent support from home, and contact students' parents at least once a quarter to update them on their students' progress.

- Once a semester, review specific emergency procedures and behavior expectations with students.

- At least once a semester, consider whether expectation levels contribute to the differential treatment of students, and use specific strategies that support academic and behavioral equity as needed.

- At least once a month, assess how the enforcement of behavior expectations, classroom design, and classroom structure create a sense of order and consistency.

The following scenario depicts how these recommendations might manifest in the classroom.

Table 6.5: Parent-Teacher Conferences

Timing	Procedure
Before the Conference	1. Send out invitations far in advance about parent-teacher conferences, the goals of the meeting, and options for scheduling. Options for dissemination of these materials include flyers and notices sent home by mail or with students, phone calls, emails, or announcements during community meetings. 2. Send out a reminder to parents about a week before the actual conference. The reminder should include the date, time, and location of each conference. You can choose to include a brief agenda for parents if desired. 3. Before the conferences, clean up the classroom and make sure it will be comfortable for incoming parents and guardians. For the meetings themselves, designate a more private space for the conferences and try to find adult chairs for parents to sit in (if they are not already present in the room). 4. Organize and review materials for each student. Create a portfolio for each student that contains relevant assignments, assessments, and grades. Create a list of topics that you want to address with parents and write down thoughts related to each. Topics may include student progress, strengths, weaknesses, growth goals, opportunities, expectations, challenges, concerns, content to be taught, upcoming school events, or parental support.
During the Conference	1. Begin the conference by giving an overview of where the student stands academically and socially. If parents are unfamiliar, explain how student progress is measured against learning goals. Focus on positive aspects of the student and provide examples of notable work the student has done. 2. Allow parents to voice their questions and concerns. Listen to parents actively and respond consciously and respectfully. If the answer to a question is unknown, tell parents that you will find an answer and follow up in a timely manner after the conference. 3. Find out information about students' backgrounds. Ask parents about what they believe to be their student's strengths, weaknesses, needs, learning style, goals, interests, and so on. Furthermore, ask parents about their goals for their student and the ways in which you can help the student achieve those goals. 4. Talk about areas that the student needs to work on. Have specific examples ready to explain these areas to parents. After noting areas of improvement, explain what actions you are taking in the classroom to help the student and provide ideas for parental support. When talking about at-home supports, make sure to avoid language that might be perceived as accusatory toward the parents. Focus on using "we" instead of "they" or "you." 5. Create action plans with parents when possible. If parents seem receptive to creating at-home supports for students, make commitments regarding what actions will be taken, how long such actions will last, and how often progress check-ins will occur. Determine preferred methods of communication (for example, phone calls, emails, letters home, and so on).
After the Conference	1. Thank parents who attended parent-teacher conferences either by phone or by note. Remind them that you are available to address questions or concerns they may have, and provide contact information. If you promised to provide specific information or resources during the parent-teacher conference, send that information promptly. 2. Follow up with parents who did not attend parent-teacher conferences and ask if they are interested in meeting at an alternative time. Ask about preferences for communication to have on hand, even if they are not interested in meeting in person. 3. Continue to stay in touch with parents throughout the year. Notify them of opportunities for students and for parents as they come up. Furthermore, communicate and celebrate students' successes with parents when possible.

Source: Marzano Research, 2016f, pp. 12–13.

Before the school year starts, a high school science teacher wants to ensure that her students feel safe. The teacher examines her classroom to identify potential dangers—for example, she determines the best place to store chemicals when they are not in use, writes extensive procedures that detail how to work safely with dangerous equipment, and creates emergency plans in the event that something goes wrong. The teacher reviews emergency procedures with students regularly and, before any lab, makes sure that students understand the procedures that support their safety. The teacher also reaches out to parents at the start of the year to establish positive relationships with them. She develops a class newsletter to keep them aware of the class's activities and makes a goal to talk to at least one parent per week. Throughout the year, she considers whether her treatment of students is fair. She regularly assesses her expectations of students and how they might contribute to differential treatment and goes out of her way to build relationships with students for whom she holds lower expectations. As she begins this work, she monitors how her perceptions of students change throughout the year.

CHAPTER 7
Physiology

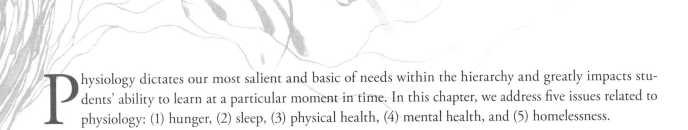

Physiology dictates our most salient and basic of needs within the hierarchy and greatly impacts students' ability to learn at a particular moment in time. In this chapter, we address five issues related to physiology: (1) hunger, (2) sleep, (3) physical health, (4) mental health, and (5) homelessness.

Hunger

Hunger can drastically affect student learning, particularly over the long term. As such, it is crucial that teachers are aware of the extent to which their students have access to adequate and nutritious food, including identifying chronically hungry students, providing food in the classroom, and programs that address food needs.

Identifying Chronically Hungry Students

The first step in combating student hunger is to identify food-insecure students. Unfortunately, this is not always as easy as directly asking students about their hunger needs. Instead, teachers should become adept at identifying signs of chronic hunger and learn how to discuss hunger with students in a sensitive and conscientious manner.

Consider the following topics when identifying these particular students: (1) differentiating between normal hunger versus food insecurity and (2) questioning students about hunger.

Differentiating Between Normal Hunger Versus Food Insecurity

Students who say they are hungry do not always suffer from food insecurity. In fact, it is probably safe to say that "growing children have an appetite and will say they are hungry at periods throughout the day" (Montana Food Bank Network, n.d., p. 1). In order to identify students who are chronically hungry, teachers should consider student behavior and physical appearance. In terms of student behavior, a teacher should keep an eye out for the following behaviors indicative of chronic hunger:

- Rushing food lines

- Extreme hunger on Monday morning

- Eating all of the food served

- Lingering around for seconds (Montana Food Bank Network, n.d., p. 1)

If a student exhibits a pattern of behavior including one or more of the previous actions, a teacher might speak directly to the student about food availability at home or to a school counselor or administrator about next steps. Not all chronically hungry students exhibit these behaviors, however. Teachers can also assess the general demeanor of students and their performance at school. Note that the following behaviors are not always caused by hunger but do serve as indicators that students may lack adequate access to food:

- Excessive absences—due to sickness or unexcused

- Hyperactive, aggressive, irritable, anxious, withdrawn, distressed, passive/ aggressive—any display of these mentioned which leads to disciplinary action

- Repetition of a grade

- Difficulty in forming friendships, getting along with others

- Sickness—sore throat, common cold, stomach ache, ear infection, fatigue

- Short attention span, inability to concentrate (Montana Food Bank Network, n.d., p. 2)

In addition to these behaviors, teachers might consider the physical appearance of their students as potential indicators for unmet food needs. Consider the following list of symptomatic physical characteristics adapted from the Montana Food Bank Network (n.d.).

▶ Extreme thinness caused by a protein or calorie deficiency

▶ Puffy or swollen skin caused by a protein deficiency

▶ Chronically dry, cracked lips caused by a protein or calorie deficiency

▶ Chronically dry, itchy eyes caused by a vitamin A deficiency

Identifying students for hunger intervention based solely on appearance is not a consistently dependable method, just as assessment based on behavior can lead to misdiagnosis. For example, weight or thinness does not always reliably identify students with unmet food needs—some students may look underweight but maintain a healthy diet or be overweight but not have access to essential nutrients due to an unhealthy diet. Instead, teachers should use students' behaviors and physical appearance as an indication of the need for further evaluation and assessment.

Questioning Students About Hunger

Teachers can ask students about the availability of food at home and notify school administrators if they have doubts about students' access to food. Teachers can use the following questions to gauge whether students may suffer from chronic hunger or are just experiencing normal hunger.

- Are you hungry? If so, why?
- Do you have enough food in the house?
- What did you have for breakfast? Did it make you feel full?
- What did you have last night for dinner? Did it make you feel full?
- Are you part of the free or reduced-price breakfast or lunch program (if eligible)? If so, do you use it each day?

When questioning students, teachers should make sure to do so privately and tactfully. Students, particularly at the middle and high school levels, often are embarrassed to be associated with free or reduced-price lunch programs or to acknowledge their unmet needs, especially in the presence of their peers (Pogash, 2008). Teachers should also keep in mind that even when alone, students may not be completely honest when responding to teachers' queries. As such, teachers should try to use their best judgment when parsing the responses of students, and in the event of uncertainty, notify school counselors or administrators about their concerns.

Providing Food in the Classroom

Teachers might take it upon themselves to ensure that chronically hungry students have some access to food throughout the day. No Kid Hungry (2013) estimated that teachers across the country, on average, spend thirty-seven dollars a month feeding students in their classes. These acts of generosity are especially admirable considering that many teachers pay for supplemental school supplies for their classrooms while also juggling their own personal expenses. When providing food in class, teachers should not single out specific students. Rather, teachers should provide snacks to all students when financially feasible or establish a way to provide snacks to hungry students privately or in a predetermined manner. For example, a teacher may establish a bin that holds fruit for students to take when they are hungry or let students who may need extra food know they can come to class a few minutes early to pick up a snack before the majority of the class arrives.

Teachers should also consider the type of food they offer to students. In 2010, the Healthy, Hunger-Free Kids Act (HHFKA) passed, which mandated that schools provide more whole grains, fruits, and vegetables and reduce high-fat and sugary foods served in cafeterias (State of Obesity, n.d.). Despite controversies surrounding the HHFKA, the intent of the bill was to help students make healthier food choices. This is particularly important when one considers the fact that "in 2012, more than one third of children and adolescents were overweight or obese" (Centers for Disease Control and Prevention, 2015). As such, it is counterintuitive for teachers to provide students who may already lack a healthy diet with snacks that schools have actively removed from their menus for being unhealthy. Instead, teachers should provide healthy options, such as fruits, vegetables and low-fat dips, cereal bars made with whole grains, or individually packaged bags of nuts, when possible.

Connecting Students With Programs That Address Food Needs

While providing food directly to students temporarily addresses their unmet food needs, it is generally not a sustainable solution for food-insecure students. Rather, teachers can connect students and their families with existing programs that supply substantial quantities of food to those in need. Here we describe four possible programs: (1) free breakfast and lunch, (2) school food pantries, (3) weekend backpack programs, and (4) summer meal programs.

Free Breakfast and Lunch Programs

Students from food-insecure homes generally qualify for free or reduced-price meals at school. In addition to lunch programs, some schools offer free and reduced-price breakfast as well as after-school snacks. Many qualified families are not aware of the existence of these programs or their children do not get to school early enough or stay late enough to take advantage of them. Teachers might find out what resources are available at their schools and pass this information on to families. Families with incomes at or below 130 percent of the poverty level qualify for free lunches, and families with incomes between 130 and 185 percent of the poverty level qualify for reduced-price meals (U.S. Department of Agriculture, 2016). For example, for the 2016–2017 school year, the poverty level was established at $24,300 annual income for families of four. Thus, students from families of four whose total income was $31,590 or below were eligible for free meals, and students from families of four whose total income was between $31,590 and $44,955 were eligible for reduced-price meals (U.S. Department of Agriculture, 2016). Additionally, any student whose family receives Supplemental Nutrition Assistance Program (SNAP) benefits automatically qualifies for free meals at school (U.S. Department of Agriculture Food and Nutrition Service, 2015).

Some families believe the timeframe for application to such programs is limited to the beginning of the school year. As teachers identify potentially food-insecure students, they can direct the students' families to government websites or print out resources for them; the United States Department of Agriculture Food and Nutrition Service provides information about free and reduced-price meals, a letter for parents, and a household application in both English and Spanish on its website (see www.fns.usda.gov/school-meals /applying-free-and-reduced-price-school-meals for details).

School Food Pantries

Some schools, particularly schools with high populations of students who qualify for free or reduced-price lunch, have established onsite food pantries. Feeding America's School Pantry Program "serves more than 21 million meals to nearly 110,000 children nationwide" by setting up school pantries with "set distribution schedules [that] offer ongoing food assistance services" (Feeding America, n.d.b). While Feeding America has established food pantries across the country, teachers interested in establishing similar programs in their schools can speak with school administrators and leaders of local food banks. If a school food pantry seems implausible, teachers can organize food drives for food-insecure students and their families. Along with talking to local nonprofits, teachers can reach out to local businesses to see if they are willing to donate non-perishable supplies. Food drives can occur throughout the year, though they are particularly important around vacation periods—such as Thanksgiving, winter, or spring break—as students may struggle to find alternative sources of food during these times.

Weekend Backpack Programs

Teachers may notice that food-insecure students tend to act out more frequently on Mondays but become increasingly well behaved over the course of the week. This pattern of behavior can often be attributed to students' distress from not having their food needs met over the weekend. *Backpack programs* are food programs that send backpacks filled with easily prepared food home with food-insecure students on Friday afternoons. The Feeding America BackPack Program is the largest example of such a program and partners with over 160 food banks to serve 450,000 children across the United States (Feeding America, n.d.a). Teachers can investigate existing programs in the area by reaching out to local nonprofits or developing their own backpack programs. The following nine steps are from the Hunger Free Colorado's (2011) Backpack Food Program Starter Toolkit.

1. Assess the school and its level of need.
2. Schedule a meeting with the principal of the school.
3. Talk with other school teachers and staff.
4. Plan the specifics of the program.
5. Make a budget considering all of the necessary resources and materials.
6. Recruit volunteers.
7. Plan food bags and purchase food.
8. Confirm a start date and launch the program.
9. Measure the success of the program.

The Backpack Food Program Starter Toolkit (Hunger Free Colorado, 2011) breaks down each of these steps and also provides prefabricated resources, such as letters for parents to opt in or out, sample descriptions of programs, teacher information, and surveys to ease the process of creating and implementing such a program.

Summer Meal Programs

Though many students look forward to summer vacation and the end of classes, students who come from food-insecure homes often dread it, as they may rely on school as their primary source of food. Students and their families may be unaware of state and nonprofit programs that exist to provide free summer meals. Specifically, although "more than 20 million U.S. children . . . rely on free or reduced-price lunch during the school year, only around 3 million receive a free meal in summer" (Felling, 2013, pp. 59–60). After researching local summer programs designed to provide food to eligible students, teachers can create resource guides for students to take home at the end of the school year to ensure they are aware of the available programs. For example, the USDA created the Summer Food Service Program, which has locations throughout the United States (to find a location nearby, see www.fns.usda.gov/summerfoodrocks), that provides meals to food-insecure students throughout the summer. Teachers can also find other local resources through school administrators, guidance counselors, or local charity organizations.

Sleep

Sleep is a physiological need that increasingly goes unmet, particularly for older students. To address this phenomenon, a growing number of schools across the United States have delayed their start times and have seen significant improvements in students' academic performance, mood, and health (Adolescent Sleep Working Group, Committee on Adolescence, & Council on School Health, 2014; Owens, Belon, & Moss, 2010; Wahlstrom et al., 2014). While individual teachers do not have control over the amount of sleep students get at home nor the time school begins, they can emphasize the importance of sleep to students and encourage appropriate sleeping schedules outside of school. Teachers can also express their concerns about students' unmet sleep needs to parents and administrators and work to create specific behavioral interventions as needed. In terms of classroom actions, teachers can consider how they react to students who fall asleep in class and whether their reactions truly support students' needs.

Most teachers, at some point during their careers, will encounter at least one student who regularly falls asleep during class. When students fall asleep, it is important for teachers to consider their interpretation of the situation before responding. Some teachers may have a tendency to become angry; often, these educators consider sleeping in class to be an act of defiance or disrespect. However, becoming angry with sleeping students rarely results in the most positive outcome and "distorts our thinking in the short term" (Marzano & Marzano, 2015, p. 17). Instead, teachers should not necessarily view sleeping in class as a disciplinary problem but rather a symptom of underlying causes—namely that students are attempting to fulfill their unmet sleep needs and cannot focus on anything else.

Once teachers consider their interpretations, they can assess the best course of action. Educators seem to be divided on whether to wake up sleeping students, with one group believing that teachers should always wake up students and the other believing that there are situations in which students should be allowed to sleep. For example, if a student falls asleep and such behavior is uncharacteristic, it may be worthwhile to let the student sleep, then follow up with him or her at the end of class. Alternatively, the teacher could wake up the student and ask if he or she is all right. Depending on the response, the student might be sent to the nurse if it is clear that the sleep is needed or asked to rejoin class after getting a drink of water (Shore, n.d.b). If students repeatedly fall asleep during class, teachers can consider implementing the following strategies, identified by Kenneth Shore (n.d.b), as preventative measures.

▶ **Call on students unexpectedly:** When teachers establish that they will call on all students at any time, students are more likely to stay alert. As students seem to become drowsy, teachers can ask them questions to keep them engaged. However, as Shore (n.d.b) noted, "Your goal is to heighten [their] alertness, not humiliate . . . , so ask a question you are confident [they] can answer."

▶ **Consider the placement of students' desks:** When students are in closer proximity to their teachers, they are less likely to fall asleep. Alternatively, fresh air and natural light can keep students alert. As such, students who repeatedly fall asleep in class can be assigned seats near the front of the class or by windows to help them stay awake.

▶ **Keep students active:** Teachers should incorporate frequent movement breaks into their class periods to keep all students alert. If students seem to be dozing off, teachers can ask them to briefly walk down the hall to get a drink of water.

> ▸ **Make it hard for the students to sleep:** When students frequently fall asleep in class, teachers can find ways to make it more difficult for them to fall asleep. For example, teachers can give students clipboards and move the students away from their desks so they cannot easily rest their heads to sleep.

Teachers should follow up each time students fall asleep in class. These meetings can be used to determine the best course of action for dealing with particular students when they fall asleep. This is also an appropriate time for teachers to express that they are not angry with or trying to embarrass these students but, instead, are concerned for them. Teachers might also offer students the option of extended deadlines for assignments so that they can catch up on sleep, with the qualification that they refrain from sleeping during class in the future.

Physical Health

Outside of students' physiological needs related to food and sleep, students have specific needs related to staying physically healthy. Here, we briefly discuss the following three aspects of physical health: (1) illness, (2) hygiene, and (3) exercise.

Illness

Throughout the year, students will get sick with short-term illnesses such as colds or the flu. These sicknesses commonly occur during the colder months as students spend more time indoors in close contact with one another. Teachers can take the following preventative measures—adapted from a list by Colleen Story (2012)—to reduce the spread of sickness among students.

> ▸ **Encourage hand washing:** Keep hand sanitizer in an easily accessible area of the classroom. For younger students, teach them the importance of preventing the spread of germs through proper handwashing techniques.

> ▸ **Sanitize the classroom:** Develop a cleaning schedule in which surfaces that are regularly touched (such as countertops, desks, computer keyboards, phones, faucet handles, doorknobs, and cupboard handles) are disinfected. Keep adequate cleaning supplies on hand in the classroom.

> ▸ **Teach preventative behaviors:** Teach students to properly cover their mouths when coughing and sneezing, and make tissues easily accessible. Help students understand what is appropriate to share and why certain items are best kept for personal use.

However, even with these considerations, students will inevitably get sick. Teachers should encourage students to stay at home, as illnesses with symptoms of sneezing, fever, or coughing are often contagious. When students are sick in class, they should be sent to the nurse's office to wait away from other students before going home. Teachers may also want to send home a sickness policy at the beginning of the year informing parents that they prefer that students stay home if they are sick, especially when students have fevers.

Teachers should also establish a clear procedure for how students should collect and return make-up work when absent. For example, figure 5.4 (page 113) contains an example standard operating procedure that outlines how absent students can determine what they missed. The procedure should also include what students are responsible for and the timeframe for the completion of missed assignments. Teachers should keep track of daily classwork and homework and place this information in an easily accessible location. Teachers could also place photocopies of other students' notes from class here as well. When students return to class, teachers can find times to meet with them to review missed content, especially if the content is particularly important for understanding future lessons. If students have long-term illnesses that require they miss extended periods of school, teachers should work with the students, their families, administrators, and school counselors to create plans that prevent the students from falling too far behind during their absence.

Hygiene

Some teachers may encounter students with poor hygiene—for example, body odor, unkempt hair, bad breath, or dirty clothes. Though addressing such topics may be difficult or uncomfortable, teachers should talk to students with poor hygiene and work to resolve any issues. Teachers should talk to students directly and honestly, though also emphasize that such conversations are motivated out of concern for the student. Shore (n.d.a) suggested the following four recommendations for elementary school teachers with students struggling with poor hygiene.

1. **Make hygiene a regular part of the curriculum:** Teachers can directly teach students about positive hygiene behaviors and their importance. For example, a teacher might spend time outlining steps for proper handwashing and explain how this behavior prevents the spread of sickness.

2. **Talk with students privately:** When students have poor hygiene, teachers can meet with them to give them instructions for specific behaviors that support good hygiene. However, this should be done away from the class to avoid embarrassing these students.

3. **Monitor students' hygiene:** After meeting with students about hygienic behaviors, teachers should reinforce positive changes in their behavior. Teachers can also ask students to keep journal entries that track their hygienic behaviors, if necessary.

4. **Have hygiene items handy:** In some cases, students' hygiene problems are the result of a lack of resources. In such occasions, teachers can consider keeping hygiene items—such as toothbrushes, toothpaste, combs, brushes, shampoo, deodorant, or feminine products—in their desks to provide to students in need.

For students at higher grade levels, teachers should still talk to students directly and honestly and offer hygiene items if students do not have them at home. Teachers may also work with administrators to arrange for students to use onsite resources, such as gym showers, if necessary.

Exercise

Exercise is an important part of students' physical and mental health. Teachers should remind students of schoolwide programs, such as walk- or bike-to-school days, intramural sports, school field days, and extended recess periods (for elementary schools), when applicable. Individually, teachers can model behaviors that emphasize the importance of exercise by getting involved with school athletics, talking about favorite physical activities, and directly teaching students about the benefits of physical activity.

Teachers can incorporate physical activity into class time through *physical activity breaks*—time in class that encourages students to move. Researchers have found that physical activity breaks "may increase physical activity, improve student behavior and on-task behavior, and improve some measures of health" (Active Living Research, 2013, p. 6). Activities can be related to the content being taught or allow students to take a break from class. Table 7.1 provides examples of both content-driven and nonacademic activities, which can be modified based on the grade level of students.

Table 7.1: Content-Driven and Nonacademic Physical Activity Breaks

Content-Driven Activities	Nonacademic Activities
• **Academic Games:** When playing academic games, incorporate prompts that require physical movement (for example, boxing jabs, jumps, push-ups, triceps dips using their chairs, arm circles, jumping jacks, or elbow to opposite knee touches), and have the entire class perform that action. • **Acting Out:** Read a paragraph or page of a book, and every time an action verb comes up, have students act it out. • **No Stress Test:** Make it a classroom tradition to have a five-minute walking break before a test to help everyone unwind and relax. • **Quiz Me:** While reviewing for a test, ask students a series of true-or-false questions. Assign movements to each response. For example, if a student thinks the question is true, he might jump in place, whereas if a question is false, he might touch his toes. • **Walk and Talk:** Break students into groups of two or three, and assign a topic for students to discuss while taking a five-minute walk. Have students report their findings as a class after. • **Write It Out:** When introducing or reviewing vocabulary, have students stand up and write a term using their index finger in large letters in front of them. Repeat using a different body part (for example, big toe, belly button, head, knee, or shoulder) for a different vocabulary term.	• **Calm Down:** Lead students in stretches, and have students hold each pose for fifteen to twenty seconds. Stretches might include reaching for the sky, touching your toes, making arm or neck circles, or doing lunges. • **Classroom Workout Circuit:** Create multiple stations around the room designated by signs depicting different physical activities (for example, boxing jabs, running in place, jumping on both feet, jumping jacks, or sit-ups). Divide students into groups, assign them to a station, and have them do the action. Students rotate stations after a given amount of time. • **Future Trainer:** Have a student lead a brief physical activity break using movements of his or her choice. • **Pick-Me-Up:** Have students place an object on the floor (for example, a pen, notebook, or ID) and try to pick it up with different body parts (for example, elbows, feet, forearms, knees). • **Play Cards:** Using a standard card deck, assign an activity to each of the four suits (for example, jumping in place, running in place, sit-ups, squats). Pass out a card to each student and have them do the activity for that suit for thirty seconds. Alternatively, students can perform the activity the number of times designated on the card (with face cards indicating ten times). Students can trade cards with one another to continue this activity. • **Task Master:** Give students a series of tasks to be completed as quickly as possible. Tasks might include bumping elbows with eight different classmates, touching each of the chairs in the classroom, doing twenty leg lifts while sitting, or jumping on each foot fifteen times. When finished, have students raise their hands.

Source: Adapted from the American Heart Association, 2016.

Mental Health

Mental health is another important aspect of students' physiological well-being. School guidance counselors often have resources about supporting students' mental health and can meet with students as issues arise in the classroom. Here, we discuss mental illness and worry.

Mental Illness

Determining how to best serve students with mental illness is not a simple process, as such issues manifest differently from person to person. Types and examples of mental illnesses are shown in table 7.2.

Table 7.2: Common Mental Illnesses

Type of Mental Disorders	Definition	Sample Illnesses
Anxiety disorders	Anxiety disorders involve excessive amounts or inappropriate expressions of uneasiness and apprehension.	• Obsessive-compulsive disorder • Post-traumatic stress disorder • Panic attacks
Behavioral disorders	Behavioral disorders involve repeated patterns of disruptive conduct.	• Attention-deficit hyperactivity disorder • Conduct disorder • Oppositional defiant disorder
Eating disorders	Eating disorders involve disturbances in typical eating behavior.	• Anorexia nervosa • Bulimia nervosa • Disordered eating
Learning disabilities	Learning disabilities involve difficulties in mastering basic or higher-level thinking skills.	• Dyscalculia • Dysgraphia • Dyslexia
Mood disorders	Mood disorders involve feelings of sadness or happiness outside typical variations in mood.	• Bipolar disorder • Depression • Self-harm
Personality disorders	Personality disorders involve atypical patterns of thought and behavior.	• Antisocial personality disorder • Borderline personality disorder • Paranoid personality disorder
Psychotic disorders	Psychotic disorders involve incorrect perceptions of reality, such as hallucinations and delusions.	• Schizophrenia

The illnesses shown in table 7.2 represent only a small segment of mental illnesses with which students may be diagnosed. When working with students suffering from mental illness, teachers should always remember that they are not there to judge or diagnose these students. In a literature review on mental illness and stigma, Angela M. Parcesepe and Leopoldo J. Cabassa (2013) found:

> Children and adults endorsed stigmatizing beliefs of people with mental illness, especially the belief that such individuals are prone to violent behaviors, and stigmatizing actions, in the form of social distance. Stigmatizing beliefs about the dangerousness of people with mental illness have increased over time. Beliefs of shame, blame, incompetency, punishment, and criminality of people with mental illness are common. (p. 12)

As such, teachers should consider their own perceptions of mental illness and how these beliefs may contribute to unfair and inequitable differential treatment of students (see Fairness, page 125).

Teachers should also reflect on their knowledge of mental health. Anthony F. Jorm (2012) found

> deficiencies in (a) the public's knowledge of how to prevent mental disorders, (b) recognition of when a disorder is developing, (c) knowledge of help-seeking options and treatments available, (d) knowledge of effective self-help strategies for milder problems, and (e) first aid skills to support others affected by mental health problems. (p. 231)

If teachers find that they are not knowledgeable in one or more of the previous categories, they can research mental health independently or talk with school counselors or nurses to clear up misconceptions and fill any gaps in knowledge. If teachers are aware that students in their classes are suffering from mental illness, they should talk with the appropriate staff to better understand the mechanisms of their conditions and how they affect students' behavior. Such meetings are also an appropriate time to seek suggestions on how to make the classroom a positive learning environment for these students. To address mental illnesses that affect student learning, teachers can ask school counselors about individualized learning plans and the development of presentation, response, setting, timing, scheduling, organization skills, assignment, or curriculum accomodations (Strom, 2014).

Teachers can also use the following list, adapted from the U.S. Department of Health and Human Services (n.d.), to identify warning signs in students of potential mental health issues.

- Behavior that actively harms themselves or others
- Difficulty concentrating or staying still
- Involvement in class disruptions or fights
- Irregular eating patterns (for example, loss of appetite)
- Mood swings
- Extreme moods (for example, sadness lasting over two weeks)
- Regular use of drugs or alcohol
- Uncharacteristic changes in behavior or personality

If a student reaches out to a teacher or if a teacher believes that a student in his or her class is exhibiting warning signs of a potential mental health issue, the teacher should notify school counselors or administrators as well as the student's parents to make them aware of the situation (U.S. Department of Health and Human Services, n.d.).

Worry

While mental illness may only affect a few members of a class, teachers may also want to consider the negative effect that worrying can have on all students' mental health. While worry is certainly not a mental illness, excessive worry can drastically affect students' mental health. Students, even young ones, worry much more than many teachers might realize. Younger students may worry about their academic performance, relationships with their peers, family members' health, and local or world events. Older students continue to worry about these things in addition to worrying about more complex social dynamics and decisions that affect their future after high school. Teachers can use the following strategies, adapted from Daniel B. Peters (2013), to reduce the amount that students worry.

▶ **Ask students to verbalize their worries:** Students who worry incessantly may find comfort in writing their worries down or saying them aloud, as this highlights how many are unrealistic. Teachers can also have students consider the probability of the outcome occurring and behaviors to mitigate their occurrence. For example, a student might recognize that she is most worried about not getting into college, consider under what circumstances that would occur, and relate those circumstances to her own behaviors (for example, applying to a mix of schools in terms of difficulty of acceptance, keeping her grades up, or committing to working hard on her college essays).

▶ **Be supportive of the student, not the worry itself:** Teachers should be supportive of students as they voice their worries. However, teachers should also recognize the difference between being supportive and reinforcing students' fears. For example, language such as, "I hear you and what you're saying," has a very different effect from "That is very scary," or "I can see why you think that."

▶ **Differentiate various levels of worry:** Teachers can explain to students the difference between healthy and unhealthy worry. To start, teachers can note that all people worry and that it is a natural human response. Teachers can then differentiate between healthy and unhealthy worry by asking students to compare the amount of time they ruminate on specific worries versus other subjects.

▶ **Externalize the worry:** For younger students, teachers can externalize their worries through the fictional character, the Worry Monster. Teachers can introduce students to the Worry Monster as a bully who makes people feel bad. Just by talking about the Worry Monster frequently, students may begin to understand that their worries are separate from themselves.

▶ **Teach students about the physiology behind fear:** One way to minimize students' worry is to explain worry as a neurological process that naturally occurs. For younger students, teachers can relate worry to fight-or-flight responses, whereas for older students, teachers can explain more complex neurological responses.

In addition to these strategies, teachers can also introduce students to the concepts of explanatory style (page 66) and thought revision (page 67) as a means to recognize and control excessive worrying.

Homelessness

Homeless students are defined as those who "lack a fixed, regular, and adequate nighttime residence. . . . A wide range of living situations [are recognized] as homelessness, such as frequent mobility or living in shared housing . . . motels, cars, parks, makeshift housing, or shelters" (Mizerek & Hinz, 2004). In 2013, close to two and a half million children in the United States experienced homelessness, representing one out of every thirty children (Bassuk, DeCandia, Beach, & Berman, 2014). With such statistics, it is critical that teachers understand how they can best serve students who are homeless.

While it is certainly true that teachers cannot fully alleviate students' unmet needs related to homelessness, teachers can be aware of students' circumstances and strive to make the classroom as comfortable for them as possible by taking note of the following considerations articulated by Tony Evers (2011).

▶ **Assess and stabilize students' basic needs:** Consider whether students' needs related to physiology and safety are taken care of, and if not, meet with appropriate administrators and staff to ensure that they are.

▶ **Avoid unnecessary punishment when possible:** Homeless students may not have access to reliable transportation or alarm clocks. As such, teachers should avoid penalizing these students for being late unless discussed previously. Furthermore, teachers should directly teach the behaviors they want students to exhibit and should recognize that homeless students may not know socially acceptable behaviors that other students may have internalized during school.

▶ **Consider students' privacy:** When discussing homeless students' situations, take care to do it away from other students to avoid embarrassment.

▶ **Determine students' academic ability:** Because homeless students may have changed schools frequently in the past, teachers should meet individually with such students to determine their abilities with mathematics, reading, and writing. Teachers can develop individualized learning plans as needed.

▶ **Emphasize positive experiences at school:** When possible, teachers should take actions to make students without homes feel competent (page 71), significant (page 82), and recognized (page 89). Teachers can also arrange for certain fees to be waived so that all students can have school pictures or attend field trips.

▶ **Plan to avoid assigning homework:** When scheduling assignments, teachers can avoid asking students to bring work home with them. If this is unavoidable, teachers can create flexible due dates or provide school supplies, books, and clipboards to students if they do not have access to these resources. Furthermore, teachers should not ask students to bring in food, photos, or other items from home if it seems that this may exclude some students.

▶ **Set up community supports:** Teachers can set up check-in programs (page 100) that require that students find time at least once a day to meet with them. Teachers might also consider assigning such students "buddies" to help them become familiar with the school. If necessary, teachers can work with administrators, counselors, and community resources to find tutors or therapists for students at no cost to them.

▶ **Work with parents:** Teachers can use previous strategies for successful interactions with parents (page 134) and regularly contact parents to ensure students have consistent transportation to school. In the event of repeated absences, teachers should reach out to parents immediately to prevent students from falling through the cracks.

As teachers work with students without a secure home, they should consider how homelessness may affect students' other needs. For example, if a homeless student repeatedly falls asleep in class or is often late, teachers should consider that an unstable life at home may be the root of the issue. Although teachers cannot guarantee a homeless student a secure place to live, teachers can attend to such students with compassion and consideration.

Summary and Recommendations

This chapter discussed students' physiological needs related to hunger, sleep, physical health, mental health, and homelessness. We differentiated between normal hunger and food insecurity and provided strategies for providing food and information about programs that address unmet food needs to students. The chapter also examined how teachers can best serve students struggling with unmet sleep needs, aspects of mental or physical health, and homelessness.

Although teachers can use the strategies in this chapter in a variety of ways, we recommend the following.

▸ At least once a month, teachers assess the needs of students related to hunger, sleep, mental health, physical health, and homelessness.

▸ Use specific strategies as needed.

The following scenario depicts how this recommendation might manifest in the classroom.

A second-grade teacher in a school with a high percentage of students eligible for free or reduced-price lunch commits to meet his students' physiological needs to the best of his ability. Throughout the school year, he reflects on students' behavior to see if any exhibit symptoms of unmet physiological needs. He finds that some of his students are regularly hungry when they come to class. He begins providing food by giving out snacks in the afternoon to all students and establishing a pantry in his classroom, eventually working with administrators to create a more permanent food pantry in the school. He also meets with students individually when possible to check in on their physical and mental well-being, and, if repeated problems arise, reaches out to parents or administrators to solve problems before they escalate.

Epilogue

The purpose of education is not simply to teach and reinforce academic knowledge and skills. Rather, it is also to awaken in students the motivation and inspiration to become productive, satisfied human beings who not only add value to their own lives but the world at large. This requires a new vision of what constitutes "good teaching."

We have presented a framework for instruction that is based on a hierarchy of needs and goals. Metaphorically, the framework assumes that at any point in time, students are asking themselves the following questions.

- ▶ **Level 1:** "Am I physiologically comfortable in this situation?"
- ▶ **Level 2:** "Does this situation make me feel safe?"
- ▶ **Level 3:** "Does this situation make me feel like others accept me?"
- ▶ **Level 4:** "Does this situation make me feel like I am valued?"
- ▶ **Level 5:** "Does this situation make me feel as though I am living up to my potential?"
- ▶ **Level 6:** "Does this situation make me feel like I am a part of something important?"

When students answer the first four levels of questions affirmatively, they are most likely paying attention and engaged, at least in the short term. However, they are not motivated and inspired unless they answer the last two questions affirmatively.

In the previous chapters, we have identified specific teacher actions that address all six levels of the hierarchy. It is our firm belief that if individual teachers address all six levels, they will see unprecedented improvement in not only students' academic abilities but also their motivation and inspiration, ultimately leading to enhanced self-efficacy. At a more general level, we believe that if schools or (better yet) districts were to address all six levels systematically, we would see a veritable transformation of the nature and power of K–12 education.

Appendix:
Obtaining Feedback

While this book provides specific strategies for teachers to ensure that students' needs are met in their individual classrooms, teachers can take a more holistic view of students' experiences at school to support not only engagement and attention but also motivation and inspiration. Teachers can accomplish this by using surveys that assess students' needs at each level of the hierarchy, such as the reproducible provided on page 158. Teachers should be aware that this survey is designed to assess students' experiences at school in general. Therefore, teachers and administrators should work together when considering students' responses to determine changes that best support the needs of all students in a school.

Teachers can administer the survey on page 158 to students, which should take no more than about ten minutes and include all students available at the time. The eighteen items found in the survey are strongly skewed toward the top two levels of the hierarchy of needs and goals. To illustrate, table A.1 presents the distribution of the survey items across the levels of the hierarchy.

Table A.1: Distribution of Items Across the Hierarchy of Needs and Goals

Items	Levels of the Hierarchy
1, 2	Physiology and safety
3, 4, 5, 6, 7, 8	Belonging and esteem within a community
9, 10, 11, 12, 13, 14, 15, 16, 17, 18	Self-actualization and connection to something greater than self

As seen in table A.1, the survey primarily assesses the top two levels of the hierarchy, as these levels are the engine of motivation and inspiration. This is not to say that levels 1 through 4 of the hierarchy are unimportant—as described in previous chapters, they are foundational to motivation and inspiration. However, multiple items assessing specific elements of these levels would render the survey quite long, and, as the title of the survey indicates, the survey is meant to be a snapshot of the needs of students in a school. Surveys that address more specific aspects of levels 1 through 4 can be found in a variety of sources (for example, Marzano, Warrick, & Simms, 2014).

The survey relies on the scale shown in table A.2.

Table A.2: Survey Scale

1	2	3	4	5
Strongly disagree	Disagree	Neutral	Agree	Strongly agree

Typically, the survey data are reported formally, like those in table A.3. The first three columns to the right of the survey items in table A.3 depict (respectively) the mean (M), the standard deviation (SD), and the number of students who responded to a particular item (n). Educators often only look at the mean and standard deviation when determining whether survey results are favorable. In the results shown in table A.3, all items except for three had a mean greater than 4 (agree). This might lead one to conclude that students believe that their school tends to meet their needs at all six levels of the hierarchy. Indeed, even the three items that had a mean below 4 (items 1, 3, and 5) had values closer to 4 (agree) than to 3 (neutral). When considering the mean of each item, teachers often also take into account the standard deviation of each response, which quantifies the variance of student responses. The larger the standard deviation, the more students disagree across their responses to that item. Unfortunately, it is difficult to ascertain just how large a standard deviation has to be before one considers it important when drawing conclusions about survey results.

Examining the mean and standard deviation of each item is not the only form of analysis that educators should conduct if they are truly interested in students' perceptions of the school. Instead, teachers can use the next four columns (under the larger *percentage* column) in table A.3 to better understand the student response patterns for each item. These columns report the percentage of students who responded at each level of the scale for each item. This paints a somewhat different picture from an analysis based on the mean alone. Consider responses of 1 (strongly disagree) when they are viewed as a percentage. Item 1, *This school is a clean and pleasant place to be,* had a percentage of 1.6, indicating less than two students out of one hundred strongly disagreed with it. When reviewing this answer, it may not warrant alarm on the part of educators. However, consider item 3, *I'm not worried about being bullied or pushed around in this school,* which a little more than twelve students out of one hundred strongly disagreed with. In contrast to item 1, this percentage should probably be a cause for concern and directly addressed by teachers and administrators.

Another approach to assessing these surveys is to combine responses of strongly disagree and disagree as well as the responses of agree and strongly agree—that is, combine the number of students who responded 1 (strongly disagree) and 2 (disagree) as well as students who responded 4 (agree) and 5 (strongly agree). This is depicted in table A.4 (page 156).

Table A.3: Formal Survey Results

	Survey Item	M*	SD*	n	Percentage				
					1	2	3	4	5
1	This school is a clean and pleasant place to be (for example, it's not too hot or cold; it's not messy).	3.92	1.12	249	1.6	12.4	19.7	24.9	41.4
2	I feel safe in this school.	**4.37**	0.92	249	1.6	2.4	14.1	21.7	60.2
3	I'm not worried about being bullied or pushed around in this school.	3.66	1.42	250	12.4	11.6	13.6	22.0	40.4
4	If I have problems, there are adults at school who I know and can go to for help and guidance.	**4.27**	1.05	250	4.8	1.6	11.2	26.4	56.0
5	The other students in this school treat me with respect.	3.85	1.18	250	5.2	8.8	20.8	26.0	39.2
6	In this school there is at least one adult who I know likes me.	**4.33**	1.10	240	5.4	2.1	10.0	19.2	63.3
7	The adults treat me fairly in this school.	**4.26**	1.04	242	3.7	4.1	9.1	28.1	55.0
8	The adults in this school know who I am.	**4.20**	0.99	249	2.8	2.0	17.7	26.9	50.6
9	This school helps prepare me for things I want to accomplish in the future.	**4.18**	1.06	245	3.3	5.7	11.8	27.8	51.4
10	This school teaches me how to set goals for myself.	**4.18**	0.96	249	1.6	2.8	20.5	26.1	49.0
11	This school teaches me how to overcome problems I encounter when I am having trouble learning.	**4.04**	1.11	248	6.0	2.8	14.1	35.1	41.9
12	This school teaches me how to work with other students to accomplish things together.	**4.23**	0.93	244	1.2	3.3	17.2	27.9	50.4
13	This school helps me believe that my future is bright and promising.	**4.07**	1.05	244	2.0	7.0	18.9	26.6	45.5
14	This school gives me tools and strategies that help me when I'm discouraged.	**4.05**	1.06	246	2.8	7.7	13.4	33.7	42.3
15	This school helps me recognize the positive things about myself.	**4.06**	1.10	246	4.9	4.5	15.0	31.3	44.3
16	This school helps me understand the things I might need to change about myself if I want to accomplish my goals.	**4.01**	1.11	245	3.7	7.3	17.1	28.2	43.7
17	This school makes me believe that I can make life better for other people.	**4.20**	1.05	243	4.5	2.5	12.8	28.8	51.4
18	This school helps me understand that what I do in life is important.	**4.30**	0.99	240	2.5	2.5	15.4	21.3	58.3

Note: 1 = Strongly disagree; 2 = Disagree; 3 = Neutral; 4 = Agree; 5 = Strongly agree; *M* = Arithmetic mean; *SD* = Standard deviation; *n* = Valid response count.

Item means greater than 4.00 appear in boldface type.

Table A.4: Combining Strongly Disagree and Disagree and Combining Agree and Strongly Agree

Item	Strongly Disagree and Disagree	Neutral	Agree and Strongly Agree
1	14	19.7	66.3
2	4	14.1	81.9
3	24	13.6	62.4
4	6.4	11.2	82.4
5	14	20.8	65.2
6	7.5	10	82.5
7	7.8	9.10	83.1
8	4.8	17.7	77.5
9	9	11.8	79.2
10	4.4	20.5	75.1
11	8.8	14.1	77
12	4.5	17.2	78.3
13	9	18.9	72.1
14	10.5	13.4	76
15	9.4	15	75.6
16	11	17.1	71.9
17	7	12.8	80.2
18	5	15.4	79.6

With strongly agree and disagree responses combined, there are a number of areas of concern indicated by the survey data.

▶ Fourteen percent of students disagreed with the statement, *This school is a clean and pleasant place to be* (item 1).

▶ Twenty-four percent of students disagreed with the statement, *I'm not worried about being bullied or pushed around in this school* (item 3).

▶ Fourteen percent of students disagreed with the statement, *The other students in this school treat me with respect* (item 5).

▶ Almost 11 percent of students disagreed with the statement, *This school gives me tools and strategies that help me when I'm discouraged* (item 14).

▶ Eleven percent of students disagreed with the statement, *This school helps me understand the things I might need to change about myself if I want to accomplish my goals* (item 16).

With this analysis, teachers can address students' needs at levels of the hierarchy not initially identified by solely considering the mean of each item.

Some educators like to combine the responses of 1 (strongly disagree), 2 (disagree), and 3 (neutral) responses when interpreting survey data. This can be justified, as these scores all indicate that respondents could not respond positively to an item. This is depicted in table A.5.

Table A.5: Combining Strongly Disagree, Disagree, and Neutral

Item	Strongly Disagree, Disagree, and Neutral	Agree and Strongly Agree
1	33.7	66.3
2	18.1	81.9
3	37.6	62.4
4	17.6	82.4
5	34.8	65.2
6	17.5	82.5
7	16.9	83.1
8	22.5	77.5
9	20.8	79.2
10	24.9	75.1
11	22.9	77
12	21.7	78.3
13	27.9	72.1
14	23.9	76
15	24.4	75.6
16	28.1	71.9
17	19.8	80.2
18	20.4	79.6

The results in table A.5 identify even more areas within the school that could use improvement. Specifically, in thirteen of the eighteen items, 20 percent (or more) of students could not respond positively about a specific aspect of their experience at school. Additionally, one-third of students could not respond positively to the following statements.

▶ *This school is a clean and pleasant place to be* (item 1).

▶ *I'm not worried about being bullied or pushed around in this school* (item 3).

▶ *The other students in this school treat me with respect* (item 5).

Thus, with these interpretations, teachers and administrators might recognize that there is more work to be done within the school than initially identified by an analysis of solely the mean and standard deviation of each item.

Awaken the Learner Snapshot Student Survey

Please rate your agreement with the following statements on a scale of 1–5.

1	2	3	4	5
Strongly Disagree	Disagree	Neutral	Agree	Strongly Agree

	1	2	3	4	5
1. This school is a clean and pleasant place to be (for example, it's not too hot or cold; it's not messy).	☐	☐	☐	☐	☐
2. I feel safe in this school.	☐	☐	☐	☐	☐
3. I'm not worried about being bullied or pushed around in this school.	☐	☐	☐	☐	☐
4. If I have problems, there are adults at school who I know and can go to for help and guidance.	☐	☐	☐	☐	☐
5. The other students in this school treat me with respect.	☐	☐	☐	☐	☐
6. In this school there is at least one adult who I know likes me.	☐	☐	☐	☐	☐
7. I am treated fairly by the adults in this school.	☐	☐	☐	☐	☐
8. The adults in this school know who I am.	☐	☐	☐	☐	☐
9. This school helps prepare me for things I want to accomplish in the future.	☐	☐	☐	☐	☐
10. This school teaches me how to set goals for myself.	☐	☐	☐	☐	☐
11. This school teaches me how to overcome problems I encounter when I am having trouble learning.	☐	☐	☐	☐	☐
12. This school teaches me how to work with other students to accomplish things together.	☐	☐	☐	☐	☐
13. This school helps me believe that my future can be bright and promising.	☐	☐	☐	☐	☐
14. This school gives me tools and strategies that help me when I'm discouraged.	☐	☐	☐	☐	☐
15. This school helps me recognize the positive things about myself.	☐	☐	☐	☐	☐
16. This school helps me understand the things I might need to change about myself if I want to accomplish my goals.	☐	☐	☐	☐	☐
17. This school makes me believe that I can make life better for other people.	☐	☐	☐	☐	☐
18. This school helps me understand that what I do in life is important.	☐	☐	☐	☐	☐

References and Resources

Active Living Research. (2013). *Do short physical activity breaks in classrooms work?* Accessed at http://activelivingresearch .org/files/ALR_Brief_ActivityBreaks_Feb2013.pdf on July 7, 2016.

Adolescent Sleep Working Group, Committee on Adolescence, & Council on School Health. (2014). School start times for adolescents. *Pediatrics, 134*(3), 642–649.

Adversity Advantage. (n.d.). *About Paul Stoltz and Erik Weihenmayer.* Accessed at www.adversityadvantage.com /weihenmayer.html on July 7, 2016.

Alderfer, C. P. (1969). An empirical test of a new theory of human needs. *Organizational Behavior and Human Performance, 4*(2), 142–175.

American Heart Association. (2016). *Teacher resources.* Accessed at www.heart.org/HEARTORG/Educator /FortheClassroom/NFLPlay60Challenge/Teacher-Resources_UCM_453019_Article.jsp on July 7, 2016.

Amos, L. (2014, March 20). *50 community service ideas for teen volunteers* [Blog post]. Accessed at www.teenlife.com /blogs/50-community-service-ideas-teen-volunteers on July 7, 2016.

Aronson, E. (n.d.). *Jigsaw in 10 easy steps.* Accessed at www.jigsaw.org/#steps on July 7, 2016.

Barnes, V. A., Bauza, L. B., & Treiber, F. A. (2003). Impact of stress reduction on negative school behavior in adolescents. *Health and Quality of Life Outcomes, 1*(10), 1–7.

Bartlett, M. Y., & DeSteno, D. (2006). Gratitude and prosocial behavior: Helping when it costs you. *Psychological Science, 17*(4), 319–325.

Bassuk, E. L., DeCandia, C. J., Beach, C. A., & Berman, F. (2014). *America's youngest outcasts: A report card on child homelessness.* Waltham, MA: National Center on Family Homelessness. Accessed at www.homelesschildrenamerica .org/mediadocs/282.pdf on July 7, 2015.

Berger, F. R. (1975). Gratitude. *Ethics, 85*(4), 298–309.

Biography.com. (n.d.). *Eleanor Roosevelt biography.* Accessed at www.biography.com/people/eleanor-roosevelt-9463366 on July 7, 2016.

Cameron, V. (2003). *Clue mysteries: 15 whodunits to solve in minutes.* Philadelphia: Running Press.

Canfield, J., Hansen, M. V., Hansen, P., & Dunlap, I. (Eds.). (2007). *Chicken soup for the child's soul.* Deerfield Beach, FL: Health Communications.

Canfield, J., Hansen, M. V., & Kirberger, K. (Eds.). (1997). *Chicken soup for the teenage soul.* Deerfield Beach, FL: Health Communications.

Centers for Disease Control and Prevention. (2015, April 24). *Childhood obesity facts.* Accessed at www.cdc.gov /healthyyouth/obesity/facts.htm on July 7, 2016.

Chernyak, N., & Kushnir, T. (2013). Giving preschoolers choice increases sharing behavior. *Psychological Science, 24*(101), 1971–1979.

Clay, R. A. (2006). Helping kids care. *American Psychological Association Monitor on Psychology, 37*(11), 42. Accessed at www.apa.org/monitor/dec06/kids.aspx on July 7, 2016.

Cohen, J., Cardillo, R., & Pickeral, T. (2011). Creating a climate of respect. *Educational Leadership, 69*(1). Accessed at www.ascd.org/publications/educational-leadership/sept11/vol69/num01/Creating-a-Climate-of-Respect.aspx on July 7, 2016.

Colwell, R. J., & Hewitt, M. P. (2016). *The teaching of instrumental music* (4th ed.). New York: Routledge.

Conrad, H. (2005). *Historical whodunits.* New York: Sterling.

Conrad, H. (2007). *Kids' whodunits: Catch the clues!* New York: Sterling.

Conrad, H. (2009). *Kids' whodunits 2: Crack the cases!* New York: Sterling.

Conzemius, A., & O'Neill, J. (2006). *The power of SMART goals: Using goals to improve student learning.* Bloomington, IN: Solution Tree Press.

Conzemius, A., & O'Neill, J. (2002, 2014). *The handbook for SMART school teams: Revitalizing best practices for collaboration.* Bloomington, IN: Solution Tree Press.

Costa, A. L., & Kallick, B. (2008). *Learning and leading with habits of mind: 16 essential characteristics for success.* Alexandria, VA: Association for Supervision and Curriculum Development.

Council on Foreign Relations. (2016). *Martin Luther King's speech: "I have a dream."* Accessed at www.cfr.org/united -states/martin-luther-kings-speech-have-dream/p26070 on July 7, 2016.

Crocker, J. (2002). The costs of seeking self-esteem. *Journal of Social Issues, 58*(3), 597–615.

David Lynch Foundation. (n.d.). *Research.* Accessed at www.davidlynchfoundation.org/research.html on July 7, 2016.

Deci, E. L., Vallerand, R. J., Pelletier, L. G., & Ryan, R. M. (1991). Motivation and education: The self-determination perspective. *Educational Psychologist, 26*(3&4), 325–346.

Doenim, S. (1997). The most mature thing I've ever seen. In J. Canfield, M. V. Hansen, & K. Kirberger (Eds.), *Chicken soup for the teenage soul* (pp. 266–269). Deerfield Beach, FL: Health Communications.

Dweck, C. S. (2006). *Mindset: The new psychology of success.* New York: Ballantine Books.

Elias, M. J. (2014, August 27). SMART goal setting with your students. *Edutopia.* Accessed at www.edutopia.org/blog /smart-goal-setting-with-students-maurice-elias on July 7, 2016.

Elliot, A. J., & Church, M. A. (1997). A hierarchical model of approach and avoidance achievement motivation. *Journal of Personality and Social Psychology, 72*(1), 218–232.

Enright, R. D. (2001). *Forgiveness is a choice: A step-by-step process for resolving anger and restoring hope.* Washington, DC: American Psychological Association.

Enright, R. D., & Fitzgibbons, R. P. (2000). *Helping clients forgive: An empirical guide for resolving anger and restoring hope.* Washington, DC: American Psychological Association.

Evers, T. (2011). *How teachers can help students who are homeless.* Madison, WI: Department of Public Instruction. Accessed at https://dpi.wi.gov/sites/default/files/imce/homeless/pdf/teach_help_hmls_stud.pdf on July 7, 2016.

Fabes, R. A., Fultz, J., Eisenberg, N., May-Plumlee, T., & Christopher, F. S. (1989). Effects of rewards on children's prosocial motivation: A socialization study. *Developmental Psychology, 25*(4), 509–515.

Feeding America. (n.d.a). *Backpack program.* Accessed at www.feedingamerica.org/about-us/we-feed-children/backpack-program/ on July 7, 2016.

Feeding America. (n.d.b). *School pantry program.* Accessed at www.feedingamerica.org/about-us/we-feed-families/school-pantry-program/ on July 7, 2016.

Felling, C. (2013). Hungry kids: The solvable crisis. *Educational Leadership, 70*(8), 56–60.

Ferlazzo, L. (2012, May 16). Fostering relationships in the classroom. *Edutopia.* Accessed at www.edutopia.org/blog/fostering-classroom-relationships-larry-ferlazzo-katie-hull-sypnieski on July 7, 2016.

Fletcher, A., & Kunst, K. (2006). *Guide to cooperative games for social change.* Olympia, WA: CommonAction. Accessed at https://freechild.org/wp-content/uploads/2016/01/gamesguide.pdf on July 7, 2016.

Flora, S. R. (2000). Praise's magic reinforcement ratio: Five to one gets the job done. *The Behavior Analyst Today, 1,* 64–69.

Frankl, V. E. (2006). *Man's search for meaning.* Boston: Beacon Press. (Original work published 1959)

Franklin D. Roosevelt Presidential Library and Museum. (n.d.). *Biography of Eleanor Roosevelt.* Accessed at www.fdrlibrary.marist.edu/education/resources/bio_er.html on July 7, 2016.

Friedel, J., Marachi, R., & Midgley, C. (2002, April). *"Stop embarrasing me!": Relations among student perceptions of teachers, classroom goals, and maladaptive behaviors.* Paper presented at the annual meeting of the American Educational Research Association, New Orleans, LA.

Froh, J. J., & Bono, G. (2012, November 19). *How to foster gratitude in schools.* Accessed at http://greatergood.berkeley.edu/article/item/how_to_foster_gratitude_in_schools on July 7, 2016.

Garner, R. (2016, February 23). *Dr. Robert H. Goddard, American rocketry pioneer.* Accessed at www.nasa.gov/centers/goddard/about/history/dr_goddard.html on July 7, 2016.

Gassin, E. A., Enright, R. D., & Knutson, J. A. (2005). Bringing peace to the Central City: Forgiveness education in Milwaukee. *Theory Into Practice, 44*(4), 319–328.

Ghazvini, S. D. (2011). Relationships between academic self-concept and academic performance in high school students. *Procedia Social and Behavioral Sciences, 15,* 1034–1039.

Glasser, W. (1969). *Schools without failure.* New York: Harper & Row.

Glasser, W. (1986). *Control theory in the classroom.* New York: Harper & Row.

Glasser, W. (1990). *The quality school: Managing students without coercion.* New York: Harper & Row.

Gordon, T. (1970). *P.E.T., parent effectiveness training: The tested new way to raise responsible children.* New York: Peter H. Wyden.

Harlacher, J. E. (2015). *Designing effective classroom management: The classroom strategies series.* Bloomington, IN: Marzano Research.

Harmin, M. (with Toth, M.). (2006). *Inspiring active learning: A complete handbook for today's teachers* (2nd ed.). Alexandria, VA: Association for Supervision and Curriculum Development.

Harrill, S. E. (n.d.). *Self-worth: Recognizing signs of high and low self-esteem.* Accessed at www.innerworkspublishing.com/news/vol40/selfesteem.htm on July 7, 2016.

Hecker, L., Simms, J. A., & Newcomb, M. L. (2015). *Teaching reasoning: Activities and games for the classroom.* Bloomington, IN: Marzano Research.

Hunger Free Colorado. (2011). *Backpack food program starter toolkit.* Accessed at www.hungerfreecolorado.org/wp-content/uploads/2012/08/HFC-Toolkit-for-Starting-Backpack-Food-Program.pdf on July 7, 2016.

Insel, P. M., & Roth, W. T. (2012). *Wellness worksheet 20: Maslow's characteristics of a self-actualized person—Wellness worksheets* (12th ed.). New York: McGraw-Hill.

Isaacson, W. (2007). *Einstein: His life and universe.* New York: Simon & Schuster.

J. Paul Getty Museum. (n.d.). *Claude Monet.* Accessed at www.getty.edu/art/collection/artists/257/claude-monet-french -1840-1926/ on July 7, 2016.

Jacobs, J. E., Lanza, S., Osgood, D. W., Eccles, J. S., & Wigfield, A. (2002). Changes in children's self-competence and values: Gender and domain differences across grades one through twelve. *Child Development, 73*(2), 509–527.

Jennings, P. A. (2015). *Mindfulness for teachers: Simple skills for peace and productivity in the classroom.* New York: W. W. Norton.

Johnson, D. W., & Johnson, R. T. (1987). *Creative controversy: Intellectual challenge in the classroom.* Edina, MN: Interaction Book Company.

Johnson, D. W., & Johnson, R. T. (1991). *Teaching students to be peacemakers.* Edina, MN: Interaction Book Company.

Johnson, D. W., Johnson, R. T., Dudley, B., & Burnett, R. (1992). Teaching students to be peer mediators. *Educational Leadership, 50*(1), 10–13.

Jorm, A. F. (2012). Mental health literacy: Empowering the community to take action for better mental health. *American Psychologist, 67*(3), 231–243.

Kaufman, S. B. (2011, November 8). Why inspiration matters. *Harvard Business Review.* Accessed at https://hbr.org /2011/11/why-inspiration-matters on July 7, 2016.

Kesler, C. (2013, March 29). *What is genius hour?* Accessed at www.geniushour.com/what-is-genius-hour/ on July 7, 2016.

Keyes, K. M., Maslowsky, J., Hamilton, A., & Schulenberg, J. (2015). The great sleep recession: Changes in sleep duration among US adolescents, 1991–2012. *Pediatrics, 135*(3), 460–468.

Khan Academy. (2015). *Hour of drawing with code: Making drawings with code.* Accessed at www.khanacademy.org /computing/hour-of-code/hour-of-drawing-code on July 7, 2016.

Kirp, D. L. (2014, January 12). Meditation transforms roughest San Francisco schools. *San Francisco Chronicle.* Accessed at www.sfgate.com/opinion/openforum/article/Meditation-transforms-roughest-San-Francisco-5136942.php on July 7, 2016.

Kohli, S. (2015, May 14). The economic importance of teaching coding to teens. *The Atlantic.* Accessed at www .theatlantic.com/education/archive/2015/05/the-economic-importance-of-teaching-coding-to-teens/393263/ on July 7, 2016.

Koltko-Rivera, M. E. (2006). Rediscovering the later version of Maslow's hierarchy of needs: Self-transcendence and opportunities for theory, research, and unification. *Review of General Psychology, 10*(4), 302–317.

Lambert, N. M., Clark, M. S., Durtschi, J., Fincham, F. D., & Graham, S. M. (2010). Benefits of expressing gratitude: Expressing gratitude to a partner changes one's view of the relationship. *Physiological Science, 21*(4), 574–580.

Lee, S., & Oyserman, D. (2009, December 23). *Possible selves theory.* Accessed at www.education.com/reference/article /possible-selves-theory/ on July 7, 2016.

Luskin, F. M., Ginzburg, K., & Thoresen, C. E. (2005). The efficacy of forgiveness intervention in college age adults: Randomized controlled study. *Humboldt Journal of Social Relations, 29*(2), 163–184.

Ma, X. (2003). Sense of belonging to school: Can schools make a difference? *Journal of Educational Research, 96*(6), 340–349.

Markus, H., & Nurius, P. (1986). Possible selves. *American Psychologist, 41*(9), 954–969.

Marzano Research. (2016a). Acknowledging adherence to rules and procedures [Folio]. *Marzano Compendium of Instructional Strategies.* Accessed at www.marzanoresearch.com/online-compendium/acknowledging-lack-of -adherence-to-rules-and-procedures on July 7, 2016.

Marzano Research. (2016b). Acknowledging lack of adherence to rules and procedures [Folio]. *Marzano Compendium of Instructional Strategies.* Accessed at www.marzanoresearch.com/online-compendium/acknowledging-lack-of -adherence-to-rules-and-procedures on July 7, 2016.

Marzano Research. (2016c). Demonstrating value and respect for reluctant learners [Folio]. *Marzano Compendium of Instructional Strategies.* Accessed at www.marzanoresearch.com/online-compendium/demonstrating-value-and -respect on July 7, 2016.

Marzano Research. (2016d). Demonstrating withitness [Folio]. *Marzano Compendium of Instructional Strategies.* Accessed at www.marzanoresearch.com/online-compendium/demonstrating-withitness on July 7, 2016.

Marzano Research. (2016e). Establishing rules and procedures [Folio]. *Marzano Compendium of Instructional Strategies.* Accessed at www.marzanoresearch.com/online-compendium/establishing-rules-and-procedures on July 7, 2016.

Marzano Research. (2016f). Understanding students' backgrounds and interests [Folio]. *Marzano Compendium of Instructional Strategies.* Accessed at www.marzanoresearch.com/online-compendium/understanding-students -backgrounds-and-interests on July 7, 2016.

Marzano Research. (2016g). Using verbal and nonverbal behaviors that indicate affection for students [Folio]. *Marzano Compendium of Instructional Strategies.* Accessed at www.marzanoresearch.com/online-compendium/using-verbal -and-nonverbal-behaviors on July 7, 2016.

Marzano, R. J. (2000). *Transforming classroom grading.* Alexandria, VA: Association for Supervision and Curriculum Development.

Marzano, R. J. (2006). *Classroom assessment and grading that work.* Alexandria, VA: Association for Supervision and Curriculum Development.

Marzano, R. J. (2007). *The art and science of teaching: A comprehensive framework for effective instruction.* Alexandria, VA: Association for Supervision and Curriculum Development.

Marzano, R. J. (2009). *Designing and teaching learning goals and objectives: The classroom strategies series.* Bloomington, IN: Marzano Research.

Marzano, R. J. (2010). *Formative assessment and standards-based grading: The classroom strategies series.* Bloomington, IN: Marzano Research.

Marzano, R. J. (2012). *Becoming a reflective teacher: The classroom strategies series.* Bloomington, IN: Marzano Research.

Marzano, R. J., & Heflebower, T. (2012). *Teaching and assessing 21st century skills: The classroom strategies series.* Bloomington, IN: Marzano Research.

Marzano, R. J., & Kendall, J. S. (1996). *A comprehensive guide to designing standards-based districts, schools, and classrooms.* Alexandria, VA: Association for Supervision and Curriculum Development.

Marzano, R. J., & Marzano, J. S. (2015). *Managing the inner world of teaching: Emotions, interpretations, and actions.* Bloomington, IN: Marzano Research.

Marzano, R. J., & Pickering, D. J. (2011). *The highly engaged classroom: The classroom strategies series.* Bloomington, IN: Marzano Research.

Marzano, R. J., & Simms, J. A. (2014). *Questioning sequences in the classroom: The classroom strategies series.* Bloomington, IN: Marzano Research.

Marzano, R. J., Warrick, P., & Simms, J. A. (2014). *A handbook for high reliability schools: The next step in school reform.* Bloomington, IN: Marzano Research.

Marzano, R. J., & Yanoski, D. C. (with Paynter, D. E.). (2015). *Proficiency scales for the new science standards: A framework for science instruction and assessment.* Bloomington, IN: Marzano Research.

Marzano, R. J., Yanoski, D. C., Hoegh, J. K., & Simms, J. A. (with Heflebower, T., & Warrick, P.). (2013). *Using Common Core standards to enhance classroom instruction and assessment.* Bloomington, IN: Marzano Research.

Maslow, A. H. (1943). A theory of human motivation. *Psychological Review, 50*(4), 370–396.

Maslow, A. H. (1954). *Motivation and personality.* New York: Harper & Row.

Maslow, A. H. (1969). The farther reaches of human nature. *Journal of Transpersonal Psychology, 1*(1), 1–9.

Maslow, A. H. (1970). *Motivation and personality* (2nd ed.). New York: Harper & Row.

Maslow, A. H. (1979). *The journals of A. H. Maslow* (R. J. Lowry, Ed., Vols. 1–2). Monterey, CA: Brooks/Cole.

McClelland, D. C. (1987). *Human motivation.* Cambridge, England: University of Cambridge.

McCullough, M. E., Kimeldorf, M. B., & Cohen, A. D. (2008). An adaptation for altruism? The social causes, social effects, and social evolution of gratitude. *Current Directions in Psychological Science, 17*(4), 281–285.

McEwan, B., Gathercoal, P., & Nimmo, V. (1997, March). *An examination of the applications of constitutional concepts as an approach to classroom management: Four studies of judicious discipline in various classroom settings.* Paper presented at the annual meeting of the American Educational Research Association, Chicago, IL. Accessed at http://eric.ed .gov/?id=ED418031 on July 7, 2016.

McKay, M., Davis, M., & Fanning, P. (2011). *Thoughts and feelings: Taking control of your moods and your life* (4th ed.). Oakland, CA: New Harbinger.

Mizerek, E. A., & Hinz, E. E. (2004, May). Helping homeless students. *Principal Leadership Magazine, 4*(8). Accessed at www.naspcenter.org/principals/nassp_homeless.html on July 7, 2016.

Montana Food Bank Network. (n.d.). *Identifying chronically hungry children.* Missoula, MT: Author. Accessed at http:// mfbn.org/wp-content/uploads/2012/11/DefChronHungryKids.pdf on July 7, 2016.

Nidich, S., Mjasiri, S., Nidich, R., Rainforth, M., Grant, J., Valosek, L., et al. (2011). Academic achievement and transcendental meditation: A study with at-risk urban middle school students. *Education, 131*(3), 556–564.

No Kid Hungry. (2013). *Hunger in our schools: 2013.* Washington, DC: Author. Accessed at www.nokidhungry.org/pdfs /NKH_TeachersReport_2013.pdf on July 7, 2016.

No Kid Hungry. (2015). *Hunger in our schools: 2015.* Washington, DC: Author. Accessed at http://hungerinourschools .org/img/NKH-HungerInOurSchoolsReport-2015.pdf on July 7, 2016.

NPR Staff. (2011, May 20). Forgiving her son's killer: 'Not an easy thing.' *StoryCorps.* Accessed at www.npr.org/2011 /05/20/136463363/forgiving-her-sons-killer-not-an-easy-thing on July 7, 2016.

Odyssey of the Mind. (2013). *2013–2014 long-term problem synopses.* Accessed at www.odysseyofthemind.com /materials/2014problems.php#p1 on July 7, 2016.

Owens, J. A., Belon, K., & Moss, P. (2010). Impact of delaying school start time on adolescent sleep, mood, and behavior. *Archives of Pediatrics & Adolescent Medicine, 164*(7), 608–614.

Oyez at IIT Chicago-Kent College of Law. (2016). *Sandra Day O'Connor.* Accessed at www.oyez.org/justices/sandra_day _oconnor on July 7, 2016.

Parcesepe, A. M., & Cabassa, L. J. (2013). Public stigma of mental illness in the United States: A systematic literature review. *Administration and Policy in Mental Health and Mental Health Services Research, 40*(5), 384–399.

Paul, G., Elam, B., & Verhulst, S. J. (2007). A longitudinal study of students' perceptions of using deep breathing meditation to reduce testing stresses. *Teaching and Learning in Medicine, 19*(3), 287–292.

Peixoto, F., & Almeida, L. S. (2010). Self-concept, self-esteem and academic achievement: Strategies for maintaining self-esteem in students experiencing academic failure. *European Journal of Psychology of Education, 25*(2), 157–175.

Peters, D. B. (2013, December 11). *10 steps for parents and kids to tame the worry monster* [Blog post]. Accessed at www.huffingtonpost.com/daniel-b-peters-phd/10-steps-for-parent-and-kids-to-taming-the-worry-monster_b _4345171.html on July 7, 2016.

Peterson, C. (2008). What is positive psychology, and what is it not? *Psychology Today.* Accessed at www.psychologytoday .com/blog/the-good-life/200805/what-is-positive-psychology-and-what-is-it-not on July 7, 2016.

Pintrich, P. R. (2003). A motivational science perspective on the role of student motivation in learning and teaching contexts. *Journal of Educational Psychology, 95*(4), 667–686.

Pogash, C. (2008, March 1). Free lunch isn't cool, so some students go hungry. *The New York Times.* Accessed at www.nytimes.com/2008/03/01/education/01lunch.html on July 7, 2016.

Polyson, J. (1985). Students' peak experiences: A written exercise. *Teaching of Psychology, 12*(4), 211–213.

Pruyser, P. W. (1976). *The minister as diagnostician: Personal problems in pastoral perspective.* Philadelphia: Westminster Press.

Purkey, W. W. (1991). *What is invitational education and how does it work?* Paper presented at the annual California State Conference on Self-Esteem, Santa Clara, CA.

Purkey, W. W., & Novak, J. (1988). *Education: By invitation only.* Bloomington, IN: Phi Delta Kappa Fastback.

Purkey, W. W., & Novak, J. (1996). *Inviting school success: A self-concept approach to teaching, learning, and democratic process* (3rd ed.). Belmont, CA: Wadsworth.

Rachel's Challenge. (2015). *Saved by a story: Letters of transformation and hope.* San Bernardino, CA: Author.

Robers, S., Zhang, A., Morgan, R. E., & Musu-Gillette, L. (2015). *Indicators of school crime and safety: 2014* (NCES 2015–072). Washington, DC: National Center for Education Statistics. Accessed at http://nces.ed.gov /pubs2015/2015072.pdf on July 7, 2016.

Rogers, K., & Simms, J. A. (2015). *Teaching argumentation: Activities and games for the classroom.* Bloomington, IN: Marzano Research.

Romano, L., Papa, L., & Saulle, E. (n.d.). *How to help students set and reach their goals.* Accessed at www.teachhub.com /how-help-students-set-and-reach-their-goals on July 7, 2016.

Scott, C. G., Murray, G. C., Mertens, C., & Dustin, E. R. (1996). Student self-esteem and the school system: Perceptions and implications. *The Journal of Educational Research, 89*(5), 286–293.

Scott, D., & Marzano, R. J. (2014). *Awaken the learner: Finding the source of effective education.* Bloomington, IN: Marzano Research.

Scott, R. (n.d.). *My ethics, my codes of life* [Unpublished essay].

Seligman, M. E. P. (2006). *Learned optimism: How to change your mind and your life.* New York: Vintage Books.

Shindler, J. (2010). *Transformative classroom management.* San Francisco: Jossey-Bass.

Shore, K. (n.d.a). *Assisting a child with poor hygiene.* Accessed at http://drkennethshore.nprinc.com/for-teachers/assisting -child-poor-hygiene/ on July 7, 2016.

Shore, K. (n.d.b). *Sleeping in class* [Blog post]. Accessed at www.educationworld.com/a_curr/shore/shore005.shtml on July 7, 2016.

Smith, S. (2003). *Five-minute mini-mysteries.* New York: Sterling.

Sobol, D. J. (1967). *Two-minute mysteries.* New York: Scholastic.

Solomon, R. C. (1993). *The passions: Emotions and the meaning of life.* Indianapolis, IN: Hackett. (Original work published 1976)

Soul Surfer. (2015). *Bethany Hamilton profile.* Accessed at http://bethanyhamilton.com/profile/ on July 7, 2016.

Sowislo, J. F., & Orth, U. (2013). Does low self-esteem predict depression and anxiety? A meta-analysis of longitudinal studies. *Psychology Bulletin, 139*(1), 213–240.

Spitzer, R. C. (1951). Inspiration beats exhortation. *The Journal of Education, 134*(5), 136–137.

Spradlin, C. (2015, April 13). Make a Difference Day Awards: Teen helps homeless. *USA Today*. Accessed at www.usatoday.com/story/news/2015/04/13/make-a-difference-day-awards-shreveport-louisiana/25538935/ on July 7, 2016.

State of Obesity. (n.d.). *School foods and beverages*. Accessed at http://stateofobesity.org/school-foods on July 7, 2016.

Steinmayr, R., & Spinath, B. (2009). The importance of motivation as a predictor of school achievement. *Learning and Individual Differences, 19*, 80–90.

Stets, J. E., & Burke, P. J. (2014). Self-esteem and identities. *Sociological Perspectives, 57*(4), 409–433.

StopBullying.gov. (n.d.a). *Bullying definition*. Accessed at www.stopbullying.gov/what-is-bullying/definition/ on July 7, 2016.

StopBullying.gov. (n.d.b). *Risk factors*. Accessed at www.stopbullying.gov/at-risk/factors on July 7, 2016.

Story, C. (2012). *Preventing the flu at school*. Accessed at www.healthline.com/health/cold-flu/preventing-flu-school on July 7, 2016.

Strom, E. (2014, January 3). *Common modifications and accommodations*. Accessed at www.understood.org/en/learning -attention-issues/treatments-approaches/educational-strategies/common-modifications-and-accommodations on July 7, 2016.

Tanner, M. A., Travis, F., Gaylord-King, C., Haaga, D. A. F., Grosswald, S., & Schneider, R. H. (2009). The effects of the transcendental meditation program on mindfulness. *Journal of Clinical Psychology, 65*(6), 574–589.

Taran, R. (2013, April 26). Building social and emotional skills in elementary students: Empathy. *Edutopia*. Accessed at www.edutopia.org/blog/project-happiness-empathy-randy-taran on July 7, 2016.

TeachThought. (2013, September 26). *10 team-building games that promote critical thinking*. Accessed at www.teach thought.com/critical-thinking/10-team-building-games-that-promote-critical-thinking/ on July 7, 2016.

Thrash, T. M., Elliot, A. J., Maruskin, L. A., & Cassidy, S. E. (2010). Inspiration and the promotion of well-being: Tests of causality and mediation. *Journal of Personality and Social Psychology, 98*(3), 488–506.

Travis, R., Grosswald, S., & Stixrud, W. (2011). ADHD, brain functioning, and transcendental meditation practice. *Mind & Brain, The Journal of Psychiatry, 2*(1), 73–81.

Treat, L. (1981). *Crime and puzzlement: 24 solve-them-yourself picture mysteries*. Jaffrey, NH: Godine.

Treat, L. (1982). *Crime and puzzlement 2: More solve-them-yourself picture mysteries*. Jaffrey, NH: Godine.

Treat, L. (2010). *You're the detective! 24 solve-them-yourself mysteries*. Jaffrey, NH: Godine.

Trent, B. (2005, July). *Cooperative and adventure games*. Presentation given at the Health and Physical Activity Institute at James Madison University, Harrisonburg, VA.

Turk, D. C., & Winter, F. (2006). *The pain survival guide: How to reclaim your life*. Washington, DC: American Psychological Association.

U.S. Department of Agriculture. (2016). Children nutrition programs: Income eligibility guidelines. *Federal Register, 81*(56), 15501–15504.

U.S. Department of Agriculture Food and Nutrition Service. (2015, June 16). *National School Lunch Program (NSLP): Applying for free and reduced price school meals*. Accessed at www.fns.usda.gov/school-meals/applying-free-and -reduced-price-school-meals on July 7, 2016.

U.S. Department of Health and Human Services. (n.d.). *For educators*. Accessed at www.mentalhealth.gov/talk/educators /index.html on July 7, 2016.

Vallerand, R. J. (1997). Toward a hierarchical model of intrinsic and extrinsic motivation. In M. P. Zanna (Ed.), *Advances in experimental social psychology* (Vol. 29, pp. 271–360). New York: Academic Press.

Vallerand, R. J. (2000). Deci and Ryan's self-determination theory: A view from the hierarchical model of intrinsic and extrinsic motivation. *Psychological Inquiry, 11*(4), 312–318.

Vallerand, R. J., & Ratelle, C. F. (2002). Intrinsic and extrinsic motivation: A hierarchical model. In E. L. Deci & R. M. Ryan (Eds.), *Handbook of self-determination research* (pp. 37–63). New York: University of Rochester Press.

Wahlstrom, K., Dretzke, B., Gordon, M., Peterson, K., Edwards, K., & Gdula, J. (2014). *Examining the impacts of later school start times on the health and academic performance of high school students: A multi-site study.* St. Paul: Center for Applied Research and Educational Improvement, University of Minnesota.

Warneken, F., & Tomasello, M. (2008). Extrinsic rewards undermine altruistic tendencies in 20-month-olds. *Developmental Psychology, 44*(6), 1785–1788.

Warneken, F., & Tomasello, M. (2013). The emergence of contingent reciprocity in young children. *Journal of Experimental Child Psychology, 116*(2013), 338–350.

Wesson, S. (2011, August 16). *Langston Hughes' drafts of "Ballad of Booker T.": Exploring the creative process* [Blog post]. Accessed at https://blogs.loc.gov/teachers/2011/08/langston-hughes%E2%80%99-drafts-of-%E2%80%9Cballad-of -booker-t-%E2%80%9D-exploring-the-creative-process/ on July 7, 2016.

WGBH Educational Foundation. (2005). *Who was Chiune Sugihara?* Accessed at www.pbs.org/wgbh/sugihara/readings /sugihara.html on July 7, 2016.

White, E. B. (1952). *Charlotte's web.* New York: Harper & Brothers.

Wiseman, T. (1996). A concept analysis of empathy. *Journal of Advanced Nursing, 23,* 1162–1167.

Witvliet, C. V., Ludwig, T. E., & Vander Laan, K. L. (2001). Granting forgiveness or harboring grudges: Implications for emotion, physiology, and health. *Psychological Science, 12*(2), 117–123.

Zakrzewski, V. (2013, November 19). *Gratitude activities for the classroom.* Accessed at http://greatergood.berkeley.edu /article/item/gratitude_activities_for_the_classroom on July 7, 2016.

Index